Self-Coaching

*How to Heal Anxiety
and Depression*

Joseph J. Luciani, Ph.D.

John Wiley & Sons, Inc.

New York • Chichester • Weinheim • Brisbane • Singapore • Toronto

ISBN 0-471-38737-1

10 9 8 7 6 5 4 3 2

Dedicated
to my wife, Karen
my son, Justin
and my daughter, Lauren
—my raison d'etre

Contents

Acknowledgments   vii

Introduction   1

Part I   **What Is Self-Coaching?**

1. A New Self-Therapy   9
2. The Seven Principles of Self-Coaching Healing   19

Part II   **The Problems Self-Coaching Can Heal**

3. Getting to the Root of Your Problem   27
4. Depression   37
5. Anxiety   50
6. The Control-Sensitive Personality   60
7. The Control-Insecurity Connection   74

Part III   **Self-Coaching: The Program and How to Do It**

8. Self-Talk   87
9. The Three Easy Steps of Self-Talk   97
10. Self-Talk: Follow-through   114
11. Motivation   129

Part IV   Self-Coaching: Healing Specific Personality Types

12. Self-Coaching for Worrywarts   141

13. Self-Coaching for Hedgehogs   152

14. Self-Coaching for Turtles   168

15. Self-Coaching for Chameleons   187

16. Self-Coaching for Perfectionists   206

17. Self-Coaching for Guilt-Sensitive People   224

Part V   Self-Coaching for Life

18. Self-Coaching and Letting Go   245

Appendix: Training Log Format   253

Index   259

Acknowledgments

Self-coaching began twenty-three years ago when my friend and mentor, Dr. Alan Gettis, introduced me to jogging and marathon running. This experience provided the spark for seeing therapy in a less traditional way.

No one was more instrumental than Jane Rafal in helping with the nuts and bolts of getting this book into print. Not only has Jane contributed much editorially to this project, but she has become an ongoing source of direction and hope. She is a valued friend and coach.

I had the good fortune to begin working with my agent, Jean Naggar. As rough as my early project was, Jean was able to see its merit. An agent of Jean's caliber makes getting published seem easy.

My editor, Tom Miller, whose instincts are nothing less than inspired, was able to take my proposal and steer it in the right direction.

Throughout these years of synthesis, there have been my patients. Together we have struggled to find meaning and solace. The answers we sought weren't in the books lining my office shelves—they were an inherent part of each struggle. To all my patients, I express a profound gratitude for helping me see more clearly.

Finally there is my family. They serve as my anchor. My daughter and fossil buddy Lauren's zest for living shows how joyful life can be. She is truly gifted with happiness, and an ongoing source of inspiration for me. My son, Justin, like me, wants to know "why." His innate goodness and love for others have confirmed my belief in optimism.

I'm also thankful to him for his daily emails of encouragement, support and feedback, despite the rigors of his Princeton schedule. My wife, Karen, has believed in me since we met in high school. She has never allowed me to give up. There can be no greater gift than someone who believes in you and loves you. She is my gift.

Introduction

As far back as Joe can remember, he worried. When he was very young, about five or six, he mostly worried about his parents dying. An only child, Joe couldn't imagine life without them. He worried in school, too. What if he got into trouble or didn't do well? Some things, such as his parents dying, he couldn't control. Other things, such as school, he could.

At least he thought he could—until fourth grade. One morning, his teacher saw Joe slouched over his desk and told him to lift his head up. Joe was caught completely off guard. Hearing a few giggles, he got upset. Then he panicked. If he raised his head to please the teacher, the kids would surely see the tear that was rolling down his cheek. Joe did nothing—he froze.

The teacher stalked to his desk and yanked his head up. Unfortunately, Joe's jaw clenched—right through his tongue. His mouth began to bleed. The teacher, seeing the blood, lost control and violently dragged Joe out of the classroom, tearing his shirt, screaming, and slapping him along the way.

Panicked and terror stricken, Joe ran from the building. The bottom had fallen out of his world. His worst nightmare had come true—his teacher obviously wanted to kill him, his classmates saw him crying, and his parents would surely be upset with him for messing up. (This was, after all, the 1950s, when parents viewed schools as ultimate authorities.) It was lunch time. Joe ran all the way home and managed to slip into his room unnoticed. He changed his torn shirt, rinsed the blood, combed his hair, and would have made it back to school if it hadn't been for his cousin, who was in Joe's class, arriving in tears at the front door.

Although what happened next was a blur, Joe does recall his parents being upset. His father was so enraged that he had to be physically held back from going to the school. A day or two passed, and when Joe returned to school, his teacher had been replaced. It didn't matter when someone told Joe the teacher had "snapped" and needed to go for help. As far as Joe was concerned, this was all his fault—and he had a lot of trouble living with that realization.

Joe, already a cautious, worrisome child, vowed to become even more vigilant, more in control. Somehow he would manage never to be caught off guard again. He would see to it. Unfortunately, it never occurred to Joe that he had done nothing wrong. Nor did anyone else make that clear to him.

Joe thought long and hard. He knew he wasn't perfect—far from it. Thankfully, he didn't have to *be* perfect—he only had to *act* perfect. Although he had always been rather finicky, it was different now. In the past he "liked" getting things just right. Now he felt he had no choice: He *had to* get things right! If, for example, he were building a model airplane and happened to smudge some glue on it, he couldn't go on—the model was ruined. If he had to make a correction on his math, rather than erase the wrong answer, he would redo the entire paper. Perfection became his shield against vulnerability.

Socially, it took a long time for Joe to feel comfortable. After all, he had been seen at his weakest moment. He gradually developed an acute sense of what any social exchange called for and managed to deliver it. He could be entertaining, silly, interesting, or serious— whatever the situation called for. He became a chameleon, a very good chameleon. As one teacher was fond of telling him, "You're a good little soldier." No doubt about it, Joe not only knew how to follow orders, but he also anticipated them.

In spite of all his newfound success, Joe's self-esteem never gained solid footing. In fact, the more success he had, the more convinced he

2

became that he had to work harder to maintain the whole charade. After all, he had a lot more to hide. Everyone thought he was so cool, the truth of just how uncool he was would certainly be a traumatic revelation. He was depleted, always looking over his shoulder, wondering what might go wrong, always fearing the "what-ifs."

It wasn't easy for Joe. I ought to know—I'm that Joe.

Finding the Answer

I lived these early years of my life fighting and clawing to keep in control. It never occurred to me to ask why I needed to be in control; it only mattered that I was. By the time I reached high school I was a veteran manipulator. I joined the football team so the kids would see me as a tough kind of guy—even though at 102 pounds, I was scared to death. I joined clubs, got elected to student council, and eventually was voted most popular. I had figured out how to be what people want.

No doubt about it, I controlled how people saw me. I never felt I had a choice; everyone had to like me. At the time, it made common sense—make people like you and they're not going to hurt you. I began to feel like one of those houses in a movie—a two-dimensional façade built to fool the audience. That's what I had become: an illusion, a house without insides.

By the time I was in college, I had had enough. My life had become tormented; I longed for relief. All the "what-iffing," the "shoulds" and the "have-tos"—I was truly driving myself crazy. I worried about everything—grades, dates, money, everything. Most of all, though, I worried about losing control—screwing up, getting into trouble, being in any situation where I would be floundering at fate's mercy.

I decided to major in psychology. Don't laugh; psychological torment makes for a good therapist. I once heard this phenomenon referred to as the theory of the wounded healer. I'll admit, that my initial motive was more self-serving than altruistic. I had become desperate enough, anxious enough, and depressed enough that studying psychology appeared to be the brake pedal I was looking for. Maybe, just maybe, there was a way out.

Self-Coaching: Opening Your Fist

My studies of psychology, as well as the years I spent in both group and individual training analysis, were helpful, but both of my hands still tightly clenched life's steering wheel. I still worried and occasionally beat myself up. I gave Freud a chance, then Jung, but nothing changed. I still worried. Once again I heard myself saying "I've had enough!" I was hungry for an insight.

I didn't have to wait long. One night not long after, on the way home from work, a very simple thought floated through my mind, "There's no reason to be so miserable!" Let me tell you, something very startling happened in that moment. It's hard to convey the magnitude of this seemingly innocent and altogether elementary revelation, but for me it started a revolution in my thinking. *Nothing* was stopping me from feeling better! *Nothing* was making me worry except the way I was thinking. The truth was that I *could* choose not to be miserable! Finally, I had the insight that I had longed for. I realized, for example, that even a stubborn mood, if challenged by a shift in thinking, quickly tumbles.

I had always considered feelings, moods, and thoughts to be infused with unconscious roots. Was it possible that feeling good could be as simple as letting go of negatives, of just opening your fist? One day, while having a root canal, I had an interesting revelation. While drawing hard on the nitrous oxide to avoid a little pain, I was trying to understand just why this torturous procedure was not generating more anxiety. What I discovered was that the nitrous oxide caused me to forget. A jolt of pain would get my attention, causing a rush of anxiety, but the very next nanosecond I was completely relaxed, separate from the previous painful memory. In contrast, my normal, non–nitrous-oxide thinking would have been the opposite experience:

Jolt of pain ◗ tense recoil ◗ anticipation of more pain ◗ worry ◗ anxiety

---

What if you could learn to let go of needless worry and anticipation of negatives, even without the aid of nitrous oxide or other drugs? What if you could actively change the channel from distressful rumination to more healthy, constructive thoughts? What would happen to your anxiety, your depression? They would vanish. Just as the amnesiac effects of nitrous oxide will pull you away from anxiety and worry about a dental procedure, Self-coaching will pull you away from the thoughts that bury you. What's more, once you learn how to direct your liberation from insecurity-driven thinking, you will have beaten anxiety and depression.

It Doesn't Have to Be Complicated

In my twenty-plus years of private practice, lecturing, and writing, I knew that all my insights were wasted unless I had an adequate means of delivering those insights to others. As far as I was concerned, traditional therapy had become too complicated and stale, but many patients still felt comforted with traditional therapy's all-knowing therapist. I often heard from patients, "You're the doctor, tell me, what's going on? What should I do?" My patients expected and sometimes demanded that I not disappoint them by being a mere mortal.

Bret, a retired high school teacher, came to me dissatisfied with the years he had spent in traditional analysis. He wasn't dissatisfied with Dr. So-and-so, only with the fact that he didn't seem to be getting any better. Bret held Dr. So-and-so in the highest esteem and felt somewhat ashamed to have been such a poor patient. Bret couldn't understand why he hadn't profited from his analysis. Had his doctor not been retiring, Bret was sure he would have eventually figured it all out.

At first, no matter what I said, all Bret wanted to know was how his problems tied in with his Oedipal complex and repressed libidinal instincts. He was convinced his problems would one day be explained away by some arcane theory. His problems weren't, after all, simple problems. His torment was worthy of only the masters, Freud or Jung (and of course Dr. So-and-so). The straightforward, problem-solving approach I was presenting seemed too simple.

I asked Bret whether he had ever heard of William of Occam, the English philosopher. Bret hadn't, but he was delighted that I was finally bringing in one of the masters. Sir William, I explained, postulated the law of parsimony, commonly referred to as Occam's razor. I told Bret, Occam's razor states that you should prefer explanations that are no more complicated than necessary for any given situation.

I wanted Bret to know that for both patient and therapist, complicating things is often nothing more than a case of vanity. The only reason Bret fought my explanation was because he wanted his problems to be anything but ordinary.

Bret isn't unique. You may have similar ideas about why you suffer and what you need to feel better. Perhaps Self-coaching doesn't sound as exciting as *psychoanalysis, analytical therapy,* or *transactional analysis.* In fact, Self-coaching doesn't sound much like a psychological approach at all. Chapter 1 will provide you with a more grounded and formal explanation, but for now, I'll just say this: Put aside your old ideas. I will prove to you that there's a simple, direct way to beat anxiety and depression. My way isn't the traditional path of traditional psychology. It's a more direct path, using simple and practical psychological tools combined with coaching and motivational strategies.

As Sir William of Occam might agree, if you want to be free from anxiety and depression, why not choose the simplest, least complicated way to do it? That way is Self-coaching. Furthermore, once you rid yourself of anxiety and depression, you can keep using Self-coaching to maintain healthy, spontaneous life. Once you get in shape—psychological shape—you'll never want to go back to your old ways again.

PART I

What Is Self-Coaching?

1

A New Self-Therapy

Why are you reading this book? Maybe you worry too much, or perhaps lately you've been struggling with panicky, out-of-control feelings that leave you anxious and frustrated. You may snap at others. Perhaps your sleep isn't what it used to be, and you always seem to be in a bad mood. Maybe you've become depressed; you feel tired, hopeless, or just plain defeated. Sometimes you want to give up.

You may feel confused, but one thing you're sure of. Life's not supposed to be this hard. You want answers—now! The last thing you want is to waste time.

So let's get started. The following self-quiz will show you how you can benefit from this book.

Is Self-Coaching for Me?

Identify each sentence as either mostly true or mostly false:

T   F   I often start my thoughts with "what if."

T   F   I usually see the glass as being half empty.

T   F   I worry too much.

T   F   I'm often fatigued.

T   F   I have difficulty concentrating.

T   F   I have trouble meeting deadlines.

T   F   I worry about my health.

T   F   I generally feel as if I'm on edge.

T   F   I'm often sad.

T   F   I have trouble falling asleep.

T   F   I have trouble trusting my perceptions (e.g., Did I lock that door? Did I talk too much?).

T   F   I have too much doubt.

T   F   I would say I'm insecure.

T   F   I wake up too early.

T   F   My worst time of the day is mornings.

T   F   I dread having things go wrong.

T   F   I'm too concerned with my looks.

T   F   I have to have things done my way.

T   F   I can't relax.

T   F   I'm never on time.

T   F   You can never be safe enough.

T   F   I exaggerate problems.

T   F   I experience panic.

T   F   I feel safest when I'm in bed.

T   F   I'm too sensitive.

T   F   I often wish I were someone else.

T   F   I fear growing older.

T   F   Life is one problem after another.

T   F   I don't have much hope of feeling better.

T   F   I constantly fidget.

T   F   I'm prone to road rage.

T   F   I have phobias (e.g., intense fear of closed spaces, bridges, open spaces, social encounters).

Total your "true" responses. A score of 12 or fewer suggests that you are a relatively well-adjusted individual. Self-coaching can teach you to shake off life's setbacks. You can expect your social and personal effectiveness to improve as you begin to become less tripped-up by emotional interference. Mostly, you can expect to enhance your already healthy personality with a more dynamic approach to life.

A score between 13 and 22 suggests that you have a moderate degree of personality erosion. Self-coaching can quickly and simply teach you to get beyond the self-limiting effects of anxiety or depression, realizing a more spontaneous, natural way of life.

If your score was above 22, you have significant difficulty with anxiety and/or depression. For you, Self-coaching needs to become a priority. With patience and practice, you can learn to live your life symptom free.

As beleaguered as you are, I don't expect you to be convinced easily. For now, just recognize that regardless of how anxious or depressed you are, something in you is managing to read these words. That something, the part of you that hasn't quit, that healthy part of your personality that's still willing to try to solve the riddle that has become your life—that's the healthy person in you that Self-coaching wants to reach.

Self-Coaching, the Program

It took me twenty-three years of clinical work to write this book. That's not because I'm particularly slow or lazy (far from it), but because it takes a long time, a really long time, to see through the deceptive mist that shrouds anxiety and depression. What's interesting, once you understand the nature of faulty perceptions, is that anxiety and depression actually begin to make sense. As irrational as your particular symptoms may feel, when you learn the punch line, the riddle becomes apparent. You'll see. These insights were the catalyst for a new form of therapy I developed to teach patients what they could do to make themselves better. (I dislike the term "patient," but I like "client" even less, so I'll use "patient" throughout the book.) I consider this method,

11

which I call Self-coaching (Self, with a capital S), my most significant accomplishment.

Symptoms of anxiety and depression are parts of normal day-to-day living. Getting uptight if you're late for an appointment or feeling upset over an argument with a friend are inescapable parts of life. The problems occur when your anxiety and depression progress to a point beyond your immediate life circumstances, so that these feelings float for days, weeks, or months.

As a psychologist, the talent I value most is my intuition. Intuition is the ability, as Carl Gustav Jung once said, to see around corners. In contrast to the intellect, intuition is much less deliberate—it just happens. When it comes to psychology, strong intuitions are about as important as a telescope is to an astronomer. Just as the surface of the moon turns into pockmarked craters under a telescope's magnification, intuition can begin to reveal the hidden aspects of anxiety or depression.

Once I had magnified my view of anxiety and depression, I found myself reacting to my patients differently. Instead of treating them in a traditionally passive way, I responded to them in an active, rather spirited way. This wasn't a conscious or deliberate strategy. I just allowed my intuition to guide me. With depressed patients, for example, I sensed that they were missing a vital energy necessary to combat their difficulties. Using my energy, my optimism, and my enthusiasm, I would model the attitude necessary to conquer the negativity, despair, and inertia. Essentially, I was reflecting what I perceived to be lacking in my patients.

With anxiety patients, I followed my intuition, too. For these patients I became the voice of encouragement and conviction. I pushed hard for courage and risk taking against life's worries and fears. Anxiety-prone people need to overcome self-doubt while building trust in themselves.

Both anxiety and depression are weeds that grow from the fertile soil of insecurity. So I became a role model of a can-do attitude. Without inner confidence, everything becomes a struggle.

I realized that my new approach was a dramatic departure from the more traditional therapeutic methods I usually employed, yet I couldn't seem to put my finger on exactly what it was that I was doing. One day, while working with a young man who had been struggling with anxiety and panic attacks, I heard myself telling him, "You keep looking to me to make your anxiety go away. I can't do that for you. Think of me more as your coach than your psychologist." There it was. I was *coaching!*—not analyzing, not passively listening, not reflecting. I was coaching strength, confidence, and a sense of empowerment. My patient quickly and easily related to this simple concept. Rather than seeing me as parent-authority-healer, he clearly understood my new, revitalized role—I was coaching *his* efforts, *his* determination, and most importantly *his* need to overcome anxiety and depression.

The ease with which my patient and I progressed convinced me that approaching problems as a coach rather than a therapist could have far-reaching implications. By coaching the healing attitude that was missing in my patients, and using a fail-safe technique I call Self-talk, they were able to stop anxiety and depression where it began, in the thoughts that preceded and fertilized these conditions. *Self-talk* is a method of replacing faulty, destructive thinking with healthy, liberated thinking. This method was first introduced in my book *Healing Your Habits,* where I called it "Directed Imagination."

It doesn't matter whether you're exercising to lose a few pounds, working to improve fitness through power walking, or preparing as a serious athlete for a big race, effective training always involves following a program of repetition and progressive effort. Psychological training is no different—requiring repetition and progressive effort. Self-talk will become the core of your training program, demanding a similar commitment—no magic, no gifts, no abracadabra insights, just plain old hard work—hard work that pays off.

As I continued to develop my program, I found that the concept of training was particularly appealing to my highly motivated anxiety-prone patients. They usually struggle with traditional therapy's passive approach, especially when they aren't seeing results. A well-thought-out training program was clearly something they could sink their teeth into.

Depressed people face a different challenge. Depression makes it hard to muster the energy to do anything. How could I motivate depressed patients to want to train? Depression is like driving a car with one foot on the gas (i.e., healthy desires) and one foot on the brake (i.e., negative distortions)—you're forever feeling stuck, frustrated, and discouraged. I knew that if my method was going to be successful, the training program had to offer release from the braking effects of depression—and that's exactly what happened. By replacing negative thoughts with more objective, reality-based thinking, Self-talk, in combination with a coached attitude of optimism, made the difference. Once patients got a taste of being unstuck, the necessary motivation for continued training was no longer a problem.

This training approach to therapy also explains why results are contingent not on therapeutic insights and aha! experiences, but on consistent, daily workouts using my Self-talk approach. If you walked into a gym expecting that ten minutes on the treadmill would take two inches off your waist, no doubt you'd be very discouraged. In contrast, what if you approached the treadmill with a more realistic attitude, combined with a genuine desire to begin training? First off, you'd realize that one treadmill session is just that, one treadmill session. Only after repeated training sessions over time would you begin to reap the accumulated benefits of your efforts—but the benefits would come. Whether in the gym or in therapy, a training approach both requires and teaches three essential things:

1. Patience
2. Realistic understanding of the dynamics of change
3. Self-reliance

This coaching/training program, using my Self-talk technique for breaking destructive thought patterns, became the heart and soul of the book you hold in your hands—with, of course, one major modification. Rather than having me be your coach, you become your own coach, directing your own liberation. Understand that the potential for healing, real healing, always resides within you. Remember, the best psychologist in the world can't make you better. No one can. Only you can, and Self-coaching will teach you how.

Becoming a Self-Coach

Noticing how quickly and easily my patients responded to coaching, I wondered how effective this method would be in a self-help format. Could what I was doing for my patients be presented in a book? Had it not been for a cousin who asked me what she could do for her anxiety, I might not have pursued this possibility. I discussed my technique of Self-talk with her and gave her a number of the handouts I had prepared for my patients, describing a few simple strategies and exercises. When she called me a few months later reporting that her anxiety was gone, I was more convinced than ever that coaching could, in fact, make the transition to Self-coaching. It didn't take me long to make my final decision to start writing, but what finally convinced me wasn't my cousin's success.

I Think I Can, I Thought I Could

Somewhere back in my late thirties I had an inexplicable urge to run the New York City Marathon. I couldn't tell you why I wanted to run it. Maybe I did because it just sounded so impossible—26 miles! Perhaps I just wanted to know whether I had it in me. Whatever the reason, I decided to give it a shot. I didn't give my training much thought. After all, I had been a recreational, couple-of-miles-a-day jogger for years, what could be the problem? You just run longer and longer distances. Right?

Fast forward six months.

The first couple of hours of the marathon were terrific. I was high-fiving the kids along Brooklyn's Fourth Avenue, enjoying the crowd, my adrenalin, and the race. Why hadn't I done this before? By the third hour however, more than halfway through the race and chugging through Queens, my high-fiving long since abandoned, I began to notice a deepening fatigue. Four hours into the race, the Bronx began to fade as all my attention became focused on the squish, squish of blisters. The fatigue that began ten miles earlier had become all consuming by the fifth hour as I entered Central Park. My mind was taken over by a survival instinct that sought only to stop the pain and cramping. Somehow, I hung on and finished, five hours and twenty minutes after I had started. I shuffled through the chutes at the end of the race, trying not to think about the preceding three hours of my life.

After recovering for a few months (months in which I vowed never, ever to entertain the notion of running another race), I began talking to a friend who had run the same marathon at a much more respectable pace. He couldn't believe that I did all my training on the track. "What, no hill work? No speed work?" I realized how terribly flawed my training had been. I also realized that some things in life aren't apparent—at least not at first.

More months passed. I came across a great book written by two former coaches and marathoners *The Competitive Runner's Handbook.* The book explained and analyzed elements of training in a comprehensive program. In spite of my resolve never to think about another marathon, I found myself devouring the book. I began to understand why my legs had become stiff, why I had cramped, why I had fallen apart the last half of the race, and even why my feet had blistered. These problems, I learned, could all be eliminated by proper training. Given the proper program to follow, it should be possible to overcome the breakdowns that I had experienced. What had been a humiliating and chaotic experience could actually be deciphered, anticipated, prepared for, and—most importantly—conquered. I liked that. I was eager to put my self-coaching to the test.

To date, I've run three marathons, and I'm currently training for my fourth. My times have dropped, not by minutes, but by hours. If I say so myself, I've learned a lot about self-coaching. My self-coached marathon experiences proved invaluable as I pondered the possibility of putting my experience coaching patients into a Self-coached format.

Whether you're anxious or depressed, Self-coaching can teach you how to do what's necessary to eliminate your problems. Our minds, as well as our bodies, deteriorate if we allow ourselves to follow destructive patterns. That's what anxiety and depression are. They are patterned, negative, self-defeating habits. Self-coaching teaches you two things: (1) how to break the destructive patterns that distort your thinking and leave you vulnerable to depression and anxiety; and (2) how to replace these thoughts with a healthy, adaptive way of living.

Self-Reliance

There are obvious advantages to having a personal coach (a.k.a., therapist), but keep in mind the distinct advantage of Self-coaching: From the start, you have only yourself to rely on; you either work hard or you don't; you either improve or you don't—and this is as it should be. Trust me on this: With anxiety and depression, it is absolutely critical to believe in your own resources to heal yourself. The sooner you take full responsibility for your program of healing, the sooner you take back your life. Anyone who insists on looking for a guru, a shrink, a pill, or even a book to do their work will ultimately fail, because no one but you can ever topple your destructive habits. When you look for someone to heal you, to take care of you, to make you better, then, like a child, you remain without the full potential power of your maturity. It is exactly this power of personal maturity that Self-coaching promotes.

At first, relying on yourself for what you need may seem like a daunting prescription—especially if you're depressed. I understand this concern clearly and have made every attempt to anticipate your inertia. Ever try to push a car that's stalled? You put your back into it, straining every muscle, pushing until finally you begin to feel a slight movement. Then a bit more, a bit faster, a bit easier. You've been straining against inertia. Objects at rest—and people, and anxiety, and depression—resist movement. Your initial efforts will be the most difficult, but with proper encouragement, motivation, and direction, inertia can, and will, yield to momentum. Momentum is that glorious feeling of movement—movement that becomes easier and easier once you get started.

❖ ❖ ❖

TRAINING SUGGESTION

Inner Experience–Outer Experience: Learning to Get Out of Your Head

Periodically throughout the day, begin to listen to your "inner talk." Whatever your thoughts are, for now, don't judge or criticize, just be aware of your thinking.

Once you've followed your thinking for a few moments, see whether you can switch from following these thoughts to participating in your world. This could be any activity: listening to music, looking at a flower, or twiddling your thumbs. Whatever you try, do it as completely as you can. If, for example, you decide to wash a dish, wash it with complete attention. Feel the soapy water, the squeak of the dish as you scour it, the dragging of your towel against the damp plate as you dry it. Rather than thinking about what you are doing, try to just feel it. Try to get out of your head and into your experience.

This exercise is an important prelude to eventual ability of learning to let go of destructive thinking.

❖ ❖ ❖

2

The Seven Principles of Self-Coaching Healing

The heart and soul of Self-coached healing can be condensed into seven basic principles. Although you've already had an overview of these ideas in Chapter 1, now, as your training gets underway, you will consolidate them into specific principles to support all your training efforts. With practical, daily use, these truths will become more apparent. For now, in preparation for the training that's ahead, it's important that you gain a feel for these principles. I recommend that you write these seven principles down on a slip of paper and keep them in your wallet or purse. Occasionally, just read through the list, allowing yourself to absorb them and reflect on them. As soon as you have a casual, working awareness of them, you're ready to begin Part II—the problems Self-coaching can heal.

Principle 1: Everyone Has a Legacy of Insecurity, the Insecure Child

Growing up human means growing up with some degree of insecurity. It's inevitable. Children are ill equipped to cope with—much less make sense of—early traumas, conflicts, misunderstandings, or loss. When children feel out of control and vulnerable, they resort to any strategy that offers relief: tantrums, whining, sulking—whatever works. These are primitive tactics designed to reduce vulnerability by gaining more control.

Over time, your strategies as a child become habits, and your personality is shaped accordingly. These habits make your here-and-now thinking—when threatened—become primitive and coarse, reminiscent of your earliest struggles. With practice, you can begin to be attuned to these simple-minded, tormented reactions to life. I call the "voice" in you that spews fear and panic the Insecure Child. Differentiating your Insecure Child's voice from your healthy thinking is the first step to a more mature, liberated, healthy life.

Chapter 3 will introduce you to a technique called Self-talk, which will teach you how to break the habit of listening to the dictates of your Insecure Child.

Principle 2: Thoughts Precede Feelings, Anxieties, and Depressions

Most people, when it comes to feeling anxious or depressed, see themselves as victims: "She called me a jerk, so of course I'm depressed. Wouldn't you be?" or "See, now you got me upset. Are you satisfied?" or "How could you stay out so late? I was worried sick." Victims feel they have no choice; someone or something is always "making" them worry, panic, get upset, or unhappy. "How can I stop worrying? With my crazy job, I have no choice!"

Sometimes, when a mood or anxiety seems to appear without rhyme or reason, you feel like a victim of fate: "I wasn't doing anything, I was just driving to work and I got this panic attack." When feeling like a victim, it never occurs to you that you can do anything about how you feel.

Once you realize that thoughts precede feelings, you can understand that you're not powerless. There is something you can do. You can change how you think and simultaneously discover that you're beginning to feel better. Self-coaching can teach you how to take responsibility for your thoughts and change that victim attitude—especially the thoughts produced by your Insecure Child. If left unchallenged, your Insecure Child will ruin your life. Learning to challenge the primitive thoughts of your Insecure Child is how you'll reclaim your life.

Principle 3: Anxiety and Depression Are Misguided Attempts to Control Life

When insecurity leaves you feeling vulnerable and helpless, anxiety and depression are nothing more than misguided attempts to regain control. Anxiety does this through an expenditure of energy (worry, panic, rumination, "what-iffing," etc.), depression by a withdrawal of energy (isolation and withdrawal, fatigue, avoidance, not caring, etc.). Unfortunately, rather than helping, anxiety and depression become part of the problem, a big part.

It may seem strange to view anxiety and depression as coping strategies trying to protect you from perceived harm. Rather than coping strategies, you can view them as "controlling strategies." Anxiety mobilizes all your anticipatory resources trying to brace (i.e., control) you for a collision. Depression, on the other hand, controls through disengagement from what you perceive as a threat. Whether you wind up depressed or anxious really isn't important—either way, you lose. Either way, you're being duped by your Insecure Child.

Principle 4: Control Is an Illusion, Not an Answer

Insecurity creates a feeling of vulnerability. When you feel vulnerable, wanting to be in control seems like a natural, constructive desire. It may start out as a constructive desire, but a controlled life always invites anxiety and depression. Insecurity is greedy: The more control you have, the more you seek. Nothing ever makes you feel secure enough. You're doomed to chase control's carrot. As you grow desperate and pursue your "carrots" with increased agitation, you can't help but notice that depression and anxiety are becoming permanent fixtures in your life.

The truth is that life cannot be controlled. What confuses most is the fact that control does give temporary relief. If you've managed to manipulate or cajole life into appearing tamed and controlled, you do feel relief—for the moment. When you're desperate, this temporary relief is spelled with a capital "R." If you're honest, however, you know that control is only and always an illusion. Like the eye of a hurricane, it's a false sense of calm before the remainder of the storm.

If controlling life is an impossibility—nothing more than a dangling carrot—then what's the answer? The answer is to resurrect a feeling of self-trust and confidence so that instead of controlling life, we are courageous enough just to live it.

Principle 5: Insecurity Is a Habit, and Any Habit Can Be Broken

You weren't born insecure; you learned it. Because children are ill equipped to adequately cope with early traumas, conflicts, misunderstandings, or loss, some amount of insecurity is inescapable. We learn self-doubt and self-distrust, and if these destructive attitudes are reinforced, they become habits. Habits are difficult to break because, like any muscle, given enough exercise, they grow in strength.

Self-coaching will give you the strength, technique, and willpower to break your habits of insecurity. Start convincing yourself now that what you learned can be unlearned. No question about it—any habit can be broken. All that's needed is a plan, a little patience, and a Self-coached determination.

Principle 6: Healthy Thinking Is a Choice

You may not realize it (not yet), but you have a choice not to be hammered by anxiety or depression. Perhaps you can't control thoughts from popping into your mind, but you don't have to follow them around like an obedient puppy. If, for example, you have the thought, "I can't do it; I'm going to fail," you're obviously being challenged by your Insecure Child. Here is where you have the choice. Do you continue with this thought, "What if I fail? What will I do? This is terrible . . . ," or do you stop the Insecure Child in her or his tracks? If you realize you have a choice, then you can insist, "This is my Insecure Child talking, and I refuse to listen. I *choose* not to be bullied by these thoughts." Self-talk will make it crystal clear how you build the necessary muscle to choose healthy thinking.

Principle 7: A Good Coach Is a Good Motivator

The best coach in the world must also be a good motivator. Technique, skill, and conditioning will get you so far, but without proper motivation, your results will be disappointing. Nowhere is this more important than in Self-coached healing. If you're suffering from anxiety or depression, then your Insecure Child has all the muscle (i.e., habit strength). This puts your emotional health at a grave disadvantage. Why? Because your Child has been constantly undermining your attempts to feel better. In order to turn the tide—building healthy muscle/habit to resist the distortions of insecurity—you must keep yourself pumped up for the challenge.

You're going to learn to disregard your Insecure Child's resistance, using Self-coaching tools to bring out the best in yourself. Fighting the good fight requires two things: the right attitude and proper motivation. Attitude is simply having the right, positive frame of mind, and motivation is infusing this can-do attitude with energy. Motivation is what allows you to sustain your efforts and go the distance. Start shifting that attitude right now. Begin with some positive affirmations—"I'm going to beat this."

✤ ✤ ✤

TRAINING SUGGESTION

Because anxiety and depression have a tendency to confuse and disorient you, be sure to write down these seven principles on a slip of paper.

You might find it helpful in moments of stress or struggle to read through the list. These principles will become your mantra for success. Read and repeat them to yourself often.

✤ ✤ ✤

PART II

The Problems Self-Coaching Can Heal

3

Getting to the Root
of Your Problem

Most people think of anxiety and depression as two totally separate, unrelated problems. They're not. Although anxieties and depression are very dissimilar experiences, they are in fact closely related. Once you see this relationship, you will understand your problems more fully.

Anxiety can exist alone, as can depression. At other times, anxiety can lead to depression, or a depression can be mixed with anxiety components. I have had patients who could be frantically anxious one moment, and then shut down with depression the next. Worry, self-doubt, rumination, insecurity, fear, apathy, and fatigue. The question remained, How could these very different experiences have so much in common? Rather than attempting to describe these apparent dissimilarities, I will first illustrate it. Take a look at the figure on page 28. What do you see? A vase or two faces? If you saw a vase, go back and see whether you can find the two faces. If you saw two faces, go back and find the vase.

This illustration highlights what psychologists call figure and ground. What catches your eye first, what you see in the foreground, is called the figure. The background is the field on which *your* figure (whether the vase or the faces) rests. If you saw the vase first, you probably didn't see the two faces in the background. Now go back and look again. Try seeing the vase, then switch to seeing the two faces. Notice how whatever you're seeing seems to come forward and what you're not seeing seems to recede.

If you're anxious, then anxiety is in your foreground. It's what you see. Although you may not suspect that depression can be a background contributor to your difficulties, it can still be part of the overall, less than conscious, picture. On the other hand, if depression is in your foreground, suspect anxiety lying behind it. Why? Because both anxiety and depression come from the same underlying source of insecurity. They're two different strategies that attempt to protect you from harm. Anxiety does this through an expenditure of energy, depression by a withdrawal of energy.

Ken, a forty-year-old lawyer, experienced an anxiety-depression cocktail just a few days after he landed a high-profile court case. After weeks of intense suffering, Ken was desperate to know what was going on. He'd been waking up each morning feeling shaky and nervous. "My skin felt like it was crawling. I had this terrible feeling of apprehension and panic. The panic was always followed by this 'down' feeling. I mean really down! I began staying home, going back to bed. I only wanted to be left alone."

Ken had been waiting all his professional life for this kind of break. Now, he would finally be in the spotlight. But some old insecurities began to percolate, and what would have been the challenge of a lifetime turned out to be his undoing. It began with crippling doubts about his abilities and quickly escalated into a hornet's nest of panicky "what-ifs." His anxiety and depression were last-ditch efforts to control a situation that Ken's insecurity had labeled hazardous.

It may seem odd that anxiety and depression are actually attempts to attain control, but Ken's reaction clearly supports this notion. If he couldn't leave his house, then he would have to resign from the case (which he did, unfortunately)—and once he was off the case, there was no longer any danger of losing control. Because Ken did resign from the case, thereby eliminating any chance of public embarrassment (i.e., loss of control), we could say that his anxiety and depression did, in fact, protect him from his fears. The end of the case was not the end of his anxiety, however. In fact, he became more depressed, and he came to me for therapy.

Self-Coaching Reflection
If you allow insecurity to steer your life, then
don't expect to have a life.

Whether you suffer from anxiety, depression, or symptoms of both, you—like Ken—are simply trying to survive what you perceive as a threat to your security. Now, however, you don't need to rely on primitive, ineffective, destructive strategies any longer. Self-coaching will not teach you to control your problems; it will teach you to live without them.

Misguided Helpers

How you see the world, how you interpret your experiences, and even your philosophy of life are all the result of your unique background. Just as the path of a mountain stream reflects the land it traverses—a boulder, a rise, a stand of trees—your background experiences, positive and negative, have shaped, bent, and ultimately decided the course of your psychological life. A child who experiences rejection, trauma, family discord, neglect, or divorce may develop an anxious or depressed view of life. For this child, there is never enough safety. In contrast, a child brought up with only minor mishap in the loving embrace of family and friends may develop a gregarious appetite for stimulation and adventure. For this secure child, ain't no mountain high enough—same world, different interpretations.

Early wounds, whether physical (accidents, illnesses, hospitalizations, etc.) or psychological (rejections, frustrations, broken homes, neglectful or abusive parenting, etc.), are unavoidable. From these wounds, insecurity sends its roots deep into your psyche, setting the stage for destructive patterns of thinking and perceiving. Over time, these insecure thoughts can whittle away at your psychological stamina, leaving you feeling out of control and susceptible to emotional problems. Anxiety and depression are natural—albeit misguided—attempts to handle this perceived loss of control.

As far as defenses go, anxiety and depression may be ugly, but when you're caught off balance, without any suitable alternative, well, any port in a storm. If you suffer from anxiety or depression, you've run out of constructive alternatives—until now—because Self-coaching *is* the alternative!

Self-Coaching Reflection
Life doesn't create anxiety or depression; you do.

Stress: It's All in the Eyes of the Beholder

Touch a hot stove, and you reflexively recoil in pain. Similarly, anxiety and depression seem more like simple reflex reactions to stress than defenses designed to ward off insecurity. If life presents you with a traumatic experience, isn't "life," like that hot stove, creating your anxiety and depression? Isn't a trauma just as traumatic for everyone? Sometimes, but not always. Most people would find an IRS (Internal Revenue Service) audit traumatic, but not everyone reacts the same way.

The same is true of a car accident or the loss of a job. Even though you may have been quick to react reflexively in the past, Self-coaching will teach you that life isn't a hot stove, and getting caught up in destructive emotions isn't automatic. Before you go around feeling victimized by anxiety and depression, learn an important lesson from Tom's story:

> Tom, a middle-aged man who had lost a hand in an industrial accident only months before, came to therapy for marital advice. He and I had had a few sessions dealing with some frustrations he felt with his wife. When Tom made no mention of his accident, I felt he might be in denial, trying to avoid facing his tragedy. I asked him how he felt about his loss and he told me, "It doesn't bother me, I've got another one." As it turns out, he wasn't kidding! Months later, therapy confirmed that the loss of his hand had little to do with his problems. As you may suspect, when it comes to such a traumatic loss of control, Tom is truly the exception to the rule. In contrast to Tom was a patient who became depressed over the loss of a *molar*.

Tom is living proof that what constitutes a trauma has more to do with what you tell (or don't tell) yourself about what happens than what actually happens. Granted, Tom is an extreme example, and most people would be profoundly traumatized by the loss of a hand, but keep in mind that it's not *what happens* in life that traumatizes you; it's *how you interpret* what happens. No one but you decides what's good or bad, friend or foe, dangerous or safe, difficult or devastating.

Depression and Anxiety Are Choices

Once established, insecurity dictates not only how you see the world, but also how you see yourself. In time, you may start believing that you're a nervous person—or perhaps a moody person, or irritable, or inadequate. Make no mistake, anxiety and depression, whether mild or severe, will always diminish the quality of your life. Many people just shrug their shoulders, accepting their plight as inevitable, "Nothing ever turns out right for me, so why bother?" they say. Others may frantically look for some control over their lives, "If I had that job (car, promotion, boyfriend, degree, house, etc.), then I'd feel better." Some do nothing, as they passively try to adjust, but who adjusts well to a life of frustration and torment? Maybe you've come to recognize that you're living only half an existence, but what choice do you have?

The operative word here is *choice.*

Chances are, you never realized that you have a choice not to be depressed or anxious. Just as a dog constantly feels its desires frustrated by the tug of a leash, your thinking has frustrated you into accepting a lifestyle of distress. Self-coaching will teach you that you have a choice. Regardless of how long you've been besieged by your habits of insecurity, once you learn to exchange insecure, sloppy thinking for more mature, responsible thinking, your anxiety and depression will no longer be able to contaminate your life.

"Me, think differently!" Sound impossible? That's how my daughter felt about running the mile on her eighth-grade track team. The first few times she and I went out for a jog, she developed a side stitch and had to walk. Discouraged, she questioned whether she could ever race a mile. I tried to reassure her, discussing the importance of proper training and letting her know that it was only natural for her body to resist being pushed to such extremes of exhaustion. In order to run that mile, she would have to train her body to do something that—at first—felt very unnatural.

She began training. We analyzed her efforts carefully, and within a couple of weeks, she was running a nice, easy-paced mile. In order to develop more respectable times, she needed to build both endurance and speed, two more aspects to be addressed in her training. Using my own experience from marathon running, we put together a program adding longer workouts, some hill work, and some speed work. Through training, we began shaping her body into handling what, only a few weeks earlier, seemed impossible. Her first track meet is coming up. She's nervous, but she's ready—and she's well trained.

Self-coaching's training program will provide the winning formula for you, too. Sure, it's going to feel unnatural to do things differently. "What, you want me to be more trusting? I've always been suspicious!" Nonetheless, your persona, your image, what you're identified with is nothing more than habit—a habit that reflects the sum total of your entire life experience. Because your persona was learned, then according to Self-coaching, it can be challenged, unlearned, and replaced with more healthy alternatives.

Neurotic self-perceptions are shaped during your early, formative years. That's why your anxiety or depression often reflect such primitive and childish characteristics.

Take a look at Eric's fears:

> I'm driving myself crazy! All I do is worry. If someone has a cold, I'm afraid I'm going to catch it. If I hear about a celebrity getting cancer, I start feeling anxious. I worry about my boss criticizing my work. I don't want to get yelled at. I feel so vulnerable, so scared. I just want to be safe. It seems like the world is a big ugly place and I'm no match for it. I feel I'm going to get chewed up and spit out. I'm such a baby. If my wife heard me talking she'd die. I hide my fears from her. She thinks I'm just this normal guy. The truth is I'm anything but normal!
>
> When I was young I had this serious kidney disease and had to stay home from school for my whole third grade. After my illness, my mother continued to worry about me. She made damn sure no one was going to hurt me. You should have seen her go after my Little League coach when he yelled at me for flubbing a play. Once, when a bully at school said he was going to beat me up, she demanded—and got—a written apology from the boy and from his parents! I'll admit, I was overprotected, but I never had to worry either. I know it's sick, but I long for that safety. I didn't have a care in the world; it was great.

Sometimes, when things get really upsetting and I find myself getting into a panic—I've never told anyone about this—I find myself sucking my thumb! I feel really sad admitting this; I feel like crying right now. It just seems like I was never meant to grow up.

Eric is what we call a Puer Aeternus, a grown man who never grew up.

Look at your own anxiety and depressive expressions. How childish are some of your reactions? They're childish because they were designed by a child—you, way back when. Although you've grown and changed in many ways, when it comes to your habits of insecurity, nothing's changed. They're just as primitive and distorted today as they were years ago. You've become so used to living with your outdated insecurities, you never think to challenge or update them. You live your life diminished by insecurity because it's never been any other way. It actually feels natural being neurotic. It may feel natural, but not pleasant.

Considering that habits of control and insecurity are deeply ingrained, and it's a fact that habits aren't easy to break, then what's the prognosis for change? The prognosis is *excellent!* Why? Because of a secret weapon at your disposal—truth! It's really quite simple. Anxiety and depression are based not on truth but on false and distorted perceptions—perceptions such as "I'm unlovable," "I'll never succeed," or "I'm a loser." The truth, the real truth, however, will slay the dragon of insecurity. You may feel like a loser, for example, but that's the child's view of reality—not the mature view, and certainly not the truth!

Learning the truth about your life and living your truth is a major goal of Self-coached training. It may seem unnatural at first, but trust me, living according to your truth will quickly replace your old, worn-out destructive habits and perceptions. You'll find that living effectively in the present is a completely natural and comfortable experience. Skeptical? I assure you that all the patients I've ever worked with, once they move from childish thinking to mature living, have never wished to go back to their old habits.

Ruling Out Physical Causes

The next two chapters discuss anxiety and depression in detail, but before moving on to this discussion, there's one caution I should mention. Although the majority of these problems are psychological in origin, some depressions and anxieties can be triggered by physical problems. These include hyper- and hypothyroidism, hypoglycemia, endocrine disorders, cardiovascular conditions, respiratory conditions, metabolic conditions, neurological conditions, viral infections, fatigue, reactions to medication, and the abuse of alcohol, caffeine, and other drugs.

Before beginning any self-help program, you should first rule out the possibility that your anxiety or depression may have a physical/ biological basis. One simple rule of thumb is to see whether your symptoms are accompanied by distorted, negative thinking, recent trauma, loss, or a chronic stressor. If not, the possibility exists that your problem may have a physical origin, and you should consult a physician. If you have any doubt, by all means, arrange to have a thorough physical.

❖ ❖ ❖

TRAINING SUGGESTION

Before learning about anxiety and depression in the next two chapters, take a few minutes to go through some of your more disturbing behaviors or feelings. Decide whether your struggles are rooted in anxiety, depression, or a combination of the two. As a simple guideline, remember that anxiety is a defense of excessive psychic energy, and depression is a defense based on the withdrawal of energy. You may want to make a chart like the example on page 36. After reading the next two chapters, see how accurate your intuitive perceptions were.

Describe troublesome behavior or thinking	Depression	Anxiety	Anxiety & Depression
1. I found myself sulking all day. Why did she treat me that way?	☑	☐	☐
2. I couldn't get to sleep last night. Maybe he really doesn't love me. What will I do? I'm such a loser.	☐	☐	☑
3. I can't believe I actually said that to him! What's wrong with me? What if he thinks I was serious? What if he's told everyone . . . ?	☐	☑	☐

❖ ❖ ❖

❖ ❖ ❖

TRAINING SUGGESTION

Follow Up

After filling in your chart, take a second to look at your troublesome behaviors. See whether you can notice any primitive childish tendencies. This recognition will eventually be very important to your Self-coaching program.

❖ ❖ ❖

4

Depression

Mention that you feel depressed, and anyone will know what you're talking about. Feeling down in the dumps, miserable, negative, overwhelmed, or worthless—these feelings are all symptoms of what we commonly refer to as being depressed. Certainly, we've all shared these symptoms from time to time. That's because getting depressed is a normal, inescapable part of being human. Getting depressed is not the same as clinical depression.

Traditionally, *clinical depression* refers to any depression that meets specific, clinical criteria described in the *Diagnostic and Statistical Manual* published by the American Psychiatric Association. Far from being something imagined or "all in your head," clinical depression is a whole-body problem, with both biochemical and emotional underpinnings. With symptoms such as sadness, crying, fatigue, appetite disturbances, decreased sexual desire, worry, fear, concentration difficulties, and feelings of hopelessness, it's obvious that clinical depression can be a serious problem if left untreated. Yet, as devastating as clinical depression can be, it's often left untreated.

The reason is that for some, "depression" is a shameful label. They feel embarrassed and humiliated because they feel they can't cope or because they're just too weak. They say, "I should be able to handle this," or, "There's no reason for me to be depressed. If I wait long enough, I'll just snap out of it." Yet for others, it's just a matter of ignorance, as they perceive their depression to be an inevitable part of life.

37

Take a look at Peggy, a thirty-four-year-old, stay-at-home mother of three who was depressed. Because her functioning was adequate, she didn't realize she needed help:

> I've been feeling kind of blah for a long time. At first I thought it was the routine—getting up, getting the kids off to school, cleaning, shopping, cooking, homework. Every day, never a break. Lately I've been more fatigued and just feeling down. I never gave it much thought. I just felt that I had no choice. I saw my life as a burden and, well . . . that's life! It's funny, but that old song by Peggy Lee, "Is That All There Is?" keeps popping up in my head. Guess it's not that funny.
>
> Lately I've had a few crying episodes. They come from out of the blue. I'll just find myself crying. I put on a show for the kids and my husband, but lately it's become more difficult—especially with my husband. I have absolutely no interest in sex. The things I used to enjoy—reading, going out to dinner, having friends over—are all too much of an effort. I just want to be left alone. But that's impossible. I'm beginning to feel more and more detached. The one thing that scares me most is that my kids don't bring any joy to my life. That kills me!

Peggy is obviously depressed—right? Well, it wasn't obvious to her. It took her more than six months of suffering to realize it. Another common reason that depression is often overlooked is because we have a tendency to adapt to our declining mood—our habit of depression. It begins to feel natural—crummy, but natural. Like sunglasses, after you have them on a while, the darkened view becomes natural. At first, Peggy thought she was just one of those ineffective people. She, unlike other mothers, was too weak to handle the demands of motherhood. This distorted shameful self-perception was enough to solidify her already formidable insecurity and push her into clinical depression.

How Depressed Am I?

When Peggy started counseling, her functioning had deteriorated substantially. Because of the pressing responsibilities she felt at home, she was eager to explore the possibility of antidepressant medication. Within a month of starting medication, Peggy began to feel more tolerant and optimistic. Her functioning improved significantly, as did her overall effectiveness.

Feeling less pressured, Peggy was able to use counseling to finally stop the erosion caused by her insecurity. She learned that she had allowed herself to become a victim of circumstances. Overwhelmed, out of control, and too insecure to explore her needs, Peggy had capitulated. She also learned that once you surrender, it's almost impossible to avoid feeling depressed. She felt hopelessly trapped, never realizing she had choices. Her first step toward health was the realization that she was, in fact, depressed and in need of help. Self-coaching, along with the relief she experienced from medication, quickly allowed Peggy to start making healthy choices.

Like Peggy, you need to accurately evaluate how depressed you feel. If your functioning is deteriorating and you find your thoughts growing more dark and overwhelmed, you should explore the possibility of medication. If, on the other hand, you find yourself holding your own and managing your life in spite of a mild, or even moderate depression (as long as you're managing), then by all means, a self-managed program may be all you need to begin to turn the tide of your malaise.

Because depression can be a serious, life-threatening condition, let's begin with the following self-quiz to assess whether you might be struggling with clinical depression. Take a look at the following checklist. In the boxes on the left, check any symptom that you've experienced for more than two weeks.

☐ I feel depressed, sad, and/or irritated most of the day, nearly every day.

☐ Things that once gave me pleasure don't interest me any longer.

☐ I've noticed a decrease or increase in my appetite, with a change in my weight.

☐ I sleep either too much or too little.

☐ I'm fatigued and drained all the time.

☐ I feel worthless or have intense guilt most of the time.

☐ I can't concentrate like I used to, and I find it difficult to make decisions.

☐ I feel restless, agitated, or slowed down physically.

☐ I think of death often. I've thought of or tried to commit suicide.

If you've experienced four or fewer of the preceding symptoms, you may be dealing with a mild depression (assuming you didn't check the last box and aren't suicidal). Keep in mind, however, that even a mild depression needs your attention. A dysthymic disorder, for example, is one particularly troublesome form of low-grade depression that can last for years, with chronic feelings of sadness and hopelessness. Another, rather elusive form of mild depression, called atypical depression, can be difficult to evaluate because you may feel fine one day and down the next. Self-coaching alone or Self-coaching along with counseling can make a real difference in these struggles. In some cases, antidepressant medication may also be helpful. If you choose a Self-coaching approach, retake this quiz periodically to make sure your depression is, in fact, subsiding.

If you checked five or more of these symptoms, you may be experiencing a major depressive episode and should consult a mental-health professional or your physician. The need for antidepressant medication should be explored, especially if you've had suicidal thoughts or fantasies. If you've had suicidal thoughts and feel out of control, you should call a health-care person immediately. Don't hesitate! If you don't have a person to contact, call your nearest hospital emergency room.

Pinning Down Depression

The exact cause of depression is unknown. What is known is that there are some common factors that may trigger depression and depressive symptoms. The following five factors may be related to your depression:

1. *Physical illness* can be associated with depression. Diabetes, thyroid disorders, cancer, congestive heart failure, Parkinson's disease, and chronic, incurable, and painful conditions (spinal cord injury, acquired immunodeficiency syndrome [AIDS], etc.), or even a simple virus can contribute to your becoming depressed. Because many medical conditions may contribute to a depression, should you have any physical concerns, arrange to have a complete physical.

2. *Medications, over-the-counter drugs, and illegal drugs* can all have side effects associated with depression. Prescription drugs (including hypertensive medications, tranquilizers, steroids, and codeine), alcohol and other drug intoxication, and alcohol and other drug withdrawal can all cause depression. If you think your depression is caused by medicine you are currently taking, you should not hesitate to call your physician.

3. *Family history* can contribute to depression. Depression is 1.5 to 3 times more common among siblings, parents, or other close relatives. Discuss the importance of this information with your relatives, encouraging them to be candid with you.

4. *Environmental stress* can contribute to depression. Losses such as death, divorce, breakup of a significant relationship, or job loss, as well as difficult living conditions such as poverty, danger, or uncertainty, can all provide significant stress and precipitate a depression. Some current research shows how stress—environmental or

social—actually changes the shape, size, and number of neurons in the brain. Keep in mind, it's not just the stress that affects us; it's how we interpret and handle stress in our lives. (Self-coaching can teach you how.)

5. *Psychological factors* also influence depression. Most depressions are triggered by stress and anxiety. Research suggests that early childhood experiences set the stage for a sensitivity and susceptibility to depression. Simply stated, this means that insecurity sets the stage for distorted, negative thinking. It's this habit of insecure thinking that supports your depression. Depression is predominantly a recurrent problem. Eighty percent of those having one episode will eventually have another-unless they change their habit of distorted thinking. (Self-coaching can change that habit for you.)

Self-Coaching Reflection
Thoughts change chemistry. Unless you change your habit of insecure, negative thinking, you will remain susceptible to depression or to a recurrence of a depression.

Natural and Destructive Depression

As you can see, depression has many faces and can be the source of much confusion. Self-coaching can help by simplifying the problem. We do this by using only two broad categories of depression: natural depression and destructive depression. A third depression is listed here, but this is merely a designation for a natural depression that progresses into a destructive depression.

Natural Depression   A natural depression is a proportionate reaction to loss, frustration, or tragedy. Natural depression dissipates in a timely manner. The death of a loved one, for example, can certainly bring on a debilitating depression with such symptoms as intense sadness, insomnia, poor appetite, inability to concentrate, and a general malaise. As difficult as these symptoms may be, because they're a normal and expected part of bereavement, I wouldn't ordinarily suggest that the grieving widow seek therapy.

If your reactions are consistent and proportionate to a stressful or traumatic life circumstance, then depression can be seen more as a coping mechanism, one that should dissipate on its own in time.

Destructive Depression A destructive depression may be precipitated by a trauma or stressor, but it's fueled and sustained by insecurity's destructive thinking. Because your thoughts can change your brain chemistry, destructive depression can easily degenerate into clinical depression. In the upcoming chapters, you'll learn how depression is often a feeble attempt at controlling life.

Natural/Destructive Depression If people suffering from natural depression begin to fuel their depression with thoughts of insecurity, then destructive depression can develop. In the example of a widow, if her symptoms were to last for more than two months or if her insecurity were to begin to create symptoms not associated with her bereavement—such as guilt, worthlessness, prolonged functional impairment, or thoughts of suicide—we might conclude that her natural depression is progressing into destructive depression.

Relatively Speaking, Just How Depressed Am I?

To evaluate depression, aside from assessing your mood, we also need to assess any change in your behavior. Mild depression, for example, may be experienced as an apathy toward your job. "I can't explain it, I just don't have the desire to go to work anymore." Using the same example, moderate depression may cause this same person to begin to miss work, calling in sick more often, or just taking off for no reason. In moderate states of depression, some functioning is sacrificed. In severe depression, functioning is markedly impaired. Again, using our example, not only would work become impossible, but so too would simple day-to-day tasks such as grooming, relating, or even eating. Severe depression is obviously a serious problem both emotionally and functionally.

If you have a virus and your temperature reads 99 degrees, you're less likely to be concerned than if it's 102 degrees. Another common problem with depression is deciding—as objectively as possible—just how depressed you are. Because there's no depression thermometer, I've put together a severity continuum to help you visualize the intensity of your depression. As you progress from left to right along the continuum, notice that the symptoms are cumulative—that is, moderate depression can include any or all of the mild symptoms, whereas severe depression can include any or all of the mild and moderate symptoms. Take a look at the continuum and estimate at what point you would place your depression.

Depression: A Severity Scale

1	2	3	4	5	6	7	8	9	10

Mild	Moderate	Severe
Depressed mood, apathy, lethargy, decreased performance, decline in interest or hobbies, reduced spontaneity, "blah" feeling, occasional depression, functioning may be strained but remains mostly unimpaired	Intensification of all mild symptoms, occasional bouts of crying or tearfulness, worry, mildly impaired general functioning, fatigue, anxiety, social difficulties, some appetite disturbances possible, disturbed or excessive sleep, difficulty with concentration and memory likely, diminished interest in sex, depressed most of the time with occasional periods of distraction, susceptibility to illness, low frustration tolerance, feelings of hopelessness	Intensification of all mild and moderate symptoms; functioning is minimal or completely shut down; thoughts of suicide; depressed all the time

The Not-So-Blue Blues

Are moods a form of depression? From time to time, we all find our-selves feeling down—nothing critical, nothing earth shaking, just blah. Moods, because of their transient and reactive nature, are not depres-sions. They're no fun, but they're not serious.

In contrast, destructive depression habitually saps your vital energy in an attempt to handle insecurity. The key word here is "habit." Moods are only occasional and mild skirmishes—not ongoing habits.

How did I know that the depressed mood I had an hour ago, when I was buried knee deep in paperwork and miserable from the heat, wasn't a depression? Because it lifted in a timely manner. If you're not sure, simply wait and see. If, after a few days, your mood doesn't improve, then you may suspect depression.

What about Medication?

As previously discussed, clinical depression can become a major dis-ruption to your normal, day-to-day functioning. With any severe depression, antidepressant medication may be indicated. Considering the low side-effect profile of the newer serotonin re-uptake inhibitor (SSRI) medications, which can provide an efficient, safe, nonaddictive intervention, there's no reason to struggle with this consideration. Medication alone, however, is not an effective treatment choice. The combination of medication and counseling has been shown to be the most effective strategy for working with moderate to severe depression. Remember, unless the perceptions and insecure thoughts that support your depression are removed, the chance of your depression recurring is high.

For many, the concept of taking antidepressant medication conjures up many negative reactions: "Guess I'm really screwed up if I need medication." "Medication, I'm that sick?" This is unfortunate, because anyone (not just you), given enough stress, anxiety, or depressive symptoms, is going to wind up disrupting his or her natural biochem-ical balance. Your emotions are very sensitive to any depletion of the brain chemicals serotonin, dopamine, and norepinephrine, known as neurotransmitters. Antidepressant medication can restore this bio-chemical depletion. It may seem unnatural to take a pill to feel better, but consider this: Antidepressant medication isn't going to get you high or just cover up a depression. It's going to allow you to reestablish a more natural balance. Once you're physically more fortified, your efforts, whether they be Self-coaching alone or a combination of Self-coaching and professional counseling, can be optimized. Look at anti-depressant medication as a temporary "jump-start" to your ultimate goal of self-reliance through Self-coaching.

What if you're experiencing only a few of the foregoing symptoms, or feeling them only occasionally. Are you depressed? Do you need medication? If you're functioning adequately and emotionally holding your own, then you may have a mild depression, in which case med-ication is probably not necessary—but change *is* necessary. Self-coaching will teach you to live your life free from insecurity, thereby stopping the depressive psychological and chemical drain on your system. Once you stop the leak, you'll be able to restore your chemical reserves naturally.

Beating depression with Self-coaching requires that you have

- A working understanding of what you're doing that's fueling the habit of your depression

- A progressive training program to follow

- A capacity (determined by the intensity of your depression) to maintain your ongoing training

If you can manage these three goals, then you can realistically expect to beat depression.

Types of Depression

I mentioned previously that one reason we tend to overlook being depressed is because we adapt to our declining mood. Another reason is ignorance. Depression (especially mild and moderate forms) can be deceptive, mistaken, or excused away: "I'm just bored," "Leave me alone, I just want to stay in bed. I'm tired" or "There's nothing wrong, I'm just out of sorts." The following list of more common depressions will further assist you in appreciating depression's many faces: major depression, dysthymic depression, seasonal affective depression, bipolar depression, atypical depression, and postpartum depression.

Major Depression

Major depression is one of the most serious forms of depression and is characterized by one or more major depressive episodes (see the symptoms listed in the self-quiz on page 40). Major depression is typified by a profound state of despair, hopelessness, worthlessness, dejection, loss of interest in usual activities, and so on. This type of depression is also associated with a high suicide rate. It's not uncommon for substance abuse, panic disorder, or obsessive-compulsive disorders to occur with major depression.

Major depression, although more frequent in women, can occur in any group of people, affecting one out of every ten of us. With this type of depression you should contact a mental-health professional immediately. Although medication and psychotherapy are essential, Self-coaching can be an ongoing adjunct to your treatment, as well as a long-term strategy for preventing or minimizing future occurrences.

Dysthymic Depression

A dysthymic depression is characterized by a chronically depressed mood, usually described as being always sad or down in the dumps. Dysthymia usually persists for a period of years and doesn't disable a person's functioning. It doesn't disable, but it greatly inhibits! Typically, there are low-level depressive symptoms that include poor self-esteem, low energy, sleep disturbances, poor appetite or overeating, general feelings of inadequacy, and so on.

Dysthymic depression is generally more frequent in women than in men. Although individual counseling and medication are helpful with dysthymia, Self-coaching is an extremely valuable and effective technique for helping you get out of your "blahs."

Seasonal Affective Depression

Seasonal affective depression (SAD), often referred to as "winter blues," is not a common depression. Although the specific cause is unknown, lack of sunlight during the low-light months of winter seems to be a major factor. In fact, the latitude at which you live is an important variable. Symptoms vary from mild to severe and develop in late fall and clear up in early spring.

Phototherapy (i.e., full-spectrum fluorescent light therapy) has been proven an effective treatment. Self-coaching can be very effective in controlling the negativity, guilt, and inertia of SAD.

Bipolar Depression

Bipolar depression (formerly referred to as manic depression) is characterized by alternating cycles of high-energy periods of wildly unrealistic activity, lasting from several days to months, followed by a severe depressive phase consisting of feelings of inertia, low self-esteem, withdrawal, sadness, suicidal risk, and so on. In either phase, there is a susceptibility to alcohol or other drug abuse. These episodes are not precipitated by a clear-cut environmental or situational cause.

Heredity and psychological factors seem to play a major role in bipolar depression. There is a higher incidence in patients with relatives who have suffered from this disorder. A mental-health professional should be consulted as soon as possible. Self-coaching, used in conjunction with professional treatment, can be a valuable tool for achieving long-term stability.

Atypical Depression

This type of depression is described as not having the usual, steady down reactions of other depressions. A person may be fine one day and then down or depressed the next, often without any obvious trigger or incident. Self-coaching can be of great assistance with atypical depressions.

Postpartum Depression

Mild moodiness isn't uncommon after childbirth. If, however, these symptoms become more severe and last for more than a few days, postpartum depression must be suspected. Postpartum depression can be severe, threatening both mother and child, and it appears to be caused by hormonal imbalances.

Help should be sought immediately. Self-coaching, along with formal therapy, can be particularly helpful in fighting off distorted perceptions and feelings and maintaining an optimistic outlook.

❖ ❖ ❖

TRAINING SUGGESTION

Using the descriptions in this chapter, see how many depressive symptoms you recognize in your day-to-day struggles. Make a list of these symptoms, then use the depression severity scale to estimate the severity of your depression.

The reading from this severity scale will serve as a baseline for your training. Once you begin your more formal training, once a week, you may want to repeat your listing and evaluation of your symptoms. One reason for this exercise is to make sure that your depression isn't progressing. Your results will also serve as a useful source of feedback and encouragement.

❖ ❖ ❖

5

Anxiety

I'm going to have a heart attack. Trust me, I know I am. Sometimes you just know certain things—in your gut. Lately, I've been afraid to go to work. When I do go, I'm constantly looking for any opportunity to rest and not get my heart rate up too high. I went for a physical and was told that my pressure was mildly elevated. Listen, if it were that mild he would have told me to lose a few pounds, not prescribe medication! I think he's trying not to alarm me. He started me on some beta blockers, and now all I'm thinking about is that my heart is going to explode.

I was worried before I knew about my high blood pressure, and now I worry about how much damage has been caused. They call high blood pressure the silent killer, but I'm telling you mine isn't silent. I can actually feel my blood pressure! I feel like a balloon that's been overinflated and about to burst.

My doctor says to relax, that I'm "healthy as a horse." I know he wouldn't tell me the truth because he knows how much I worry. And anyway, doctors can't tell what's going on from a few tests. I'm telling you my heart is going to explode! I'm afraid to have sex because of the exertion. My wife thinks I'm crazy. My kids want to know why I won't play catch with them anymore. I'm getting more nervous; I'm not sleeping. Lately, when I'm trying to go to bed, I can feel my heart racing and that's where I really panic . . . I start sweating. Last night I actually hyperventilated. My heart can't take much more of this. I should be relaxing, but instead I'm driving myself to the grave.

I think I need to be in a hospital. I'm worried all the time. It's all I think about. I can't stand thinking about it, but I can't *not* think about it. I'm driving myself crazy. All I see is me riding in an ambulance, the pain. I don't want to die.

Sal was suffering from anxiety and panic, a terrible, terrifying combination. Essentially, his insecurity wouldn't permit him to trust life. The organ most associated with life is the heart, and this became Sal's hook for projecting his insecurity. Because he couldn't trust his heart, he couldn't trust life. His only choice was to live in chronic dread. Self-coaching taught Sal to challenge these distortions. It wasn't life or his heart that was the problem; it was his long-standing habit of insecurity and distrust that had to be challenged. With the insights we established in counseling, Sal began to fight back.

Sal never had a bad heart. In fact, Sal's monologue came from what he said more than five years ago. I recently saw Sal at a local baseball game. He was managing the team and was walking off the field after infield practice. He saw me and approached me with a big smile, telling me, "Hey, Doc, guess you could say the old ticker's doing well, huh?" We laughed. If only Sal could have seen this result five years earlier.

Anxiety, whether mild or as severe as Sal's panic attacks, can have profound effects on your body. Some of the possible effects of anxiety are

- A rise in blood sugar
- Muscular tension

- Dry mouth
- Rapid heartbeat or palpitations
- Headaches
- Fatigue
- Impotence
- Colon spasms
- Diarrhea or constipation
- Insomnia
- Poor concentration
- General feeling of apprehension and dread

Blame It on the Saber-toothed Tigers

Anxiety is a vestige of what scientists call the fight-or-flight response. During our evolutionary past, this response would have been a crucial reason we survived as a species. Let's face it, as humans, we're not equipped with lightning speed, daggerlike teeth, sicklelike claws, or even protective coloration. The truth is we're pretty vulnerable; we needed all the help our genes could muster in order to avoid extinction.

The fight-or-flight response is a generalized protective strategy that quickly pumps up your body with energy by releasing hormones and other chemicals. Thus fortified, we are in a much better position to fight off danger, or to flee from it. Either way, our juiced-up body is prepped and ready. Your genes don't care whether you're a coward or a hero—just that you survive.

Quicksand and Other Life Challenges

Throughout human history, the fight-or-flight response made sense. It still makes sense today—particularly in moments of crisis. I remember being alone on a fossil dig at a phosphate mine in North Carolina. I accidentally found myself sinking in a marl-like quicksand. When I was up to my thighs and sinking, everything about my usual consciousness shifted. Aware only of my very shallow (oxygen rich) breathing, I spread my upper body flat on top of a digging rake I had—fortunately—taken along. With strength I have never felt before or since, I used my upper body muscles to remain splayed out on my rake while simultaneously pulling my legs free from the marl's incredible suction. Slowly I advanced. After about a ten-minute struggle, which seemed like ten years, I reached more stable ground and collapsed, completely exhausted. I gulped down the remains of what water I had left, while frantically unwrapping a candy bar I had—luckily—packed with my lunch. I was famished, absolutely depleted, and for quite some time unable to slow down my pulse or my breathing.

What did I learn from my near-death experience? A few things. For one thing, the body is a magnificent machine. My instincts knew it was do or die (in this case, my only option was to fight in order to flee). Every system in my body cooperated to pull me free from a rather horrific ending. All this expenditure of instinctual energy was necessary to survive. Afterward, I felt as if I had run a couple of marathons, and it took a good night's rest before I felt like my old self again.

Here's my point: As intense as my experience was, I can tell you I've had patients who, suffering from intense anxiety, panic, or phobias, describe virtually the *same* reaction—without the quicksand! The reason for this is really quite simple: Anxiety doesn't differentiate between real danger and imagined danger. If, for example, you interpret an IRS audit as the end of the world, then your body will respond in the only way it knows how—fight-or-flight, all or nothing, do or die. All it takes is distorted, insecurity-driven thinking to get your adrenal glands to start pumping stress hormones into your bloodstream, and once anxiety begins, it can become one hell of a steamroller.

Natural and Destructive Anxiety

As with depression, I divide anxiety into two general categories: destructive anxiety and natural anxiety. Sal's panic was a clear example of destructive anxiety. *Destructive anxiety* is driven by insecurity, disproportionate to the circumstance, always exaggerated, and persistent. Its purpose is to try to control life with an intense flurry of mental gyrations (worrying, rumination, obsessing, etc.).

Natural anxiety, unlike destructive anxiety, is normal, proportionate to the circumstance, not exaggerated, and time limited. Like depression, natural anxiety is an inescapable part of life. What my wife and I went through a few years ago anticipating her surgery serves as a good example. We found ourselves worrying about lots of things—the anesthesia, the outcome, the physical therapy—but finally (at my wife's insistence), we decided to put our faith in the hands of God and the surgeon. We actively chose—and struggled—to let go of our worries. Up to this point, though, I remember a few sleepless nights, headaches, ruminations, worries, difficulty concentrating at work—all anxiety symptoms, yes, but all natural anxiety (i.e., proportionate concern and worry, not exaggerated, and time limited).

Just because natural anxiety is a normal part of life, this doesn't mean you can't deal with it. Self-coaching can help you know when enough is enough, and how to let it go. Why suffer needlessly, even if it is natural?

Negative Patterns

Although Self-coaching can be a useful tool for dealing with transient, natural anxiety, when it comes to wrestling with destructive anxiety, it's indispensable! Let's take a look at the most common destructive patterns: general anxiety disorder, panic attacks, obsessive-compulsive disorder, and social anxieties and phobias.

General Anxiety Disorder (GAD)

General anxiety disorder (GAD) is characterized by the following symptoms:

- Excessive worry and anxiety
- Feeling restless, keyed up, or edgy
- Fatigue
- Difficulty concentrating or forgetting
- Feeling irritable, testy, grouchy much of the time
- Muscle tension

- Sleep difficulties (difficulty falling or staying asleep, restless, non-restorative sleep)

People with GAD worry all the time. They're not picky about what they worry about. Big problems, small problems, it makes no difference. Someone with GAD is always feeling out of balance and out of control. Worry is an ongoing, persistent attempt to figure out how to regain control and avoid vulnerability. Unfortunately, worrying, rather than lessening vulnerability, generates more anxiety, which increases feelings of vulnerability. A vicious cycle begins:

❖ ❖ ❖

Vulnerability/insecurity ▶ loss of control ▶ worry (attempt to gain control) ▶ increased anxiety ▶ increased feeling of vulnerability and loss of control ▶ increased, persistent worry ▶ increased, persistent anxiety ▶ etc.

❖ ❖ ❖

Panic Attacks

Panic attacks are characterized by the following symptoms:

- Palpitations
- Sweating
- Trembling or shaking
- Shortness of breath
- Chest pain or discomfort
- Nausea
- Lightheadedness or faintness
- Fear of losing control
- Fear of dying
- Numbness or tingling
- Chills or hot flushes

People who suffer from panic attacks experience periodic, intense rushes of uncomfortable physical symptoms combined with thoughts of impending disaster and doom. Panic attacks are usually unpredictable and disorienting. These attacks can be so traumatic that a person begins to live in dread of future occurrences.

Panic usually occurs in two stages: (1) an *anticipation stage* of mounting anxiety, where insecurity begins to dominate the thinking; and (2) a *fight-or-flight stage* of physical reactivity. This experience is so intense and disorienting that many people report feeling crazy or losing control.

Obsessive-Compulsive Disorder (OCD)

Obsessive-compulsive disorder (OCD) has two components:

- Recurrent, persistent, intrusive thoughts that cause an increase in anxiety
- Repetitive behavior or thoughts that the person feels compelled to perform in order to regain a sense of control

OCD sufferers are victimized by ruminative, exaggerated worry. The thought, "Did I turn off the stove?" may generate a momentary bit of concern for most of us, but for someone with OCD, it's never this simple. People with OCD are driven to ruminate and obsess, on and on, "Did I set the alarm? I think so, but I can't remember. Did I? I can't be sure. I remember going into the kitchen. I think I did. Maybe I didn't . . ."

OCD is insecurity driven. It's the inability to trust yourself, your actions, or your thoughts. Because you can't trust yourself, then you can't possibly trust your recollections. Never feeling safe (i.e., in control) is what generates the anxiety.

Compulsions are an attempt to reduce the anxiety generated by obsessions. Take the example, "Did I set the alarm?" This question would be followed by checking to see whether, in fact, the alarm was set properly. Unfortunately, it doesn't stop there. Because of the basic distrust, a person with OCD must then question once again, "Am I sure I set it?" Again the alarm will be checked, not once, not twice, but sometimes countless times before it can be left. OCD sufferers get some anxiety relief from their compulsions, but little, if any, satisfaction.

Obsessive-compulsive behavior is closely related to superstitious behavior. Both have to do with controlling some aspect of behavior in order to feel more in control (knocking wood, not stepping on cracks, etc.). OCD rituals are, in fact, superstitious attempts at warding off insecurity by controlling fate. A seventeen-year-old OCD patient of mine had just begun driving. She told me, "If I tap my car door handle six times before getting in the car, I won't have an accident. I tried not giving in to this 'silly' behavior, but my anxiety went through the roof when I tried to drive. I had to stop the car, get out, and do my six touches!"

Having a set number of repetitions is a rather common aspect of these compulsions (three taps on a door before entering, buckling and unbuckling a seat belt five times before driving off, etc.). Over time, a very exacting sequence can develop, with very rigid demands.

OCD sufferers are not crazy. They will, in fact, tell you that they know their compulsions are silly—even ridiculous, but because these rituals reduce anxiety, they're reinforced.

Social Anxieties and Phobias

Social anxieties and phobias are characterized by

- A persistent, excessive fear that is unreasonable and connected to the anticipation of a specific object, situation, or experience.

Some people experience specific situations that bring on anxiety and panic. Fear of bridges, tunnels, public speaking, elevators, and flying are all examples of phobic responses. Essentially, social anxieties and phobias are anxiety and panic attacks that are connected to a hook experience. Any experience that has been imbued with a projection of insecurity (e.g., I can't breathe in this elevator) can become a hook for future anxiety and panic. The excessive fear and anxiety usually produces avoidant reactions (referred to as phobic avoidance), as the person tries to avoid any circumstance that will produce this intense, debilitating reaction. With social anxiety, the fear/hook has a social link. For example, fear of disapproval, public speaking, public bathrooms can all be seen as possible catastrophes.

Physical and Medical Considerations

Although anxiety is typically an emotional disorder, it's important to rule out any medical condition that may be causing it. Problems with your adrenal gland, thyroid gland, heart disease, respiratory disease, or hypoglycemia are all possible underlying physical causes. If things are going well in your life and you can't identify any stressors or reason for concern, and especially if you suspect there may be a physical problem, it can't hurt to have a thorough physical examination. Also keep in mind that many prescription medications, over-the-counter medications (especially nasal sprays and stimulants to lose weight), and other chemicals (caffeine, illicit drugs, etc.), can also cause anxiety. Ask your physician about whether any medication you're taking may cause anxiety.

Whether or not you need to consider antianxiety medication requires a close look at your functioning. If the intensity of your anxiety or panic is significantly interfering with your ability to work, relate, and relax, then exploring the possibility of medication is usually a wise choice. Don't struggle alone with this evaluation. If you're in doubt, any mental-health professional can help you decide whether medication is an appropriate choice.

There are many medications available for anxiety and, depending on the type of anxiety you suffer from, some may have specific benefits. BuSpar, for example, works very well for general anxiety disorder (GAD), while Xanax, monoamine oxidase (MAO) inhibitors and tricyclic antidepressants work well for panic disorders. The benzodiazepines, beta blockers, tricyclic antidepressants, MAO inhibitors, SSRIs, mild tranquilizers, and anticonvulsants have all been successfully employed in the treatment of anxiety. As with medication for depression, keep in mind that medication alone is not nearly as effective as medication along with a therapeutic program to follow.

Whether you're in counseling for intense, debilitating panic attacks, taking medication for a general anxiety disorder, or just curious about handling day-to-day natural anxieties, Self-coaching will significantly reduce or eliminate the anticipatory, insecurity-driven anxiety that is the base of all anxiety disorders.

❖ ❖ ❖

TRAINING SUGGESTION

Using the descriptions in this chapter, see how many anxiety symptoms you can recognize in your day-to-day struggles. Make a list of these symptoms, including both destructive and natural anxieties. Keep this list for future reference. Periodically, throughout your training (about once a month), update this list to monitor your progress.

Use a simple chart like the one suggested here to record your symptoms. Your goal is to eventually eliminate or minimize all entries under the "Destructive Anxieties" heading. Under the "Natural Anxieties" heading, you'll always have a few symptoms—this is normal. Eventually, however, you'll want to see whether you're falling prey to certain patterns of anxiety. Understanding these patterns will help you know when enough is enough!

Destructive Anxieties	Natural Anxieties
1. Intense fear of talking to the opposite sex	1. Feeling a bit anxious about getting your wisdom teeth pulled
2. Heart palpitations, sweating, or panic while caught in traffic	2. Nervousness when a man walks up to your car asking for money
3. Inability to fall asleep, worrying about whether you are going to succeed	3. Worry about your loved one's illness

❖ ❖ ❖

6

The Control-Sensitive Personality

Rather than prejudice your thinking, let's start out with the following short quiz:

T   F   I tend to be compulsive.

T   F   I get very upset when things go wrong.

T   F   The more chaotic a situation, the more anxious and tense I feel.

T   F   I worry a lot.

T   F   I've been accused of being a black-and-white thinker.

T   F   I'm always in my head, figuring, thinking, ruminating, and so on.

T   F   I find it hard to trust.

T   F   I tend to be suspicious.

T   F   I like for things to be done just so.

T   F   I can't say "no."

T   F   I typically have trouble being on time.

T   F   I like to be the one driving the car.

T   F   I'm often rigid and inflexible.

T   F   I'm a doer.

T   F   I go out of my way to avoid confrontations.

T	F	I'm often too sensitive.
T	F	I like to have the last word in any argument.
T	F	I always have a reason or excuse for what I do.
T	F	I would say I'm a better talker than a listener.
T	F	I'm very impatient with other people's mistakes.
T	F	I always feel that I'm right.
T	F	I'm too vulnerable.

Total your "true" responses. A score of 10 or fewer suggests that you are not overly control sensitive. Self-coaching can teach you to cultivate an even deeper sense of self-trust and spontaneity.

A score between 11 and 16 suggests that you have a moderate degree of control sensitivity. For you, control is a more limiting aspect of your life. Self-coaching can make a noticeable difference in your overall feeling of well-being and sense of personal security.

A score of 17 or more suggests that you are particularly sensitive to control. For you, life is significantly compromised by a need to maintain control. Self-coaching is going to change your perspective. You don't need more control; you need more self-trust.

When Control Gets Out of Control

Most people like being in control. It's normal and healthy to want to be in control of life. Avoiding injury, anticipating danger, dressing for inclement weather, or learning to get along with people are all aspects of healthy control. From an evolutionary standpoint, the desire to maintain control certainly seems to have adaptive significance. Losing control, particularly in our ancestral past, would almost certainly have led to personal, familial, or tribal harm. Survival depended on *not* being vulnerable. It made sense to want to be in control during the Ice Age. It still makes sense. We human beings just hate to feel out of control.

Obviously, the desire for a less vulnerable, more controlled life isn't a problem. On the other hand, when insecurity, doubt, distrust, or fear cause you to see danger in safe places, to anticipate only what can go wrong in life, or to feel convinced that you are doomed to failure, then the need for control changes from a healthy desire, "I *want* . . . ," to a compulsive declaration, "I *have to* be in control."

People vary in their sensitivity to a perceived loss of control. On one end of the continuum we have people who are not only insensitive to a loss of control, but even totally oblivious to it. Remember Tom, the man who lost a hand in an industrial accident? You can't get more insensitive than not missing your own hand.

Assuming you're not like Tom, and you do struggle with anxiety or depression, chances are you're what I call a *control-sensitive person.* Simply put, a control-sensitive person reacts strongly to any loss of control, or perceived loss, with symptoms of anxiety or depression (fears, apprehensions, worries, etc.). This sensitivity may be learned or it may simply be your nature—your predisposition.

A psychological predisposition is an innate tendency toward certain reactions or behavior. Ever spend an hour at a nursery school? If so, you probably noticed a whole array of psychological dispositions: leaders, followers, talkers, thinkers, introverts, extroverts, criers, pouters, all destined to one day shape each tyke's eventual adult personality. We know, for example, that children of parents with panic disorder are seven times more likely to be anxious themselves. These children may have an inherently lower threshold to anxiety, which makes them more susceptible to insecurity and depression. They are predisposed to anxiety. Similarly, children of parents that have suffered from a major depressive episode are 1.5 to 3 times more likely to develop depression. You don't need a predisposition to anxiety or depression to develop a control-sensitive personality, however. Stressful life circumstances, especially loss, can initiate the same reaction. Anyone, given enough insecurity, is susceptible to developing a control-sensitive personality.

Whatever their origins, however, anxiety and depression can be stopped where they begin, in the insecure thoughts that *you allow* to float unchecked in your head. Keep in mind that adversity, loss, even a psychological disposition, aren't necessarily life sentences; they're only tendencies toward certain behavior. Whether you know it or not, it's up to you to decide whether you're going to fan the flames of insecurity. You always have a choice. You'll see.

In the list that follows, you will find some typical strategies of control. The list is far from complete, but it does give you a flavor of control's diversity. The tendencies listed on the left are usually more associated with anxiety, while those on the right are more typical of depression. Keep in mind, however, that there is no hard-fast rule, and your defensive profile (which you will be setting up in later chapters), will show you your unique preference(s) for maintaining control (worry, procrastination, avoidance, etc.). In the chapters that follow, you will find a full explanation of how these and other similar tendencies, rather than establishing control, wind up making you feel more out of control.

- Worry, rumination—recklessness, not caring, disregard for life circumstances
- Rigid, opinionated thinking—indecisiveness, excessive doubt
- Overcommitment—avoidance of life circumstances
- Social isolation—excessive dependence
- Excessive frugality—overspending
- Perfectionism—slovenliness
- Workaholism—lethargy
- Lack of emotion—excessive emotionality
- Excessive ambition—apathy
- Excessive risk taking—excessive fear
- Arrogance—low self-esteem
- Distrust—blind trust

An Exhausting Way to Live

Once you turn to control to combat your self-doubt and insecurity, you begin to build a life of torment. That's when, instead of living spontaneously moment to moment, you become congested by such

63

thoughts as, "What if I lose my job?" "I know he's not going to like me." "I'll never get ahead." "Why go on?" Instead of mental clarity, what you wind up with is an opaque world, clouded and distorted by perceptions of insecurity.

Anticipating life's potholes may sound appealing if you want to feel invulnerable, but don't be surprised if you become so intent on avoiding potholes that you don't see the stop sign at the intersection. I remember my very first therapy session. I was an intern, and I was nervous. Although I was in casual California, I nevertheless opted for my three-piece blue suit, white shirt, and somber tie. I entered that session feeling very "psychological." Things seemed to go well, and I was more than pleased when the hour finished. As I stood up to escort my patient to the door, something white against a dark blue background caught my eye. My first session was delivered with my fly open! So much for control.

Control requires effort, maintenance, and vigilance—it's an exhausting way to live. So why do it? By eliminating, or at least minimizing, the risks of embarrassment, failure, and rejection, control-sensitive people feel that they, not fate, control destiny. It's this heady notion of controlling destiny and sidestepping life's anxieties that becomes so habit forming. You get hooked into a treadmill-like belief that your ultimate salvation depends on having just a little more control—and more—and more.

Traps to Avoid

When the need for control becomes too important, you become particularly susceptible to certain traps—thinking traps. Without significant awareness, these traps can quickly become habits, contributing significantly to your difficulties. Recognizing these traps can alert you to danger as you proceed with your Self-coaching.

Take a look at these common traps, and begin to develop an awareness and sensitivity to these very common pitfalls: should statements, what-iffing, tunnel vision, mind reading, have-tos, black-and-white thinking, and name-calling.

Should Statements

"I should be a better daughter." "I should be more successful." "I should be smarter." "I should lose twenty pounds." "Should" statements evoke a sense of guilt and failure. By undermining who and what you are, these statements generate anxiety and depression. While it may be true that you can improve yourself in some way, when you tell yourself you "should" improve, you're telling yourself a negative—you're not good enough right now, and you can only be good enough if you do this or that.

The healthy alternative is to avoid should statements by replacing them with more positive assertions such as, "It would be a good idea to be more attentive to my mother." "I want to be more successful." "I would like to be smarter; perhaps I'll take that course at the night school." "Maybe I'll join the gym and quit eating all that fast food." These alternatives don't negate who you are now. They support growth and improvement based on who and what you are, not at your expense.

What-iffing

Another insecurity trap is what-iffing. "What if he asks me for my opinion?" "What if I don't get the job?" "What if I get too attached?" What-iffing is an attempt to anticipate problems before they happen. Why? Because you believe that if you know what's coming around that corner—before the fact—you can be braced and ready to handle yourself.

So, what's the harm in anticipating danger? Nothing, if your thinking could be limited to a few legitimate attempts at problem solving. What-iffing, unfortunately, seems to spiral quickly out of control, jumping from one "what if" to the next. Every possible solution presents you with another crisis. You wind up living with chronic worry that generates chronic anxiety, and chronic anxiety will ultimately deplete you. It's this depletion that explains why anxiety and depression are so often experienced together.

A better response to life is your natural, unrehearsed spontaneity.

It's the lack of self-trust that encourages what-iffing. The healthy alternative is to realize that what-iffing undermines your self-confidence by insisting you can be safe (i.e., in control) only if you can anticipate life before it happens. Self-coaching teaches you to be safe, not by worrying and what-iffing, but by courageously trusting your ability to handle life.

Tunnel Vision

Both anxiety and depression cause a narrowing of our perceptual field. Rather than seeing the whole picture, we see only selective aspects of a situation. For example, a depressed man may see only his own faults, overlooking his positive qualities. "I'm just a cranky old man." "I can't do anything right." These are tunnel-vision statements. Although there may be a grain of truth in them, the reality is that these gross exaggerations wind up keeping you off balance and feeling out of control.

The healthy alternative is to realize that life is rarely limited to one point of view, one option, or one solution. A more expansive view requires some practice. Depersonalization is a valuable tool that can help you see beyond your own narrow view. By asking yourself how someone else (think of someone you feel has a healthier perspective) might respond to your situation, you can experience a totally different perspective. The key is to speculate on how so-and-so would react to a situation, not how *you* think the person would react.

Mind Reading

"I know she hates me." "He does that because he doesn't care about my feelings." "People think I'm boring." Mind reading is an attempt to interpret other people's actions *as if* you know what they are thinking. You're trying to eliminate vulnerability by never being caught off guard.

When you consider how easy it is to misinterpret your own thinking, you begin to realize that reading someone else's mind is purely fiction. Why would you do it? Two reasons: first, because your negativity has convinced you that you live in a hostile world, so you need every advantage to maintain control; and second, because if you anticipate the worst before it happens, you can feel prepared (i.e., be in control).

The healthy alternative is to insist on the objective truth. Ask questions instead of guessing. As much as you may desire it, you can never know what someone else is thinking—not without asking. Recognize that mind reading is nothing more than a projection of your insecurity. Unless you're willing to ask what someone else is actually thinking, you must tell yourself, "I am not allowed to assume a negative!"

Have-Tos

"I have to finish today." "I have to succeed." "I have no choice; I must have that coat." Have-tos are traps most often employed by anxiety-prone individuals, and they represent the foundation of all compulsive behavior. Although driven by anxiety, a compulsive life quickly becomes a depressing way to live.

Have-tos are similar to tunnel vision, in that your perceptual field is narrowed down to whatever it is you feel you have to do. Whereas tunnel vision limits your perceptual choices, have-to thinking eliminates your choices altogether. You're convinced you have no choice and can be released from suffering only by getting to your goal.

Compulsive spending, cleaning, working, or even sex can all be expressions of have-to thinking that drags you around incessantly trying to sidestep anxiety. You tell yourself, "Once I achieve such-and-such, then I'll be okay." Unfortunately, have-tos are lies—one goal quickly evaporates as we are compulsively driven to the next. Have-tos greatly diminish, even eliminate, any joy or pleasure in life. Have-tos are hard work.

The healthy alternative is to understand that have-tos are feeble attempts to gain control and mastery over a dangerous world. Rather than recognizing and addressing the insecurity within, we externalize it and become convinced that we can become secure by doing this or accomplishing that. Security, however, doesn't flow from the outside in—only from the inside out.

Black-and-White Thinking

"I'll never be happy." "Life will always be depressing." "I'll never feel safe." Black-and-white thinking is impulsive thinking. When you're anxious or depressed, you become impatient. Something is either good or bad, positive or negative, always or never—end of discussion. With black-and-white thinking, you don't have to live with ambiguity.

The problem is that life isn't black and white. By eliminating life's gray choices, you eliminate a whole array of possibilities. The insecure person is more concerned with feeling in control than with being accurate. Even if it's negative, at least the issue gets settled: "That's it, I'm a failure."

The healthy alternative is to learn to tolerate some ambiguity in your life, to recognize that an impulsive decision, if wrong, only creates more problems. By insisting on a more objective perception that life is rarely black or white, you can begin to recognize that your anxiety doesn't have to dictate your thinking. Stop treating thoughts as facts, and insist on being more truthful with yourself. Find out that most of your impulsiveness is just a habit. Once you stop your reflexive responding and take a deep breath, you may surprise yourself with the options that begin to float to the surface.

Name-calling

"I'm stupid." "I'm such a wimp." "I'm too tall/short and skinny/fat." These are examples of name-calling. Name-calling is nothing more than a ploy. If you beat yourself up, you can give up. If you're a jerk, wimp, or loser, or you're dumb, then you've created an excuse for your shortcomings, and you might as well give up. Like black-and-white thinking, both anxiety and depression make you too eager to settle an argument because you're convinced you can't tolerate living with it.

As with black-and-white thinking, you need to recognize the impulsive habit involved in this behavior. The healthy alternative is to get tough and tell yourself that name-calling is not allowed. You're just not going to permit it! Name-calling is simply a ploy to avoid anxiety, so don't allow yourself to be duped. By further eroding your self-confidence, name-calling only makes your life more miserable. It's a lose-lose proposition. Stop beating yourself up. It doesn't pay.

Control-sensitive people can be very hard on themselves, especially when the quality of their lives erodes to such an extent that a flat tire or an unpaid bill can cause anguish, panic, or despair. As the strategies of control continue to fail and frustrate you, as you become more and more depleted by worry or depression, one inescapable truth begins to emerge—control is an illusion. Life cannot be controlled. The reality is that anxiety and depression are about as effective at controlling life as you are at defying gravity. Just as you'll never float through the air, your worrying and avoidance will ultimately solve nothing. The quest to control life is nothing more than an attempt to defy psychic gravity.

Self-Coaching Reflection
Control is only an illusion of safety.

All He Wanted Was to Feel Safe

At our first session at the rehab center, Henry told me he was going to rob a bank. The crazy thing about it was he didn't want the money; he wanted to get caught! Henry, you see, had been in prison most of his adult life, and now on parole he was floundering between severe bouts of depression and panic. He couldn't cope with life outside the "joint." On the outside, he had to make decisions, decisions you and I take for granted—where, when, and what to eat, what to do every evening, when to go to bed or when to wake up—normal everyday decisions.

Somewhere in the thirty-three years he had served in a federal penitentiary, Henry had surrendered his right to control his own life. He had become institutionalized. Every aspect of his life was prescribed by prison rules. He didn't have to think about anything. He became the child, the prison his parent. In prison, Henry felt safe, controlled. Out of prison, with no personal resources, he felt exposed and out of control. When I met him, he had become obsessed with one thing: He wanted to go home.

One day, Henry just disappeared. After he didn't show up for our session, I checked his room. Gone. No one at the rehab had any clue—at least no one was about to say anything. Henry and I had only a couple of sessions, barely enough time for us to get acquainted. I never heard from him again.

I'm convinced Henry's doing time right now. Somewhere in San Diego, a bank teller was probably traumatized by a scruffy-looking guy brandishing nothing more than a finger in his coat, demanding money. Why the robber walked slowly down the street after he left is probably still a mystery to the bank manager, but at least the felon was apprehended. Now, somewhere, in one of our federal prisons, Henry's finally at peace. He's starting each day at 6:15, going to breakfast, working in the laundry, stopping only for lunch, then again for supper, watching a little TV, and at 11:00 his lights are turned off for him. He doesn't have to think about anything. Henry falls asleep easily.

Don't be like Henry.

It's All Relative

Loss of control is a relative experience. For one teenager, a zit may be no big deal, while for another it could feel like the end of the world. Here are some common, everyday experiences where people report feeling a loss of control:

- Getting caught in traffic
- Forgetting someone's name

- Being late for or forgetting an appointment
- Speaking or performing in front of a group
- Getting sick
- Being unable to figure something out
- Being embarrassed or humiliated
- Having difficulty with confrontations
- Getting lost
- Not having enough money
- Failing a test
- Saying no
- Admitting a mistake

What about you? Are you one of control's victims, bullied about by anxious or depressed thoughts and fears? Like Henry, you may not realize to what extent control governs your life. Perhaps you feel a bit anxious now and then, occasionally depressed, tormented, or powerless, and you never realize that the culprit is a neurotic fear of losing control. Once you begin to understand the force behind your suffering, be it chronic or sporadic, you will realize you have a choice. Rather than compulsively seeking control's protection and insulation, you can choose to reclaim a natural, gregarious vitality for living.

Your insecurity is nothing more than a long-standing habit. As with changing any habit, whether it be smoking, or biting your nails, learning to live a secure life without anxiety and depression is first going to require that you break the habit of destructive thinking and replace it with mature, healthy, and—most importantly—objective, reality-based thinking. This is what your coaching and training will prepare you for. Keep reminding yourself, anxiety and depression aren't as ominous or mysterious as you once thought; they're just bad habits.

✤ ✤ ✤

TRAINING SUGGESTION

Logging Experiences Where You've Felt a Loss of Control

Shortly, you will be setting up a formal training log. For now, it's a good idea to get used to recording information that will become critical to your Self-coaching efforts.

Begin by recording any experience you've had where you felt a loss of control. For now, look for any experience that you would describe as producing either anxiety or depression. If you're not sure, write it down anyway. There's no harm in guessing.

You might use the following example as a guide:

Loss of Control Experience	Reaction
9:40 A.M. Driving to work. Caught in turnpike traffic.	Intense anger, frustration, feeling fidgety and nervous, started pounding steering wheel.
3:00 P.M. Boss told me to redo my report.	Strong panic feeling—I screwed up! My boss won't tolerate this behavior for long. What will I do?
7:00 P.M. Sister-in-law called wanting to borrow money.	Wanted to say "no," but couldn't. Felt bullied, out of control, and panicked. I really can't afford to give her the money!

❖ ❖ ❖

❖ ❖ ❖

TRAINING SUGGESTION

Thinking Traps

You may want to use the following template to record any thinking traps you've noticed. In a short while you'll begin to notice that you have definite preferences.

If you're comfortable sharing this with a spouse or other loved one, that person's perception of your typical traps can be invaluable. Ask—it's worth it!

Thinking Traps	Occurrences and Examples
Should statements	
What-iffing	
Tunnel vision	
Mind reading	
Have-tos	
Black-and-white thinking	
Name-calling	
Miscellaneous personal traps	

❖ ❖ ❖

7

The Control-Insecurity Connection

In the chapters that follow, you'll find that your control-sensitive disposition will always be fueled by insecure thinking. The converse is equally true: The more secure you are—or become—the less you worry, and the less anxious you are about being in control. Because insecurity can often be subtle, even unconscious, take the following insecurity quiz to help you assess your insecurity quotient. Answer each question as being either mostly true or mostly false.

T	F	I tend to be shy or uneasy with strangers.
T	F	I'd rather be at home than going out on an adventure.
T	F	I wish I were smarter.
T	F	I never have enough money.
T	F	I'm usually pessimistic.
T	F	I often wish I were better looking.
T	F	I don't think I'm as good as others.
T	F	If people knew the real me, they would think differently.
T	F	In relationships, I tend to cling.
T	F	I'm usually afraid to get too close to others.
T	F	I would be a lot happier if I didn't worry so much.
T	F	I have lots of fears.

74

T	F	I hide my feelings.
T	F	If someone's quiet, I might think they're angry with me.
T	F	I often wonder what people *really* think of me.

A score of 1 to 5 true answers indicates a tolerable degree of insecurity. You'll be using this book more for personality expansion rather than for repair. A score of 6 to 10 true answers indicates a moderate level of insecurity. Insecurity is probably undermining your capacity for effective living. You can expect this book to change significantly your view and experience of the world. If you scored 11 to 15 true answers, you may be suffering from substantial interference due to insecurity. Your self-worth has been eroded by insecurity, and it's clear you're going to need to restructure your thoughts and perceptions.

Insecurity + Control = A Toxic Mix

Maybe you've noticed yourself becoming a bit too perfectionistic, not wanting to make mistakes, or just trying too hard to avoid trouble. At other times, you may notice yourself worrying about life's what-ifs, trying hard to anticipate what life's going to throw at you. At still other times, you might catch yourself bullying your mate, such as by insisting on choosing your vacation spot. These are all expressions of how insecurity drives us.

Sometimes our need for control is minimal, especially when our lives are calm—and secure. When stress rears its ugly head and hooks up with insecurity, however, control can cause some big-time problems. Of course, some amount of insecurity is an inescapable by-product of living. If you think about the growing complexity of our world, the countless trial-and-error experiences you've had growing up, the traumas, the mishaps, and, of course, the reality that there are no perfect parents, doesn't it stand to reason that some insecurity is inevitable? From burglar alarms and karate schools to metal detectors, mace, and pepper sprays, our culture reflects this growing apprehension. We're becoming part of Generation I—Generation Insecurity.

A little insecurity isn't necessarily bad. The key word here is "little." It may be what prompted our earliest ancestors to band together in groups, defending against a hostile world—both real and imagined. In our lives, a little insecurity can also be put to good use. Anxiety about gaining a little weight or the health risks of smoking can certainly be used as motivation for positive change. It's when insecurity goes beyond a little and becomes a lot—that's when you suffer. Instead of feeling concern over losing weight or quitting smoking, you become obsessed, or depressed, or anxious about it. You may even panic as your everyday waking thoughts become filled with negativity and self-loathing.

First, before you can understand what's been undermining your life, you must recognize the degree to which you are insecure. The following progression reflects varying degrees of insecurity from normal, to anxious, to depressed. Which statement best reflects your thinking?

❖ ❖ ❖

I want to be liked ◗ I'm concerned about what people think of me. ◗ I worry about what people think of me. ◗ I know I'm going to mess up . . . I'm not going to come across well. ◗ No matter what I do, no one really cares about me. ◗ People hate me!

❖ ❖ ❖

Self-Coaching Reflection
In life, there's no absolute security and safety,
so stop acting as though there is!

It All Begins with Insight

Control-sensitive people shudder at the thought of not being able to control life. They work hard trying to become invulnerable. They insulate themselves by building walls higher and higher, always insisting, "Just a little bit more, then I'll surely be secure." Why do you think the lottery has become such a huge phenomenon? Millions of people walk into their local convenience store every morning, plop down a dollar or two, rattle off their sacred numbers, and walk out clutching that ticket, thinking, "Maybe today I'll hit the big one, then I'll never have to worry again."

If you think you can beat your insecurity from the outside in (e.g., getting a better job, making more money, buying that fancy car, attracting that special person), you're dead wrong. It's also not uncommon for control-sensitive people to assume that the answer to their problem is only a question away. Someone, anyone, may have the secret or the insight that will set them free—abracadabra! It's hard to convince people who distrust themselves to believe in themselves.

Sam, a forty-year-old computer programmer, couldn't stop asking for help. He was driving his wife crazy, as well as his friends, and even his kids. All he would say, over and over, was, "Am I getting better?" "What's wrong with me?" "Do I need to go to the hospital?" The more he asked, and the more he was reassured, the more compulsive he became. It was Sam's wife who initially called me because she and her family couldn't take Sam's hounding any longer. Sam needed to break his cycle of looking outside of himself for answers. Once he did, with a little hard work, he found what he was looking for. It was there all the time. He just needed to build up his confidence to trust it.

Alcohol and Other Drugs

Alcohol and other drugs are particularly dangerous for the control-sensitive individual. You don't have to look too far to understand why. What could be more appealing to a control-driven person than not caring—about anything! Ah, the relief of being set free. Drugs, and especially alcohol, reduce anxiety by producing a cavalier, detached attitude—an attitude in which being in control isn't nearly as important as getting high and staying high. If your life is riddled with anxiety and depression, you're a potential candidate for the devil's nectar, as an Alcoholics Anonymous (AA) friend of mine calls it.

I met Randy at an alcoholic rehabilitation center in San Diego, where I was doing one of my internships. He was an unemployed, twenty-eight-year-old electrician who had recently come to the shelter. Sober, Randy was terribly insecure, panicky, and fearful of life. Drunk, however, he saw things differently:

> When I drink I don't think about things. Nothing matters, only drinking. For a while I would hang with some friends, especially when we were doing drugs, but as I got more into booze, I just wanted to get high—alone. Everyone was a distraction. It wasn't social anymore. *All* that mattered was getting drunk. Nothing else. It didn't matter if I lied, stole, hurt, as long as I could get drunk. I know I did some terrible things, but when I was drinking, I didn't care about anything.
>
> Getting sober was another story. About six months ago, I tried to get sober, even went to a couple of AA meetings. But I had this attitude, I wasn't like that room full of drunks. I was different. I'd be able to control my drinking. Yeah, I was different! My father was on my back to go to work, I had bills, collection agencies calling . . . I couldn't take it. The worse things got, the more I wanted to drink. The last couple of months, I was managing to stay drunk all the time. A few weeks ago, I woke up here. I started drinking in Boston, and I wound up here! I have no idea how I got here. I have no idea what I've done along the way. For all I know, my picture could be hanging in the post office right now. I'm scared. Really scared.

Before turning to alcohol, Randy had been feeling anxious about being laid off. His self-esteem was so low that he avoided any socialization. At first, he found that marijuana took the edge off his anxiety, enough so that he began going out to clubs. His ritual was to get high on pot, go to a club, and drink all night. At first, he was attracted to being able to discard his woes like a snake shedding its skin. He began to live for his evenings, sleeping all day and partying all night. As Randy began to deplete his savings, he turned away from his marijuana habit and became mostly a shot-and-a-beer drinker.

For a short while, Randy thought he was on top of the world. He loved going out, partying, womanizing, playing pool, and meeting new people. He was feeling no pain, as long as he kept drinking alcohol and smoking marijuana. What he didn't count on was that the more he drank, the more the drink controlled him.

When it comes to life's insecurities, perhaps the very last place you'll find an answer is at the bottom of a whiskey bottle. Drugs such as alcohol are dangerous because they lull you away from your struggles, offering instead an anesthetized escape. Unfortunately, in order to stay in this surreal place of detachment, you have to stay high. As your life becomes more and more a shambles, the more you have to escape it. As every addict finds out, what appears to be an escape invariably becomes a prison.

There's only one acceptable way out, and that's to dismantle the engine that produces your anxiety and depression. It's an engine that's being driven by a primitive, destructive part of your personality I call the Insecure Child. The best way for you to shut down the engine is to remove the driver.

As long as your Insecure Child is left unchallenged, steering your life, you're looking for that "free lunch." Alcohol and other drugs are tempting to the Child because they require no effort, offer immediate relief, and create an illusion of invincibility. If you're drinking too much or using any illegal substance, you are contradicting your Self-coaching goals. You must stop! If you can't, you need to get into a program (there's none better than AA) or at least consult with a mental-health professional.

If you really want to beat anxiety and depression, recognize the obvious: One foot going north while the other goes south can only waste your efforts. Self-coaching will introduce you to Self-talk, a powerful technique that is compatible with both a twelve-step program and counseling. Self-coaching can train you to choose and sustain one direction, one path—life.

Self-Coaching Reflection
No one else—only you—can do what's necessary
to heal you. The sooner you realize and accept this,
the more quickly you will progress.

He's Driving Me Crazy!

Before you decide that immunity sounds pretty damn good, let me tell you about a husband who thought he was well vaccinated:

Stacy, a rather distraught wife, called me one evening, asking about marital counseling. She said that her husband, Peter, was so jealous he tried to control her literally every minute. She couldn't shop where she wanted, talk to her friends, or choose her own clothes. Peter would follow her, eavesdrop on her phone conversations, read her mail, and even check the mileage on her car each morning. He was running—and ruining—her life. She just couldn't take it anymore.

I suggested that Stacy speak with Peter about joining her for a couple's session. She called back a week later saying that Peter felt there wasn't anything wrong with the marriage. As far as he was concerned, things were fine.

On one level, Peter was no fool. He knew that coming to therapy was going to stir things up, and that could be dangerous. From his point of view, as long as his wife cooperated with him—

allowed him to control her—there were no problems. Control gave him what he wanted—the illusion of marital harmony—his illusion, not hers!

Do I Really Need to Change?

Ask yourself the following questions:

- Does the need for control consume and frustrate my life?
- Have I noticed more anxiety, desperation, moodiness, or even depression creeping into my life?
- Has my have-to-be-in-charge attitude made me rigid?
- Are my relationships showing signs of deterioration, becoming strained and quarrelsome, if not hostile?
- What about my capacity for enjoyment? Has it diminished because my mind is always somewhere else, distracted by incessant "what-ifs"?
- Is my life being wasted, pooled up in a puddle of ruminations and frantic motion?
- Does my impatience make it difficult, if not impossible, to relax and have fun? Does it take having a couple of drinks for me to loosen up?
- Does everything always have to be done my way, or no way? Has delegating responsibility always been a problem?

If any of the preceding sounds familiar, then you may have a control-sensitive personality. Don't panic; it's not a death sentence. It just means that Self-coaching is going to become a valuable tool for you.

Self-Coaching Is the Solution

All your problems begin and end with insecurity—specifically, self-doubt. Once you doubt your capacity to handle life, then you're doomed to compensate through control. The more you doubt, the more control you need to handle that treacherous world out there.

81

What if I can show you that your need to control has nothing to do with the problems you've so desperately tried to juggle for so long? What if I can demonstrate that your deficiencies—your perceived inadequacies to handle life—are gross misperceptions born out of past wounds? Most importantly, what if I can help you recognize your genuine and spontaneous capacity for responding to life in a winning way?

Consider this. Let's say you're sitting out on the deck one balmy summer evening and a hungry mosquito decides to dine on your neck. What would happen? Without any debate, you'd raise your hand and smack. Right? You wouldn't think about it, you'd just do it.

While out on one of my fossil digs in Wyoming, I came across an allosaurus tibia. Deeply engrossed in the tedious excavation, I hadn't noticed the three-inch scorpion crawling only inches from my face. Even though I had never come nose-to-claw with a scorpion in the wilds, I had an immediate recognition and split-second response. With my knife, I swiped away at the scorpion and sent it, along with a pound of sand, cascading down the cliff.

Growing up in the New York metropolitan area, I didn't get much experience with scorpions. Nonetheless, when it comes to taking care of business, we humans are formidable machines—unless, of course, insecurity and a demand for control have mucked up the works. Self-coaching can teach you to "unmuck the works" with your unrehearsed natural talent to handle life. A control-sensitive person, rather than relying on his or her natural resources to handle life's challenges, instead leans exclusively on one resource: thinking. As formidable as your intellect may be, it represents only a tiny island in a vast ocean of ability. This ocean is your genuine capacity for automatic self-preservation and protection. The nice part is that you don't need to understand your ocean; just unleash it—and then trust it.

❖ ❖ ❖

TRAINING SUGGESTION

It's important to distinguish between a normal, healthy need for control and insecurity-driven desires. Writing down your expressions of control can really help you see the difference. If you get stuck coming up with examples, look at the quiz at the beginning of this chapter, along with those in Chapters 1 and 6. They can help trigger a recognition for a particular struggle you might have had that day.

Use the following example as a guide, but keep in mind that success with this exercise will take some practice. Look especially for a certain desperate, compulsive, or rigid quality to help you spot insecurity-driven expressions (for example, a compulsive "I have to" versus a normal "I want to").

Expressions of Control	Normal	Insecurity-Driven
1. I'm always avoiding germs.	☐	☑
2. I like to please my husband.	☑	☐
3. I have to please my friends.	☐	☑
4. I can't stand it if one hair is out of place.	☐	☑
5. I'm a penny-pincher.	☐	☑

For the sake of clarity, let me show you how the preceeding expressions can switch polarities:

Expressions of Control	Normal	Insecurity-Driven
1. I don't want to catch her germs.	☑	☐
2. I have to please my husband all the time.	☐	☑
3. I enjoy pleasing my friends.	☑	☐
4. I like my hair to look nice.	☑	☐
5. I try to avoid wasting money.	☑	☐

❖ ❖ ❖

PART III

Self-Coaching: The Program and How to Do It

8

Self-Talk

When a coach sees her star pitcher begin to slump as batter after batter start to get on base, what does she do? She calls time out and walks out to the mound. Once on the mound she has one job: to calm down her rattled ace. She uses whatever coaching strategies and tools are available to her.

With a high-strung, perfectionistic kind of kid, the coach might try reassurance with a bit of objectivity, "You know you're better than this. Your confidence is rattled—no problem. Just slow down and play your game. You're my star—right?" With a more obsessive type, the coach may choose a no-nonsense, tough-love approach, "You know what the problem is? You think too much! Stop thinking, and just throw strikes." Coaches need to know how to focus their athletes.

Like a pitcher who's in a slump and throwing nothing but meat-balls, you, too, can quickly lose objectivity when your insecurity trips you up. "It's all too hard," you say. "I can't do it; but what am I going to do now? I'm such a loser." This is when you need a time-out, when you need to have a conference with your coach—but hold on a minute. Because you're both the athlete and the coach, how can you possibly be objective when you're feeling out of control? You can, if you're using Self-talk. *Self-talk* is a technique that allows you to work with yourself, even when you're riddled by insecurity and self-doubt. With Self-talk, you can actually coach yourself back to health—even when a part of you has quit and given up.

Self-Talk Basics

What's going through your mind right now? What thoughts are you aware of? Can you "hear" this inner talk? When you say, "I don't feel I'm ever going to get better," or "Why would he want me anyway, I'm such a loser," you're actually talking to yourself—not with your mouth, but with your mind. In order to be emotionally affected by your thoughts, two things have to happen: First, you—a part of you—must *listen* to what you're saying, and second, either you must accept what you hear as being the truth, or you must reject it.

A part of you talks, and a part of you listens—this may seem strange at first, but with some reflection, you can see how obvious it is. If I say to myself, "I can't lose weight, I'm just too weak," and then I find myself getting depressed, I've listened to and accepted this thought. I could just as well have chosen not to listen by insisting, "No problem, I'm going to work harder at my diet" or "Nonsense, I'm fine just the way I am." By understanding this simple concept that part of you talks and another part of you chooses either to listen or not to listen, you begin to understand the essence of Self-talk.

The part of your thoughts that gets you into trouble is what I refer to as your Insecure Child. Let me briefly highlight this important concept.

Your Insecure Child

All this talk about voices, different parts of you, and your inner child may leave you feeling a bit fragmented. First off, let me reassure you it's normal and healthy to have different levels of conscious expression and awareness. Think of consciousness at any given moment as a view from a 35mm camera. If you have a manual focus, you can turn the lens so that Fido is in focus and the flowers in the background are all a blur. Turn the lens in the opposite direction, and Fido becomes a blur and the flowers jump into crisp focus. With you, one moment, your Insecure Child may be in focus while your more mature side recedes into a blur. In contrast, Self-coaching, specifically your work with Self-talk, will teach you to stay focused on what's healthy and ignore what's unhealthy.

Imagine that someone followed you around when you were a young child and took videos of your every move. Watching these videos now, you might notice times when you became panicked about your mother leaving, or lying in your bed frightened over hearing your parents arguing in the next room. In another video, you might even notice yourself sulking and feeling sorry for yourself because you thought no one loved you. These images, captured on video, would show seminal moments of vulnerability that eventually shaped and molded the adult that you've become.

No matter how many times you watch the video, the child captured on that tape doesn't change—same fears, same panic, same doubts. Just as these images are permanently recorded on the videotape, they are also permanently recorded—imprinted—on your psyche. Along with this imprint of your Child are the misperceptions, distortions, and primitive thinking that eventually shaped your habit of insecurity.

Like the image on the psychic video, your inner child remains forever childlike. This eternal child is your Insecure Child. When your Insecure Child is allowed to be in charge of your thinking, you suffer. Why? Because your Child has only one perception of the world, the primitive, distorted, out-of-date perception captured on that old videotape. Self-talk will teach you all about your Child, but most importantly, it will teach you how to separate from the habit of adopting your Child's view of the world. It will teach you to turn off that video.

With practice, you'll begin to notice the childlike character of your troubled thoughts. Like your outer personality, the Insecure Child's personality expresses itself in many different ways. Just as any personality is composed of many traits, your Insecure Child's personality is a mosaic of many different expressions. Sometimes, you might hear yourself whining, "Nobody cares about my needs. I never get any help. Why do I have to work so hard?" Sometimes, you may hear a primitive tantrum, "No, I'm not going to give in!" or "Fine, I'll go to your mother's, but I'm not going to say a word!" At other times, you may hear a frightened, panicked child, "I can't go on, what's going to happen to me, somebody help me, please." Just as the world sees your unique outer personality, you need to recognize your other unique personality, the inner personality of your Insecure Child.

❖ ❖ ❖

Self-coaching healing principle 1.
Everyone has a legacy of insecurity, the Insecure Child.

❖ ❖ ❖

Let me introduce you to Jenna; her story will acquaint you with Self-talk's basics. Jenna, an eighteen-year-old high school senior came to therapy because of anxiety about her boyfriend:

> Michael is a great guy. I don't know why I don't trust him. I make him call me every night. He thinks it's because I miss him—actually, it's because I want to know if he's at home. He's going away this summer for football camp at his college and I just know something is going to happen. He's never been unfaithful, and he says he loves me. I know it's stupid, but I feel he's going to cheat on me. It's crazy because I've got the great boyfriend who has never done one thing wrong and I just can't trust him. I'm not eating, I worry all the time, and lately I'm getting furious with him over the smallest things.

The insecure, distrusting part of Jenna's psyche that's talking is her Insecure Child. Rather than fighting, or even challenging her Child's distortions, she accepts them without so much as a hesitation. Her Insecure Child talks, and she listens—and then she gets anxious.

Self-talk is a technique for learning to talk yourself out of negative, insecure thinking and into healthy alternatives. You build self-assurance by choosing to replace the paralyzing thoughts of insecurity with more objective, rational thinking—and that's just plain smart.

❖ ❖ ❖

Self-coaching healing principle 6.
Healthy thinking is a choice.

❖ ❖ ❖

You don't actually talk yourself out of negative thinking, well, not verbally. You talk by directing your thoughts, "I don't have to take this abuse any longer!" Most of the time, however, your thoughts are not directed; they're just part of a constant stream of semiconscious reverie, ". . . think I'll get a bite to eat . . . I'm so tired . . . I don't want to go to work tomorrow . . ."

Take a second right now to hear your inner talk. You might be sitting, thinking, "I can't go on reading much longer, I've got to make that phone call . . ." Your inner talk instigates and directs actions, precipitates reactions, and generates feelings. In the preceding example, telling yourself that you have to make that phone call might precipitate a slightly anxious feeling. You may feel a bit tense, unsettled, unable to concentrate as easily on your reading. This subtle pressure is a result of the thought/talk that innocently passed through your field of consciousness, ". . . I've got to make that phone call . . ." It was this thought that pulled you away from your tranquil reading. Instead of being in the moment, you were briefly living in an abstract future moment: thinking about getting up and making that phone call.

Self-talk is directed talk. It's talk designed to wrench your thoughts away from insecurity and to insist on more appropriate thinking. With few exceptions, most other thinking is undirected. These are simply neutral meandering thoughts: "Hmm, that coffee smells so good . . ." This, however, isn't the case with undirected thoughts driven by your Insecure Child. I'm sure you know the experience of being gripped by a panic or a sour mood. You never directed this experience ("Think I'll let that comment upset me now . . ."); it just happened to you. Anxiety and depression are reactions to undirected thoughts that are driven by your Insecure Child—thoughts that just seem to happen.

Living in the Moment

Whether you're reading a book, enjoying a sunset, listening to music, or playing with your children, once you've abandoned the moment because you've become swallowed up in insecurity, you've lost an opportunity for relaxation and true connectedness with your world. You are either in the moment or not. Anxiety-prone people, for example, can usually be found living in dread anticipation of the future, rarely in the moment. Their inner (undirected) talk might sound something like, "What if I get sick? Then I'll lose my position. All my work will be ruined. I know I'm going to get sick. . . ." Depressive people, on the other hand, typically dwell in the melancholy of past defeats and rejections. They, too, rarely live in the moment. Depressive inner talk might sound like, "If only I didn't say that. What's the use now? It's over, I'm doomed."

The irony is that the past and the future don't exist. They're nothing more than artifacts of our brain's ability to abstract. The only reality is the present. If you're anxious or depressed, your life has been pulled away from here-and-now living, leaving you floating in a netherworld of worrisome regrets or anticipations. Life has been pulled away only because you don't realize you can say no. Self-coaching is going to change all that.

❖ ❖ ❖

Self-coaching healing principle 2.
Thoughts precede feelings, anxieties, and depressions.

❖ ❖ ❖

With the exception of simple reflexes, thoughts precede actions, reactions, and—most importantly—feelings. The thoughts that we do have are based on how we perceive our world. These perceptions are the conclusions we've drawn from our unique learned experiences. An abused or neglected child will arrive at very different conclusions about life than a child reared with love and respect. A secure person, for example, may handle the silence of a therapy session calmly, thinking,

"This is an unhurried chance for me to express my concerns." An anxious person, on the other hand, might react quite differently to the same silence: "What does he want from me? What is he expecting me to say? I hate this!" A depressed person, dealing with the same silence, might conclude, "I have nothing to say. I can't even do therapy right! I'm such a failure."

I Know I Worry Too Much, But . . .

Insecurity, self-doubt, and fear all create distortions of reality. Take a look at Linda's struggle. She shows just how easy it is to become confused by the Insecure Child's distorted way of thinking. Linda is a twenty-four-year-old mother who, for years, had been struggling with panic and fear. Nonetheless, it wasn't until her daughter started school that she felt totally out of control and in need of help.

> With all that's going on in the world, I just can't stop being anxious about my daughter being in school. I know they don't lock the doors at the rear of the school. Anyone can walk in. I know I'm the only mother who stands and watches until she's inside. During the day I find myself driving past the school. I know she's all right. I just feel so nervous. I keep having these racing thoughts. "What if this . . . or what if that . . ." I know it's silly, but bad things can happen—right? How do I know they won't happen to my daughter? The only time I begin to calm down is when I see her coming out of the building after school.

Linda's thinking is somewhat extreme, but it does show how a little information combined with a lot of insecurity can begin to write a scary screenplay. Linda isn't any different from you or me. What's happened is that she allowed her concerns and normal anxieties to piggyback one on top of the other—unimpeded. She developed a habit of tortuous, insecure thinking. Notice how all her thoughts are anticipations of future chaos. As you can see, Linda clearly suffers from her distortions. If, like Linda, you begin to slide down the slippery slope of anxiety's seductive "what-iffing," then it won't be long before you'll feel like a dog chasing its tail. Anxious thoughts causing anxiety, causing more anxious thoughts, causing . . . you get the point.

❖ ❖ ❖

Self-coaching healing principle 5.
Insecurity is a habit, and any habit can be broken.

❖ ❖ ❖

Linda needed to understand that if you let insecurity dictate what's real, then you must pay a price. She paid with anxiety. Self-talk helped Linda learn that her insecurity had a unique voice. In fact, it actually had a personality—in her case, a very worried, fearful, distrusting, primitive personality. This voice, different from her more rational, healthy voice, was her Insecure Child. By using Self-talk to first help her recognize who was talking to her (i.e., healthy Linda or tortured, Insecure Child Linda), she was ready to coach herself to fight off these distortions. She did this by replacing her Child's thinking with more rational, positive, directed thinking—Self-talk. Linda chose to be healthy. Self-talk insists on more appropriate interpretations: "I'm going to risk believing that my daughter is all right—no more 'what-ifs.' When I drop her off, I'm just not going to allow myself to dwell on such silliness." Linda found out, as you will, that once you take charge and direct your thinking using Self-talk, anxiety and depression lose their power.

❖ ❖ ❖

Self-coaching healing principle 6.
Healthy thinking is a choice.

❖ ❖ ❖

It may be surprising to you that insecurity, fear, doubt, and distrust can actually have a voice and a personality. You're surprised because, over time, you've become identified with your destructive patterns. You see them not as contaminants to your persona, but *as* your persona. When you say, "I am depressed" or "I am anxious," you actually become your depression or your anxiety. On the other hand, if you were to say, a *part of me* is depressed or anxious—a very destructive part—then you can approach your symptoms with the necessary detachment to liberate yourself from them.

You are not now and never were meant to be your anxiety or your depression. Anxiety and depression, although a normal expected part of life, should never dominate your life. If you are bullied by any of these destructive symptoms, please realize that you are a victim of nothing more than misguided, insecurity-driven attempts to control life. Don't be misled by your symptoms. Habits are only habits; anxiety is only anxiety, and depression is only depression. These are not supernatural, unworldly, or beyond your ability to change—just bad habits.

❖ ❖ ❖

Self-coaching healing principle 7.
A good coach is a good motivator.

❖ ❖ ❖

Getting Started—a Tip from Super Mario

A few years back, my kids invited me to join them in one of their video games. I had observed them playing, making little Mario leap, jump, dodge, and scurry all over the screen. It seemed easy. With the controller in hand, I quickly found out otherwise. Don't forget, kids today have been brought up on video games. In my day, the only toys that moved were those you wound up. I was all thumbs.

The good-natured chiding from my kids only galvanized my resolve to develop this useless skill. Occasionally, after work, I'd slip into the basement for a few Nintendo minutes. At first, I was frustrated. Just as when I've tried to write wrong-handed, I couldn't make my Mario guy do what I wanted. It didn't matter how hard I tried. (This actually made things worse.) Then, after about a month, Mario began to do exactly what I wanted him to do! Somehow my brain, hands, and eyes all began to work together, and Mario began to become an extension of my will.

Your first attempts with Self-talk may feel like "all thumbs" to you. Just as with my Nintendo experience, you will have to learn to do things—over and over—that feel unnatural at first. Keep reminding yourself, the frustration is only temporary. Accept from the start that Self-talk takes practice—the more the better, and the sooner the better. Even if your technique is rough, go ahead and give it a shot. If you get confused or feel you've made a mistake, you're allowed. Just keep trying and learning from your efforts. You've got absolutely nothing to lose—and so much to gain.

❖ ❖ ❖

TRAINING SUGGESTION

Take any opportunity you have to practice differentiating between directed Self-talk, undirected thoughts driven by insecurity, and neutral undirected thoughts. The following chart is an example of how to log these experiences. See whether you can come up with a few examples of each category from your day.

Undirected Neutral Thinking	Undirected Insecure Thoughts	Directed Self-Talk
1. Guess it's time to call it a day; I'm tired.	1. It's too hard. I can't do it.	1. No, I'm not going to give up. I've worked too long and too hard.
2. What a beautiful sunset.	2. Why does he want to see me? What did I do? This is terrible.	2. There's nothing to be afraid of, it's just a simple cough.
3. What do I feel like eating? Guess I'm not that hungry.	3. My hair looks awful; I can't go to the dance. I want to die.	3. Enough is enough. It's time to get to work.

❖ ❖ ❖

9

The Three Easy Steps
of Self-Talk

The dictionary defines insecurity simply as a lack of confidence or assurance. Most people will tell you that it's an unsafe, doubting tension you feel from time to time. What about you, how would you describe insecurity? I would describe it as the inability to believe in yourself. It's your Insecure Child who, filling your head with doubt and fear, has made it impossible for you to trust that you can handle life. Know what? You've been duped. Your Insecure Child may have some habit strength, but trust me, your Child's not that strong. There's only one reason you've been bullied for so long: It's because you've never adequately challenged your Child—until now. In just three simple steps, you're about to put an end to the erosion that has stripped you of self-trust and personal security.

Self-Talk Step 1. Learn to Listen
Practice hearing your thoughts. Ask yourself,
"Does what I'm hearing sound mature, rational,
or reasonable? Or does it sound primitive, excessively
emotional, childish, and insecure? Is it me,
or is it my Insecure Child talking?"

Step 1 isn't complicated; it just takes practice. Using the sample workout sheet at the end of this chapter, all you need to do is start asking a simple question: Is this childish or is it mature?

Self-Coaching Tip
Whenever you sense an increase in anxiety or depressive symptoms, suspect that your Insecure Child is behind your distress.

Take a look at how Lauren, a twenty-five-year-old schoolteacher, was eventually able to apply Step 1 to her problem:

> Last week I was watching TV, and my roommate walks up to me and drops this note in my lap and then goes into her room and slams the door. The note said she couldn't go on living with my sloppiness.
>
> I just sat there. I was fuming. My first reaction was to barge into her room and give her a piece of my mind. Okay, I'll admit it's true. I am a slob, but I wasn't aware that it was an issue for Sandy. She thinks she's so perfect. Well, we'll have to see about that. As far as I'm concerned she can start looking for a new roommate! From now on, she can start taking the bus to work—the taxi service has just ended. Do you believe it—a note? She couldn't even tell me face-to-face! Now we're not talking. I just turn away when she walks into the room. I refuse to be civil. Why should I be? I'll show her. She's going to pay for this. I don't care how uncomfortable it gets. If she doesn't like it, she can leave. You'd think she was Miss Perfect. The nerve! Guess what? I haven't done a dish since Sunday, my clothes are all over the apartment and the bathroom is absolutely gross—and I'm not changing!

Does Lauren sound mature, rational, or reasonable? Of course not. Lauren's thinking is highly emotional, childish and spiteful. It's classic Insecure Child, and she's listening. Step 1 requires that she begin to evaluate her thoughts and reactions. When Lauren first challenged herself with Step 1, she found herself defending her childish position, recalling all the terrible things Sandy had done in the past. Because Lauren was feeling so anxious, however, she rightly suspected that her Insecure Child lurked behind her intense thinking. She finally admitted, "Yes, I'm acting childish. If I were more mature about it, I would have told her how much she hurt my feelings. Maybe we could have worked out a contract or something."

Lauren is a good example of what I've found time after time. When pressed, most people can tell the difference between what is mature and what is ridiculous. Trust me, child talk, if nothing else, is usually quite ridiculous.

If you get confused, as Lauren did, step back, let the dust settle on any emotionally charged incident, then just come back to your assessment again, and again, if necessary. Don't be fooled by your Insecure Child's attempt to fog the issue. In fact, you can expect it. Once you get the hang of it, you'll see it's not that hard to spot the influence of your Insecure Child. After you've seen through your Insecure Child's smoke screen a few times, you'll have no further trouble. In fact, you'll get so good at it, you'll be able to evaluate the quality of your thinking while you're thinking it.

Take a look at the following examples. See how good you are at spotting Insecure Child thinking. Read each quotation, and see whether you think it describes Insecure Child thinking (circle "Yes") or more mature, rational thinking (circle "No"). You'll find the answers following the quiz.

1. "Fine, he doesn't want my opinion, then let's see how he likes my silent treatment."   Yes   No

2. "I'm never going to get ahead, I'm such a failure."   Yes   No

3. "Nothing ever goes right for me. Everyone is against me. Why me?"   Yes   No

4. "She hasn't called in weeks. That's not at all like her. I wonder if everything is all right. Maybe I should call?"   Yes   No

5. "He didn't call yet. Something must be wrong.   Yes   No
   Maybe he had an accident. Maybe he's lying
   on the side of the road in a ditch."

Answers: Except for the fourth quotation, all of them are typical of the Insecure Child (insecure, exaggerated, hysterical, etc.). If you're not sure about number four, just contrast it to number five. The fourth one is a rational question, whereas number five starts off, not with an objective question, but with a negative, "Something must be wrong." This negative is followed up by more hysterical speculations.

Trying to come up with your Insecure Child's personality can really help. Just as you can easily recognize others in your life by what they say and do, your Insecure Child can become very predictable once you recognize your Child's personality traits. Start out using the following list to help with your identification:

- What kind of Insecure Child expressions do you encounter? Ask yourself, does your Child sound insecure; depressed, spoiled, panicked, fearful, sulky, or defiant?

- It helps to know the circumstances that typically bring about your Insecure Child—for example, stress, confrontations, free-floating anxiety or depression without external conflict, anticipation of conflict or confrontation, fear of losing control, difficulty in maintaining control, and so on.

- Find out how, specifically, your Insecure Child twists things around. What's his or her style: worry, anticipation of doom, excessive negativity, withdrawal, guilt, or hostility?

- Based on your Insecure Child's personality, see whether you can come up with a simple description or name that conveys your Child's essence (Scared Mary, Hostile Harry, Doomsday Dan, Whiny Wanda, Lonely Louise, etc.).

Long ago, I found that descriptions such as "the voice of insecurity" or "distorted thinking" are not effective in developing a working relationship with your insecurity. The more you flesh out your Insecure Child, the more intimate you become, the more quickly you will be to recognize your Child's nefarious effect on your thinking.

Keep in mind that, like your outer personality, your Insecure Child's personality expresses itself in many different ways. Your Insecure Child, for example, may act panicked one moment, impulsive the next, and helpless or desperate the next. Just as any personality is composed of many traits, your Insecure Child's personality is a mosaic of many different expressions. The following list gives you a hint of the many possible expressions you may encounter. See whether any sound familiar. The following list may help you as you characterize your Insecure Child. (Note: Descriptions in italics are characterizations you will meet in upcoming chapters.)

Panicked Child: *Chicken Littles*—believe that the sky is always falling; anxious, often with underlying depression (*Worrywarts, Turtles, Guilt-sensitives*)

Frightened Child: fearful; always worrying; the *what-iffers;* always anxious, with depression not far behind (*Worrywarts, Turtles, Guilt-sensitives*)

Manipulative Child: controlling and manipulative (*Martyrs* and *Chameleons—Swindlers, Politicians,* and *Diplomats*)

Bully Child: controlling through aggression and intimidation; black-and-white, opinionated thinkers; insensitive (*Hedgehogs*)

Hysterical Child: coming apart and waiting to be rescued; overly emotional; anxious and depressed (*Worrywarts, Control Freaks*)

Overwhelmed Child: a life-is-too-much; can't-go-on attitude; usually depressed and anxious (*Worrywarts, Guilt-sensitives, Turtles*)

Sulking Child: woe is me; "see what a pathetic wretch I am"; depressed (*Martyrs, Turtles, Worrywarts, Guilt-sensitives*)

Impulsive Child: black-and-white thinkers; impatient; need to be in control—right now; anxious (*Hedgehogs, Control Freaks*) and depressed (*Worrywarts, Turtles, Guilt-sensitives*)

Stubborn Child: my-way-or-the-highway attitude; prone to tantrums (*Politicians, Hedgehogs, Perfectionists—Stars, Control Freaks,* and *Fanatics*)

Helpless Child: overly dependent; clingers; looking to be rescued; anxious and depressed (*Worrywarts, Turtles, Guilt-sensitives*)

Hopeless Child: why bother, nothing-ever-works-for-me attitude; pessimistic; anxious (*Martyrs, Turtles*)

Self-Talk Step 2. Learn to Stop Listening
When you realize that your Insecure Child is speaking, decide not to listen. Then make yourself stop listening!

How do you stop listening to your Insecure Child? Conceptually, this isn't as hard as you might think. Imagine you're trapped in a car with a whining child. At first, you may listen to what this spoiled brat is spewing forth, but after awhile, you tune out. You know that this child is still a menace to your tranquility, but the child's words are going totally unnoticed by you. Do the same thing with your Insecure Child: Once you recognize who's doing the talking, why would you go on listening?

In real life, I know this isn't so simple. It takes practice and a reorientation in your thinking—it takes strong, directed Self-talk. For example: "There's my panicked Insecure Child telling me I'm not going to make it. I'll be damned if I'm going to subscribe to my Child's view of life." Step apart from your Child's thinking, and ask yourself what a more mature, objective view might be.

Changing Channels

Changing channels is a handy technique to assist you in ignoring your Insecure Child. Imagine that you're listening to the radio. The announcer is delivering an apocalyptic speech on the danger of global warming. You're sitting in your living room beginning to feel tense. As you continue listening, you find your mood becoming increasingly anxious. Finally, you can't take any more, you turn the dial and find another radio host talking about the expected balmy weather forecast for the weekend. You begin to relax.

Each radio announcer represents a variation of your own thinking—positive and uplifting, negative and depressing, or neutral. What you listen to on the radio is no different from what you listen to in your mind. It's your conscious ego, using the techniques of Self-talk, that learns to change the channel and tune in to an appropriate broadcast. What you choose to listen to is what will influence you. Don't like what you're hearing? Change the channel. It's that simple.

Kerry, a forty-year-old receptionist found that changing channels saved her life. I asked her whether she would document her experiences for this book:

> I've been a control freak all my life. When I went to the doctor's for my cough last winter, I was shocked to find out that my blood pressure was high—really high. My doctor wanted me to start medication immediately. "No way!" I blurted out. If I had high blood pressure, I was going to handle it on my own. I've never had a problem with self-discipline. What was the problem? I read a few pamphlets the doctor gave me, and I was off. I started walking, losing a few pounds, cutting back on my salt, and checking my blood pressure at home. Unfortunately, my readings remained high. Nothing I did seemed to help. At one point my reading was 215/120! I began to panic. Nothing I was doing was working!
>
> My thoughts would race, "I'm going to die. What am I going to do? I don't want to be on medication for the rest of my life!" The more panicked I became, the more frantic my efforts, and the more my pressure remained high. I did some yoga, stopped smoking, increased from walking each morning to jogging . . . nothing worked. I started to get more depressed. I was feeling really out of control. Thoughts of not being around to watch my daughter

grow up, never retiring. . . . I couldn't sleep, I was irritable, snapping at everyone. I was getting headaches, but I wouldn't go back to the doctor because all he wanted me to do was get on medication.

That's when I started therapy. At first, I was elated with the concept that I could do something about my anxiety. Since stress was one of the things my pamphlet mentioned as a contributor to hypertension, therapy seemed like the next step. I found your technique of changing channels was exactly what I needed. At first, I wanted to see how many channels my radio had. It only had three: a panic channel; a distracted, neutral channel; and an "I've-got-to-do-something" control channel. After learning about control and Self-talk, I recognized that I was limiting my thinking—and my channels. I added a fourth—the "fact-finding" channel.

The fact-finding channel required that I stop being so pig-headed and explore all options—not just the ones listed on channels one through three. I went to a hypertension specialist and had a consultation. I was shocked to find out that there were recent medications that had very little, if any, side effects. I had always assumed blood-pressure medication made you sleep all day and go to the bathroom all night. I told the doctor I would consider his recommendations.

Next morning, while out on my run, my panic channel came in loud and clear, "Don't give in, you can't be on medication the rest of your life . . ." I knew this anxiety was coming from my Insecure Child, and using Self-talk, I decided not to listen—I changed the channels. I switched to the fact-finding channel. "Okay, so you don't want to take medication, but what's this pressure doing to my body? While I go on not deciding, I'm hurting myself. When I get back I'm going to research that medication." Okay, that was a success. I actually switched and listened to a more rational channel. But, it was the accidental addition of a fifth channel that really surprised me.

Channel five, which I now call the "Mozart channel," was a channel of relaxation. I first realized it when, after deciding to research the medication, I felt a calmness. All of a sudden, I forgot about my panic. I actually finished my jog looking at the beautiful flowering trees! That was a first for me. I had been in my head so completely, I hadn't even noticed that spring had arrived!

Now, whenever I'm going crazy with insecurity or panic, I make myself switch to the Mozart channel. And when I tune in, I just sort of allow myself to come out of my head and observe what's around me. I've learned to pay more attention to colors, sounds, things that don't have to do with thinking.

I finally decided to try medication. I figured I would give it a month or so and then decide. I went on this ACE inhibitor medication; it was late afternoon. After dinner that evening, I took my pressure and almost fell out of my chair. After consistent readings of 200/110 and higher, I recorded a reading of 116/80! Could this be? Within hours?

I've been on that medication for over three months now. The panic channel rarely gets listened to any longer. The fact-finding channel has also gotten less play time. And I try to switch that control channel as quickly as possible. But the Mozart channel has become my favorite. I use it for lots of situations, not just panic. Sometimes, if I'm a bit down, feeling sorry for myself, or just acting out-of-sorts, I can switch channels and connect with my world.

Self-Coaching Reflection
Self-coaching relies on Self-talk to teach you how to change channels when what's going through your mind hurts you. Why put a stop to it? Because you have a choice, why not choose to feel good?

I'm Feeling a Lot Smarter Now

With a little awareness, you can't help but notice just how ridiculous your Insecure Child's twisted negativity, fear, or incessant need for control really is. Eventually, when you look back, you'll be amazed at just how gullible you were. Once you get used to rejecting your Insecure Child's voice and switching those channels, you're only a step away from completely tuning out those twisted thoughts and recognizing your true source of strength: your mature and healthy ego.

Jay, a recently retired businessman, recounted the following:

> I still keep thinking something's wrong with me. Once in a while, I catch myself imagining terrible things and make an effort not to listen. Yesterday was a good example. I was at my computer, and as I reached over to scratch my side, I was startled by a jolt of pain. My rib was very tender. I touched it again, confirming that something was really wrong. I began to tell myself that something was wrong. What if it's cancer? I was getting anxious, but somehow I realized I was taking a totally innocent soreness and making it into the worst possible scenario. I knew it was the work of my Insecure Child, panicking, getting hysterical. I took my hand away from my sore rib, and I just told myself to stop being ridiculous. I refused to listen. I made myself repeat again and again: "Stop listening. It's just your ridiculous Child." It worked! I'm not sure how many times I had to fight off the Child, but it eventually worked. I completely forgot about my rib.
>
> It was later that evening when I was taking my shirt off that I remembered my sore rib. And you know what? I remembered that I had taken a Yoga class at the gym the day before and was trying to do this impossible triangle pose. I probably stretched too much. I'm so glad I fought off that Child because I would have felt like such a fool had I gone to the doctor in a panic.

Jay is typical of many patients who need to find out that patience and perseverance pays off. The Insecure Child is used to going unchallenged. Most people, without realizing it, not only permit the Insecure Child to take over, but also actually join in the hysterics. For example, had Jay not been aware of his Self-talk training, he might have taken the thought of cancer and added a whole host of doom-and-gloom prognostications, "What else can it be; it must be cancer!" "I don't want to die!" The last thing your Child needs is your help.

Self-Talk Step 3. Direct Your Thinking
After you stop letting your Insecure Child steer your thoughts, do something about it. Direct your thinking toward a healthier perspective.

Self-talk's first step is to distinguish between healthy thinking and Insecure Child thinking, then with Step 2 you decide not to listen to your Insecure Child. Now, using Step 3, you direct your thoughts toward a more objective, healthy perspective. In the next chapter, and throughout the remainder of this book, you will be given ample instructions for enhancing your ability to direct your Self-talk. Once you separate from your Insecure Child, thinking clearly becomes a very natural process. Take a look at Mary's story.

Mary is a middle-aged woman, married with two adolescent children. She is employed as a computer programmer. She originally came into therapy because of tremendous guilt and depression she felt over an infatuation with a man she met in her karate class. She had become completely obsessed with this other man, so much so that her job, marriage, and friendships were all jeopardized.

Mary preferred using a journal, which she has allowed me to reproduce here:

JANUARY 28: Saw Ron [the man at karate class] tonight. I can only describe it as physical pain. . . . only want to be with him.

FEBRUARY 1: I've been trying to use the concept of the Insecure Child, but it's like I really don't want to spoil what I'm feeling for Ron. God, I don't want to jeopardize such a beautiful feeling. . . . I need him so much. I can't go on without him in my life.

FEBRUARY 5: I was reading my last entry and realized that it was probably my Insecure Child writing those words. I must ask myself, do "I" really need Ron? Really? Could it be the Insecure Child who does? Maybe it's my child. . . . I'm going to call the Insecure Child in me "Scared Mary." Not completely sure why, she just seems so young and frightened.

FEBRUARY 8: Scared Mary says that Ron would know how to treat me . . . not like Tom [her husband]. Okay, I admit it, I'm still listening to what Scared Mary says! I can't help it! Guess I don't want to stop. I tried asking Scared Mary why Ron was so perfect, so wonderful. No answer. Feels kind of stupid talking to myself.

FEBRUARY 13: Bad day. I just couldn't get out of bed. I'm definitely getting more depressed. I don't want to live my life without Ron. Should I tell Tom? What about the kids? My anxiety's going through the roof. . . . hard to fall asleep. Losing weight. That's okay with me. Can't do anything except think of Ron. HELP! I feel so empty.

Mary and I had a session at this point, and we discussed her journal entries. She told me in no uncertain terms that she would never break up her family and just wished that she could stop being tormented with thoughts of Ron. (Incidentally, Mary had never met or spoken a word to Ron; he was purely a fantasy.) I pointed out that as long as she indulged Scared Mary, she would suffer. She had to make a choice. If she wanted to feel better, she would have to decide who she was going to side with: Scared Mary or Mary.

FEBRUARY 15: Heard from Scared Mary today. She was feeling desperate again. She wants me to leave home and tell Ron about my feelings for him! I finally managed to take a stand. I told her to cool it. No one is leaving home. Not at first, but later that afternoon, I did begin to feel better! I spent the afternoon with the kids and didn't have one Ron-thought.

FEBRUARY 16: Yesterday was a false hope. . . . can't stop thinking about Ron—what else is new? Feel like I'm going crazy. Wait a second, I can straighten that thought out: I'm not going crazy; Scared Mary is going crazy! That's it! Scared Mary can't live without Ron! The question is, can I? Maybe? Just saying this to myself is making me feel better, less tense. Scared Mary wants romance. She just wants to float in those clouds and think about Ron all the time. I'm trying to distract myself. Sometimes I'm successful; sometimes I'm not.

FEBRUARY 20: Woke up this morning dragging myself around. I almost didn't recognize Scared Mary twisting my mind. She was very subtle this morning. I finally recognized her pathetic whimpering. I sat myself gently but firmly down, and let myself know that I don't have to be as needy as Scared Mary. I can choose not to be desperate! Okay, okay, maybe I'm fooling myself into believing all this, but, right now, I don't care. All I know is that I feel better and that's enough for now.

FEBRUARY 22: I'm beginning to realize that I don't have to run off to Never-Never Land to be happy. I have to see the opportunities that already exist. Life would be so easy if I would! Granted, Tom needs a little work—okay, maybe a lot of work—but he's a good man, and I'm sure I have a love for him. Maybe it's not fireworks, but, I admit, it is a love. I need to stay around and work it out, make it happen. Hear that, Mary?

FEBRUARY 23: I made my first attempt to be courageous. I went over and sat next to Tom and held his hand. For one precious moment I didn't know where Scared Mary was. For that one moment, I didn't feel scared.

FEBRUARY 26: Before class I overheard Ron telling another guy that all he wanted to do in life was "nail" his secretary! THANK YOU, GOD!

Self-talk allowed Mary to see clearly that there were two sides of her struggle—an irrational, impulsive, Insecure Child side characterized as "Scared Mary" and a more practical, healthy, responsible side. Mary's journal allows you to observe the evolution of her directed healthy efforts (e.g., "I can choose not to be desperate . . ." or "I don't have to be as needy as Scared Mary . . .").

Whenever you allow your insecurity to contaminate your healthy ego, you can't avoid feeling disoriented. Self-talk works because it helps you understand the separation that's necessary between you and your insecurity. Once you understand this separation, then it's just a matter of directing your thoughts until you begin to take your life back from your Insecure Child.

Are You Ready?

Self-talk is a technique that requires practice, practice, and more practice—every chance you get. There's no need to be compulsive or rigid with your workouts, though. With a catch-as-catch-can attitude, your advances and insights will accumulate over time. Don't be greedy; be patient, and try to trust the program. I can almost guarantee you that your Insecure Child will try to sabotage your efforts. Expect it. Remember, your insecurity trusts only its own neurotic attempts at controlling life—certainly not the prospect of change; and especially not the radical change I have in store for you.

If, because of depression, you feel overwhelmed and intimidated by your workouts, be patient. If anxiety leaves you panicked over whether you're progressing rapidly enough, be patient. In the chapters that follow, you'll learn many ways to motivate and sustain your daily workouts. For now, try to embrace every effort, no matter how small or how infrequent. Keep reminding yourself that it's impossible for the twisted thinking of insecurity to thrive in the cold, clear light of objective reality.

Think of your workouts as accumulating pieces of a jigsaw puzzle. Your job is the simple task of adding a piece here, a piece there—an insight, an observation, an intuition—always accumulating information about your Insecure Child's distorted, insecure thinking. Encourage yourself to stay focused on the accumulation of pieces to your personal puzzle—learn the distorted thinking that precedes your anxiety or depression. As with a jigsaw puzzle, although the picture may be hidden for quite a while, it may take only that next piece. . . . then, there it is! The picture reveals itself! Similarly, the view of your objective, healthy reality will pop through the haze of distortions. Remember, no pressure, no time line: Just stick with the program, and your real truth will be revealed.

Although you will learn much valuable information in the chapters that follow, at this point, you're more than ready to begin experimenting with Self-talk. Just as Mary did with her journal, you should feel free to personalize your approach. Some people prefer tape-recording their results at the end of the day, while others use the tape recorder to have an actual dialogue, switching voices to represent their insecure voice and their healthy voice. I had one patient who preferred sketching. Her caricatures were impressive, showing a child snarling, stamping her feet, and, on one occasion, spitting. Be creative—it can't hurt.

Self-Talk Review

Step 1. Practice hearing your thoughts. Ask yourself, "Does what I'm hearing sound mature, rational, or reasonable, or does it sound primitive, excessively emotional, childish, and insecure? Is it me, or is it my Insecure Child talking?"

Step 2. When you realize that your Insecure Child is speaking, decide to stop listening.

Step 3. After you stop letting your Insecure Child steer your thoughts, do something about it! Direct your thinking toward a healthier perspective.

❖ ❖ ❖

TRAINING ASSIGNMENT

In Chapter 11, you will be given specific instruction for setting up a training log. If you're feeling ambitious and want to get a head start, use the following chart on a daily basis. You can include these charts later in your log.

Start by recording as many anxious or depressed incidents as possible, filling in Steps 1, 2, and 3. Once you get used to spotting your Insecure Child and your Child's unique expressions, you will be able to recognize your Child immediately, without any aids.

Self-Talk Training Log

Describe any anxious or depressed incidents	**Step 1** Were you able to determine whether your thoughts were mature or childish?	**Step 2** Did you decide not to listen, and were you effective?	**Step 3** Did you direct your thinking toward a healthier perspective?
	☐ Yes ☐ No	☐ Yes ☐ No	☐ Yes ☐ No
	☐ Yes ☐ No	☐ Yes ☐ No	☐ Yes ☐ No
	☐ Yes ☐ No	☐ Yes ☐ No	☐ Yes ☐ No

❖ ❖ ❖

❖ ❖ ❖

TRAINING SUGGESTION

Changing Channels

Every so often, check out your undirected thoughts. See whether what you're thinking is neutral or negative. If you come across a negative thought, try changing the channel. Take, for example, the insecure thought, "I'll be up all night worrying," and change to a positive channel, "When I get home tonight, I'm going to take a steaming hot bath and melt away my worry." Get as much practice as you can interrupting and changing your thoughts.

❖ ❖ ❖

10

Self-Talk:
Follow-through

I learned about follow-through watching my son. Justin's a kicker and punter on the Princeton football team. After many a session with Justin and his coach, I kept hearing the same thing repeated after every kick, "head down, follow through, let your leg swing through the ball" You'd think that once your foot contacted the ball, that would be enough to send it skyward. Nope. The results depend on the leg swinging through, beyond the ball, completing the motion. In sports, follow-through means finishing your motion. In Self-coaching, once you succeed at directing your thinking away from the Insecure Child, you need to follow through, not with continued motion, but with continued insight.

Start by Asking Why

Let's say I've been feeling depressed and want to quit my job. After changing the channels on my Insecure Child's whining and sulking, and after directing my thoughts to a more rational and reasonable perception of my options, it's time to follow through. I do this by gaining insight into my Child's motives. If I can determine why my Child is so desperate, I can begin to fortify myself for my next skirmish with him by understanding what makes him tick, "My Child wants to quit because he can't handle the responsibility. Why? Because he's too scared of screwing up. My Child doesn't trust me!"

Why you're withdrawn, or why you worry all the time are shadows

114

of your past ("I'm sensitive to criticism because my mother was a control freak. Nothing I did was ever good enough!" "Sure I'm insecure. When I was young, I was overweight. Everyone teased me, even my parents."). Somewhere in your trial-and-error development, you found that certain strategies of control worked, and others didn't.

Laurel, a thirty-year-old secretary, recalled,

> My mother was a great one for using guilt. It would drive me crazy. I can remember sitting up all hours of the night crying, fretting . . . sometimes I wanted to die. I really wasn't a bad kid, but step out of line and immediately my mother would let me know how terrible I was. I was "driving her crazy." I tried to be a good girl, worked harder at school, did what I was told, but invariably, something would happen and I'd get nailed. I couldn't win.
>
> I remember one time, we were at the lake, and she asked me to go to the car and get her the suntan lotion. I must have grumbled, and with much ado, my mother gets up all in a huff and says, "fine, I'll get it myself you ungrateful, spoiled brat!" I had to do something, I was starting to feel almost dizzy with anxiety. Something clicked, I can't describe it, but I just decided that I didn't care anymore. It was like an anger toward my mother, but more. Hard to explain. I didn't like her, I didn't need her, I began to pull away from her. At the ripe old age of ten years old, I began to become independent—fiercely independent!
>
> As the years went on, I developed a complete shell around me. I found that no one could hurt me if I didn't care. Unfortunately, my shell never stopped growing, and now I'm accused by my husband of being too detached and aloof. Even my friends criticize me, calling me the "ice princess."

Laurel's withdrawal worked for her and with practice became her lifestyle.

If one strategy of control works more than another to reduce anxiety, it's likely to be repeated. A child with an alcoholic parent may, for example, develop a habit of emotional rigidity. Learning to think before reacting could prove the difference between a night of calm or a night of chaos. Considering such early circumstances, a primitive strategy like emotional rigidity might become highly effective. Once you begin to develop a habit's muscle, it can become a permanent fixture in your psychic life. In the preceding example, Laurel's mother has been dead for more than ten years, yet Laurel's turtlelike strategy of control continues to act the same way. Why? Habit—and once a habit is secure, it's usually ignored. We accept it as we do the nose on our face, or the color of our eyes—it becomes who we are.

❖ ❖ ❖

Self-coaching healing principle 5. Insecurity is a habit,
and any habit can be broken.

❖ ❖ ❖

Life Changes, but Habits Persist

First, a disclaimer: As helpful as the insights from follow-through are, they're not indispensable to your overall Self-coaching goals. The reason I emphasize this point is because in any self-exploration, when relying on memory and historical data, you're usually required to work with incomplete information. There's no doubt that follow-through can offer you a definite advantage in your ongoing skirmishes with your Insecure Child, but it doesn't replace the primary focus of your training program: Self-talk.

If you get too compulsive about every experience that may have wounded you in the past, you'll lose valuable time that can be spent working on your here-and-now Self-talk training. If you can't make any historical connection, be satisfied with a more casual explanation of the habits you do notice: "I've always been shy and withdrawn," or "I've worried all my life." Remember, the insight you gain from follow-through is just one component in your overall Self-coaching program. As important as it is, don't overemphasize it.

You can start off with some simple challenges, "Why did that compliment depress me?" Answer: "Deep down, I guess I don't feel worthy." Be particularly aware of any insecurity habit that may be driving your reactions. Also if you don't know or aren't sure, by all means, feel free to guess! For now, don't worry about mistakes; it's the workout we're after, not the accuracy.

The Ultimate Insight—Truth

Aside from asking why, there's one other aspect of follow-through that can make a big difference in your training—finding out your truth. If anxiety or depression are represented on one side of a coin, your truth is on the other. It's the realization that your life doesn't have to be driven by the habits of your Insecure Child—you actually have a choice. It's not only a recognition that healthy living is a choice; finding your truth also requires that you find the courage to pursue it. "Just because my Insecure Child says I can't handle it doesn't mean I can't. I can try, can't I?" You sure can!

❖ ❖ ❖

Self-coaching healing principle 6. Healthy thinking is a choice.

❖ ❖ ❖

Look at the following examples. The left-hand column lists passive, helpless, victim statements (Insecure Child–driven). Compare them with the statements on the right, which are proactive, constructive attempts to follow through:

Passive	Proactive
I feel guilty whenever I say "no."	Why do I feel I'm not allowed to say "no"? I don't know, maybe because I had soap shoved in my mouth when I was a kid. I'm not sure, but I do know what the truth is—I *am allowed!* What's stopping me from giving myself permission?

117

Passive	Proactive
I can't speak in front of people.	Why do I get anxious in front of people? Is it the vulnerability? Do I feel I have to be perfect? Just because my parents were never satisfied with me doesn't mean I can't learn to trust myself and not worry so much about messing up.
I'm so depressed about getting old.	Why do I feel it's so terrible to get old? Is it losing my sexual attractiveness, my looks, or my health? Maybe it's just feeling less in control of my life. I've always been able to charm people, but now I probably don't anymore. What I need is a deeper sense of security and self-worth—one that goes beyond the superficial, the physical.

Whenever you become a victim of exaggerated, mountain-out-of-molehill views like the preceding passive statements, you feel as though you're sinking. When you're clobbered with panic and anxiety, believe me, you're going down like a lead weight. You start feeling powerless and helpless, unable to do anything about it. Proactive follow-through statements, in contrast, start with the premise that a loss of control isn't fixed in stone; it's a problem that can be solved.

Just Ask Why

Just asking "why" is the key that eventually unlocks the mystery of your irrational lifestyle. You'd be amazed how many control-sensitive people just plod through each day, blindly accepting their self-imposed fate, never thinking to ask why; just accepting their perceived lot in life. When you do follow through and ask, "Why am I doing this?" on one level, you're recognizing that you have a choice. Once you understand you have a choice, you can ask, "Why am I *choosing* to do this?" You won't be a victim of control any longer—the truth shall set you free. Victims, by definition, have no choice. When you eventually understand the "why" of your control, you will begin to understand the motive of your insecurity. With this insight, you can begin to challenge this motive with here-and-now reality as you explore other, more healthy options.

Self-Coaching Reflection
Asking "why" is the first step in realizing
you have a choice.

Jane's Attack of the Frizzies

Jane, an energetic young lawyer, called me early one morning in a panic over having a "bad hair day." (I kid you not!) "I have the most important meeting of my life in three hours," she said. "You should see my hair . . . I look like a cleaning lady! I just can't go to that meeting; there's no way. This is terrible . . . I can't let anyone see me this way. What am I going to do?"

I've been awakened by many things in my professional career, but never by a bad-hair emergency. Even if you wanted to be generous, could you possibly, on any rational level, consider this a crisis? But Jane was convinced she was having a 911 day. "I don't believe it," she said. "I'm going to blow my chance because of this damn hair. I just can't go in today . . . I mean I *can't* go in! They'll be forced to give the case to Larry."

You and I, removed from Jane's panic, can certainly see that her bad-hair day was only a molehill. To her, though, it was a mountain of a problem. Sure, everyone likes to look good, and most of us get frustrated when we don't, but would you blow a once-in-a-lifetime opportunity over the frizzies? I hope not.

How about you? When was the last time you blew something out of proportion?

A History Lesson

I've mentioned that Self-coaching is only casually concerned with the history of your symptoms. Although this remains particularly true for the application of Self-talk, when you engage in follow-through, you will look for any clue—past or present—to help you gain insight into how your thoughts became distorted in the first place.

In Jane's case, by understanding a little of her history (in conjunction with her current perceptions), we could shed a lot of light on her emotional patterns. To understand Jane's obviously excessive reaction, it will help if you understand what she describes as her professional image and where it came from. For this type of historical exploration, you don't need a Ph.D., or years of therapy, just a little common sense.

Jane's parents were selfish, uncaring people whose parenting skills were neglectful at best, appalling at worst. For example, Jane's mother frequently forgot to make Jane any supper. "Oh, I'm sorry," she would say. "Mommy ate earlier and I just forgot about your dinner. I was going to get to it." Because of this neglectful environment, Jane began to experience intense and nagging feelings of inferiority that plagued her throughout her life. This inferiority wasn't buried; Jane was very conscious of it. She just accepted it as a part of life.

Growing up, her only solace came from school. With her Shirley Temple cute looks and her relentless study habits, she quickly earned a place in the hearts of her teachers. All that mattered at school was winning attention and admiration. School was truly her salvation. School gave her what she couldn't get at home: a sense of worth and pride. As long as she managed to control her image, no one had to know what she knew deep inside—how *really* worthless she was. Jane was a straight-A student who managed to graduate at the top of every class, from elementary school all the way through law school. At the law firm where she was currently employed, her popularity and stellar performance were quickly noticed, and she was given more high-profile clients to work with. She gave 110 percent effort all the time, and she took obvious pride in calling herself a "workaholic."

Regardless of her bright prospects, emotionally, Jane never progressed far from her childhood inferiority. She saw herself as a sham. When she was growing up, she believed her parents. She was convinced—even years after she had moved away—that if anyone really knew her, like her parents, anyone would certainly realize how worthless she was. At all costs, she had to prevent this secret from getting out.

No wonder Jane developed such a strong need for control. She worked hard at controlling what people knew, what they felt, what they thought, and what they saw when they looked at her. She felt all this was necessary because of her secret—her worthlessness.

Jane's call to me that morning was about losing control over her precious appearance. Without her image, she felt naked. Because everything in her life was held together precariously by thin threads of control, once she began to feel exposed, an old and all too familiar emotional avalanche began to bury her. Her fantasy was that her associates, seeing her this way, would start thinking differently of her. They wouldn't want to associate with her and eventually would wind up rejecting her—just like her parents.

Sound extreme? Of course it does, but if you combine Jane's history of insecurity with her years of patterning, you can understand how and why such extremes exist. Jane's reaction is a vivid illustration of how mountains begin their life as molehills, or in her case, bad-hair hills. Jane's history also reveals an important point about the general nature of control—it's driven by insecurity.

Insecurity is the bedrock on which control rests. Jane's insecurity clearly had nothing to do with her ability to perform. She'd been a star all her life. Her insecurity was an extension of her underlying sense of worthlessness. Her performance was simply a veneer masking her well-kept secret.

Separating Fact from Personal Fiction

In therapy, Jane's tenacity and seasoned work ethic proved to be an indispensable asset in dismantling her insecurity. Using Self-talk along with the various Self-coaching techniques discussed in this book, Jane quickly began to separate fact from personal fiction. Her new, more realistic self-image provided a comfort and security that had always eluded her. She learned a simple truth, one that would eventually set her free. She learned that she was okay. Actually, she learned that she had always been okay; she just hadn't known it.

Jane also came to understand that her molehill-to-mountain patterning made her particularly vulnerable to anxiety because of her perceived worthlessness. As a child, she obviously wasn't equipped to challenge these insecure feelings—what child is? The best she could do was try to avoid her pain by learning to control her circumstances.

As her burgeoning sense of security grew, Jane had one final challenge. Knowing that she was okay wasn't enough. That wasn't the hard part. She needed to *feel* that she was okay. In order to do this, Jane had to take an emotional leap of faith into unknown territory. Self-coaching paved the way, eliminating her confusion. Her choice became simple: Should she be ruled by twisted, sloppy thoughts or by the truth? Jane chose truth. Sure, she had to go against all her neurotic thoughts and risk believing—*really* believing—that she was okay, but once she did, the need for control began to evaporate.

Seeing and understanding your "truth" (i.e., an objective view of who you are) is half the battle; the other half is accepting and living it. Because you've been hurt for so long by sloppy thinking, expect some confusion differentiating between real truth and neurotic truth. One helpful rule of thumb is to be skeptical of any "truth" that seems too negative (e.g., I'm just a drunk and a cheat. I don't care about anyone else except myself. I don't care who I hurt. Life sucks.).

Given the right circumstances, emotional security, and straight thinking, people invariably find that their truth—their real truth—is positive and compatible with others. It's insecurity's twisted stranglehold that produces false, negative and hostile truths. For now, just trust that as you continue to straighten out distorted thinking, your truth will reveal itself to you. Like a mountaintop hidden by clouds, it patiently awaits your discovery. Here are two things to be aware of:

1. Self-talk and follow-through, by eliminating sloppy, Insecure Child thinking, will bring you to a realization of your truth.

2. Letting go of sloppy, Insecure Child thinking is 50 percent of the battle; the other 50 percent is embracing your truth.

Like Jane, you can learn to let go of excessive control and start to trust your innate capacity for handling life. You do this through your basic training. If you wanted to run a marathon, you'd have to build a foundation, or base, consisting of long weekly mileage. Without an adequate base, you would not only jeopardize your goals, but also risk injury. Psychological Self-coaching, like marathon training, requires a base—that's what Self-talk and follow-through teach you. It's this base of mental clarity on which everything else is built. Once you've established your base, you're ready to rumble.

Getting Hooked

In Jane's story, the tendency to exaggerate problems starts with a hook. Her hook was her bad-hair day. Whenever your insecurity gets hooked, it's hard to maintain any objective perspective. Once you lose perspective, a vicious cycle begins:

❖ ❖ ❖

Getting hooked ▶ becoming focused on your hook experience
(i.e., anxious thoughts) ▶ losing perspective ▶ magnifying or
exaggerating your problem (making mountains out of
molehills) ▶ further loss of perspective ▶ etc.

❖ ❖ ❖

Here are some typical hooks. Do any of these sound familiar to you?

- Do you get a knot in your stomach when the traffic light turns red? What about being caught in a traffic jam?
- Do you have a hard time accepting criticism? If someone does criticize you, do you get defensive?
- Whenever you lose, does it seem like the end of the world?
- Does it take you forever to finish a task you find distasteful?
- Do you fear being on bridges, in tunnels, in open places, or in elevators?
- Does confronting someone cause you anxiety?
- Do you find asking for help to be a real problem?
- When you get sick, is your distress magnified?
- Do you have a hard time whenever anyone is angry with you?

Any of the preceding molehills can become a hook for insecurity and can quickly become major problems (i.e., mountains).

How to Catch Clues

I hope that you're becoming convinced just how vital Self-talk and follow-through are. By eliminating your sloppy, Insecure Child thoughts, you can ensure that anxiety and depression will never rule your life again. At this point, as you begin to initiate your training, you're at the wide end of a funnel—every piece of information is potentially useful. In time, as you move closer and closer to your specific insecurity traps, you will become more discriminating. For now, however, maximize your gains by learning to catch any and all clues that may present themselves. Be curious. Remind yourself that anything that makes you feel anxious or depressed must have been preceded by sloppy, insecure thinking. Ask yourself, "Now, what exactly was I thinking before I started to get so down?"

❖ ❖ ❖

Self-coaching healing principle 2. Thoughts precede feelings, anxieties, and depressions.

❖ ❖ ❖

At first, you'll be amazed how often your Insecure Child calls the shots of your life. Sam's story demonstrates how a negative experience can become a positive opportunity:

Sam always dreaded his morning bus commute to Manhattan, particularly when crossing the George Washington Bridge, where he would experience extreme panic and disorientation. His anxiety was so severe that on Sunday nights, he would begin pacing and panicking just thinking of the work week starting up again and his bus ride in the morning. He began to consider leaving his very lucrative job for one in Jersey, just to avoid the commute. That's when he called me.

Using Self-talk, we began to reorient not only Sam's thinking, but also his approach to his thinking. Rather than looking at the bridge as a negative to be dreaded, he began to see it as an opportunity to learn, as a teacher who could offer him clues to his Insecure Child's twisted world of excessive fear and panic. Once he became curious, things quickly began to shift.

Sam went off to work each day determined to "catch" a few clues. It became almost a game for him. His curiosity began to challenge his anxiety. As soon as he became aware of any anxiety, Sam would "rewind" his thinking and hunt for twisted, Insecure

Child thoughts. No longer was he a passive victim of his anxiety. Now he was eager for the bridge to yield his secrets. Sam was delighted to find out that once he welcomed the bridge as a challenge, as an opportunity to grow as a person, his anxiety quickly diminished.

The truth was that Sam's bridge phobia was nothing more than his Insecure Child's distorted perception that he wasn't safe (i.e., in control). From this hysterical notion, his Insecure Child began to pile on images of cables breaking and falling into the Hudson River far below. Sam's Child was just looking for a hook to hang his insecurity on.

Like Sam, don't be afraid to confront the challenges of your life. Once you begin to catch some of your Insecure Child's thinking, you're in position for the final step—learning to let it go! Once you understand the downright silliness of your Insecure Child's thinking, you can teach yourself to stop paying attention to such drivel by simply changing channels.

There is one caution involved with catching clues: *Look, but don't dwell.* If you can't readily backtrack your thoughts and expose your Insecure Child, move on. You'll catch the little bugger next time, or the next. The last thing you want to do is become frustrated, causing more anxiety.

Next, we'll take a look at expanding your personal training program. For Self-talk and follow-through to be most effective, you'll need to combine it with motivation.

❖ ❖ ❖

TRAINING SUGGESTION

Each day, be on the lookout for any conflict. (Remember that conflict and struggle are opportunities to build muscle—psychological muscle.) Use a chart similar to the following one to record your responses. (These data will be an important part of your training log, which you will be learning to set up in the next chapter.)

Exercise 1: Use Follow-through Experiences

Expressions of control, which contaminate my life	Looking for any clues—past or present—to explain my Insecure Child's habits	Finding my truth and recognizing that I have a choice (Record any additional insights observed.)

❖ ❖ ❖

TRAINING SUGGESTION

Exercise 2: Get Hooked

If you experience exaggerated, "mountain-out-of-molehill" reactions, look for your hooks. Make a list of your typical hooks (e.g., traffic jams, things that make you defensive, fears). It's a good idea to become familiar with this list and not let your Insecure Child surprise you.

❖ ❖ ❖

TRAINING SUGGESTION

Exercise 3: Work with Proactive and Passive Thinking

Look for any passivity in your Self-coaching approach. Remember, passive thinking is victim thinking. Any thinking that leaves you feeling powerless, hopeless, or doubtful is usually passive.

Start off by listing your passive statements in the left-hand column. After reflecting on them, see whether you can come up with some proactive responses. Proactive responses are action-oriented, can-do, take-charge statements. Make a chart similar to the following one to be included in your training log. Going back from time to time and rereading your proactive statements will also serve as motivational reflections.

Passive Statements	Proactive Statements

❖ ❖ ❖

TRAINING SUGGESTION

Exercise 4: Catch Clues

Every conflict or struggle is also an opportunity to catch clues. Rather than viewing them as situations to be avoided and feared, reorient your thinking, and see these as opportunities and challenges.

❖ ❖ ❖

11

Motivation

Congratulations. With this chapter, you're completing the first two phases of your Self-coaching program. You now have a basic understanding of your anxiety and depression, along with Self-coaching's most powerful weapon—Self-talk. In order to *guarantee* your success, however, your training program needs to add one last *follow-through* component—motivation. Yes, you heard me right, I did say you can guarantee your success—providing you have the right attitude.

Attitude Adjustment: Throwing the Switch

In the previous chapter, you read about changing passive, self-defeating thinking into proactive, positive thinking. In this chapter, you'll learn more specifically how to accomplish this shift. It's all about finding and owning that right attitude. What's the right attitude? Very simply, it's one that demands success.

What exactly is the difference between attitude and motivation? *Attitude* is a mental orientation—an emotional position, such as "Hey, I'm a good person." Attitudes shape who and what we are. If your attitude supports anxiety or depression, then you suffer. If, instead, your attitude supports healthy, constructive ambition, then expect to start feeling better. Motivation, on the other hand, is simply the ability and energy required to sustain an attitude. If attitude is the fire, then motivation is what fans it.

Adjusting your attitude isn't necessarily difficult. It's a matter of shifting your mental position. Sometimes, this can be as easy as throwing a toggle switch. When this happens, all that was negative and frustrating gets replaced with the fire and determination to succeed. Think of times in your life when you threw that switch, times when you got fed up and decided not to take it anymore. If you can't think of specifics in your life, take a look at the list on the left, and compare it with the attitude adjustments on the right.

Insecure, One-sided Attitudes	Adjusted Attitudes
I can't do this! It's too hard. I just can't go on. Why bother?	Okay, now get a grip. The truth, the real truth is that I can go on! Sure I'm tired, but I refuse to go on living this way. Today I'm going to be tough!
How do I know I can handle life?	I've managed to survive all these years, haven't I? Guess that proves something. It's time to risk believing what I know to be true. I can do it!
What if no one likes me?	Of course I'm going to be liked. I'm going to go to that party to socialize, be cheerful, and have a terrific time. It won't kill me!
I can't. I'm too scared!	There's nothing wrong with being scared; but the truth is I *can* do it! My Insecure Child wants me to believe I can't, so I can avoid the pain. It's only impossible for my Insecure Child, not for me.
There's no hope.	I'm fed up with feeling powerless. I'm really tired of feeling crummy all the time. I deserve better.

George Carlin is credited with saying, "If you try to fail and succeed, which have you done?" Your Insecure Child is trying to fail. For your Child, failing is his or her success. Don't you allow it. Find your rebuttal, and begin living it.

Positive Attitude + Motivation = Success

An attitude reflecting hope, desire, self-belief, and trust is the first step, but without adequate motivation, you'll find it hard, if not impossible to sustain. Think of motivation as the mobilization of energy required to sustain your attitude and move you toward a healthy, productive life. The big question is this: How do you mobilize your positive energy? You start by becoming your own coach. First, two essentials:

1. You can't teach motivation; you can only instill it.
2. A good coach is a good motivator.

If your goal is to beat anxiety or depression, keep in mind that techniques and training aren't enough. Techniques and training, unless coupled with the right motivation, can sputter and run out of gas long before you reach the summit—in which case, you'll shrug your shoulders and conclude that you wasted your time. In *The Divine Comedy*, Dante is guided through the bowels of hell by his guide, Virgil. Virgil, representing human reason and understanding, has been sent to lead Dante from error. In Self-coaching, your Virgil, your guide to better understanding, is your training program. As Dante found out, however, understanding can get you only so far. Something else is necessary for the final assent out of the depths. In Dante's case, it was another guide, Beatrice, a symbol of divine hope and love. Your program will falter without your own Beatrice—that is, your attitude of hope and conviction. Virgil and Beatrice, understanding and hope, insight plus motivation—you need both. Self-talk teaches insight; you provide the motivation.

Pep Talks

Okay, let's get ready for a pep talk. Pep talks are another form of toggling your attitudes. The only difference is that with a pep talk, you're not just concerned with adjusting your attitude, you're also concerned with igniting motivation. Compared to a pep talk, a toggled attitude adjustment is more of an intellectual challenge attempting to direct your thinking toward a more healthy position. Pep talks, in contrast, are more spirited, emotional confrontations. You may remember an old TV commercial of a guy who violently slaps on some aftershave, then tells us, "I needed that." Pep talks are the attention-getting slap you need to awaken and mobilize your energy.

When successful, a good pep talk will leave you with a can-do attitude. How? By standing nose-to-nose with your Insecure Child and challenging your Child with an adjusted attitude fueled with high-octane motivation. Don't, however, minimize what you're up against. Expect your Insecure Child to challenge you with an array of distorted, constricted attitudes. Here are some examples of the narrow, constricted attitudes you may expect to encounter:

- "Yes but" statements
- "I can't" statements
- "I should" statements
- "I have to" statements
- "What if?" questions
- Put-down statements, such as "I'm not smart (strong, tall, pretty, handsome, rich, educated, or successful) enough"
- Whining statements, such as "It's too hard (too much, too confusing, too long, too complicated, etc.)"

Let's challenge each of the foregoing statements:

Constricted Attitude Statements	Pep Talk
"Yes, but . . ."	"No, not *yes but*—*yes* period! There's no 'but' about it. I can be strong enough—I will be strong enough. I don't have to undermine every positive I have. No more 'buts'! From now on, I risk saying 'yes' without doubting."

"I can't . . ."	"Who's saying I can't? Maybe my Insecure Child, but not me! I can succeed if I'm willing to risk believing in me—and, yes, I'm willing to take that shot—right now!"
"I should . . ."	"I don't have to be compulsive. If my Insecure Child doesn't like it, too bad! I can live with that. I *will* live with it."
"I have to . . ."	"Baloney! I don't have to do anything I don't want to. All I have to do is be strong enough to accept this—and I am!"
"What if . . . ?"	"I don't have to anticipate life, I just have to be strong enough to live it. I trust that I can handle what life throws at me—and I can handle it without living in constant fear all the time. Just watch me!"
"I'm just not smart enough . . ."	"I'm smart enough to know that my Insecure Child is trying to find an excuse. I don't need to be different, I need to *think* differently—positively! I'm smart enough."
"It's too hard . . ."	"It's hard, but I can handle it. I can handle whatever my Insecure Child throws at me. I can handle it because I refuse not to! I choose to succeed, and I will handle whatever it takes."

A pep talk is an opportunity to get tough. It's the only time when you want to use black-and-white thinking. You have no room for wishy-washy attitudes here. You're all business, and your job is to get the team up and ready for the challenges ahead. It may help you to play the role of a coach, rather than just to think of yourself as one person. Step out of your Insecure Child script and into your Knute Rockne script. As a coach, you know that your team needs you to be completely positive and encouraging—no room for doubts or hesitations. When giving yourself a pep talk, it's important to take as much time as necessary to settle into your coaching role. Once centered, then let the sparks fly.

Slaying Inertia with Pep Talks

The reason you need to be motivated in the first place is inertia. *Inertia* is your natural tendency to resist change. Even if you're anxious or depressed, your Insecure Child wants to protect the status quo. In order to get beyond your Child's inevitable negativity and inertia, you have to expect it. Expect it, then kick butt! Remember, you'll need to be encouraging. Do this with regular pep talks. Keep the following in mind:

- Some inertia is inevitable—doubts are normal.
- Motivational clichés are helpful. Find one that works for you, and use it!
- Visualize yourself as a "coach," prancing around the locker room getting yourself pumped up.

As your own coach and motivator, it's all up to you. When you're caught up in the throes of anxiety and depression, obviously the going can be tough. That's when you need a pep talk the most. No matter how overwhelmed or beat up you feel, just hang on, wait for a break, and then take your next shot. It's the accumulated efforts of Self-coaching that eventually topple the Insecure Child's stranglehold on your psyche. Every opportunity to resist or fight the Child is one more step toward building the strength and muscle necessary to liberate yourself.

It's Time

I wish I could be as clever as the people at Nike and offer you a "Just Do It" slogan for you to carry with you, but your motivation won't come from me. You'll find all your slogans, along with all your motivation, in your own heart. You've lived long enough with pain and suffering—and now it's time for action, time to demand the quality of life you deserve.

Your Insecure Child has no power to run your life. Only you possess that power. Your Child does what it does because you have inadvertently allowed it. Now you know better. Now you have no more excuses.

I hope my program serves you well. I've used it for years with my patients and with myself. From personal experience, I can tell you that the answers you seek aren't complicated. Actually, they're rather simple. See your goal for what it is—breaking the habits of your Insecure Child.

Putting It All Together—the Training Log

When self-coaching myself for a marathon, I find a training log to be indispensable. For example, notes reflecting distance, time, weather, physical condition, heart rate, and even mood prove to be essential for analyzing and understanding what's going on with my training. A couple of years ago, I was struggling to understand a disturbingly steady decline in my overall performance and stamina. I turned to my training log and reviewed the previous month's entries. I didn't have to look far. I found that after each Wednesday's hill workout, my times and performance dipped for at least two or three days. By the time my performance began to stabilize, it was time for the next hill workout. The conclusion was obvious, I wasn't recovering sufficiently from these strenuous workouts! I started taking the day off following a hill workout, and guess what? My performance not only rebounded, but quickly improved.

The last—and often the most important—part of follow-through is keeping an ongoing training log. Whether running a marathon or charting your Self-talk progress, a training log is an indispensable tool for gaining insight. Sometimes your log will offer startling revelations, and at other times, it will show a more subtle chipping away at your

Insecure Child's defenses. Your log will not only give you an overview of your program and your efforts, but it will also act as an ongoing source of feedback. Your log will help you make some very sensitive, day-to-day adjustments in your training. At the very least, these efforts will give you a sense of connection between your life and your struggles.

When it comes to motivation, your training log can really be an asset. What better place is there to challenge destructive attitudes? Look especially for your Insecure Child's characteristic patterns of self-defeating attitudes, phrases, or words. Your job as coach and self-motivator is to represent the opposite—healthy—point of view; even if you don't completely buy it—at first. Think of it as an exercise for eventually developing your winning attitude. When your Insecure Child says "no," you need to say "yes." When it says "black," you need to say "white." Write down your responses. Reflect on them. When you come up with a positive affirmation—such as "I can say yes!"—repeat it often. Don't ever underestimate the value of repeated, repeated repeated, positive affirmations. Remember that little train? "I think I can, I think I can."

Although I will suggest a format using the training suggestions and workouts from previous chapters, your log can be as formal or as casual as you like. If your log becomes a chore, beware. This usually means that you're not getting enough out of it. Perhaps you need to put more into it. Don't be rushed. Writing in your log is a vital synthesis of the day's events and should be seen as an integral part of your program. It's important to look back through your log often. It's this comparison of daily efforts that gives you a genuine understanding of both your progress and your areas of resistance.

The training log format I suggest includes the following three key elements:

1. A section on your Self-talk efforts

2. An ongoing review of your follow-through

3. Any significant incidents, insights, or daily observations

Anyone who has ever kept a diary can attest to the fact that revealing and sometimes startling insights are not uncommon. Writing uses a different part of the brain from thinking, especially if you try not to think too much and just let your words flow. You'll be amazed, for example, how quickly your log will expose the nuances of your Insecure Child, or how insights into your insecurity just seem to appear. The objective feedback you get from your log will also act as a catalyst for maintaining your motivation. That's why you don't want to skimp on this part of your training program.

Incidentally, because your training log will become a valuable record of your efforts, make sure you purchase a suitable binder, journal, or notebook that reflects its important function. Take a look at the sample "Training Log Format" I've included in the appendix. You can copy this format exactly or modify it to suit your unique style. You don't need to spend hours filling in every sheet each day. Instead, select the particular worksheet(s) that meets your need for that day. Let's say that today, for example, you were working very hard at "being in the moment." You may have spent a good portion of your training attempting to be more involved with your kids and less involved with your Insecure Child's demands. In this case, you would want to be sure to include and fill out the worksheet entitled "Learning to Get Out of Your Head."

I suggest that you print out a number of sheets of each workout, put them into a three-ring binder, and use one every time you have an update. Your log should never be about quantity, always quality. Be as thorough as you want, but if pinched for time, be selective and choose to record only the most important observations for that day. If, on the other hand, you find yourself getting compulsive, this is a reason to back off and relax. Challenge any compulsive, rigid, or perfectionistic tendencies. The last thing you want is for your training log to become a tool of your Insecure Child.

You can begin your log today. The sooner you begin accumulating data, the better.

❖ ❖ ❖

TRAINING SUGGESTIONS

Pep Talk

It's really important that you get familiar and comfortable with pep talks. Throughout the day, look for any opportunity to visualize yourself as your own coach delivering your stirring half-time speech. Be black and white, be tough, and—most important—be inspirational. Look for that can-do attitude, and promote it.

Find Your Coaching Style

You might model your coaching style after a strong, inspirational person from your past (a coach, teacher, priest, rabbi, etc.), a historical figure such as Knute Rockne, Eleanor Roosevelt, General George Patton (a.k.a. George C. Scott), Mother Teresa, or Dr. Martin Luther King Jr., or conjure up a fictional coach. Just choose someone that gets you hopping.

You're going to be surprised at how effective pep talks can be.

❖ ❖ ❖

PART IV

Self-Coaching: Healing Specific Personality Types

12

Self-Coaching
for Worrywarts

When I was in grammar school I remember the first time I saw a copy of *MAD* magazine at the newstand. There on the cover was this gap-toothed, freckle-faced, tousle-haired caricature of a boy with a wily grin that mesmerized me. There was something in that devil-may-care face that reflected an attitude of being totally unaffected by life's troubles. Whatever it was, it left an immediate and lasting impression on me. (Here I am referring to it almost fifty years later!)

The very thought of someone that removed, that oblivious, that liberated, made me smile. Alfred E. Neuman, the boy on that cover, knew something I couldn't even fathom. This was confirmed by his slogan, "What, me worry?" For the longest time, my slogan had been, "What, me not worry?" Unlike Alfred, I was often referred to by the very unglamorous title of worrywart.

If you've thought of yourself as a worrywart, then you're no stranger to worry. Worrying, as you know, is what your Insecure Child does best. If you consider yourself a worrier, you're also no stranger to the phrase "what if." "*What if* I need a root canal?" "*What if* she asks where I've been?" "*What if* I get caught?" "*What if* I don't do well?" What-iffing is a worrywart's first line of defense against things going awry (i.e., losing control). Such things as getting sick, making a mistake, messing up, being caught off guard, and feeling humiliated or embarrassed are just a few of the many things worrywarts worry about.

Self-Coaching Reflection
Mountain-out-of-molehill thinking distorts and
exaggerates your loss of control. Worrying is a
neurotic attempt to get it back.

What's Wrong with Worrying?

What's wrong with a little innocent worry once in a while? For most people, nothing, but for a worrywart, worry is anything but innocent—or "once in a while." Worry, especially chronic worry (which is the cornerstone of anxiety and depression), exacts a psychological price that is often exorbitant. Physically, our bodies may translate the stress and tension of worrying into headaches, stomach distress, hives, insomnia, reduced immune-system response, or even heart attacks—not to mention anxiety and depression. Whether we're warding off a common cold or being susceptible to cancer, there's no doubt our bodies abhor worry.

Emotionally, worrying is no bargain either, leaving us feeling off balance, insecure, and often quite frantic. We become glass-half-empty pessimists, wringing our hands as we try to anticipate what might go wrong and how we're going to handle it. Worrywarts worry because their world has become riddled with doubt and distrust. If you can't believe in life, you're doomed to fear it. If nothing else, worry gives you a sense that at least you're doing something to brace against life's curveballs. I guess you could say that spitting in the wind is *doing* something.

Why We Worry

Unfortunately, worrywarts feel there's little or no choice but to worry. For them, worry is the only way to survive having things go wrong. Heaven help them if they get a bit complacent, lazy, or too relaxed— WHAM! Life will deliver them a blow from which they may not recover. If you're a worrier, you're probably convinced that if you worry enough, you may be able to figure out (control) all those what-ifs and then stop worrying. In a sense, you worry so you won't have to keep worrying.

Sometimes, worry is a form of damage control: Because you're expecting the worst, you try to minimize the pain, and sometimes worry is just panic translated into thoughts. If, for example, you can't believe you'll survive that important meeting in the morning, you might find the anticipation of losing your job, being disgraced, and never—ever—having another opportunity throwing you into a Chicken Little mentality. When the sky begins to fall, don't count on getting much sleep.

Recall from earlier chapters that all forms of control—not just worrying—are attempts to counteract what you feel insecure about. Because you have so little trust in your capacity to handle life—to be spontaneously successful—you begin *what-iffing* in a twisted attempt to figure out what can go wrong before it happens. You become seduced by the notion that if you can figure out what's in store for you (fortune-telling), then you can feel less vulnerable—if not less vulnerable, then at least braced and ready. It would be like knowing the questions that are going to be asked on a test. Even Chicken Little's panic was an attempt to do something—anything—rather than let the sky keep falling.

Self-Coaching Reflection
We try to control what we feel insecure about.

Don't get me wrong—I have nothing against planning. After all, who wouldn't agree that it makes good sense to prepare for a presentation, to check the fluids in your car before a long trip, or to dress appropriately for bad weather? Anticipation of life doesn't make you a worrywart. It's when your anticipation focuses on those things that can go wrong, the negatives, that's when good common sense is exchanged for the not-so-good sense of the worrywart.

Let's say you hear that sleet is expected for the morning commute. It's good common sense to anticipate the extra drive time and get on the road a half hour earlier. No problem here. Given the same scenario, the worrywart may also hit the road a half hour earlier, demonstrating the same good common sense. Then, unfortunately, his Insecure Child starts *what-iffing:* "What if I get stuck in traffic? What if I have an accident? What if my boss doesn't believe me?"

Because *what-iffing* is based more on your child's projections of insecurity, worrying has very little to do with actual problems or their solutions. A worrywart suffers from chronic, often intense, insecurity. In the preceding example, it's not the difficulty with the morning commute that initiates the what-iffing, it's the worrier's insecure presumption that, "Nothing ever goes right for me. I can survive only if I prepare for the worst."

The Sky Is Falling! The Sky Is Falling!

Sometimes, worriers are inclined to add an element of hysteria to their worry. This can result in the devastating cocktail called a panic attack. Emergency rooms are no strangers to these attacks. When, after a battery of tests, frantic, would-be heart attack victims are told to go home, "There's nothing wrong with your heart; it's only anxiety. You're having a panic attack," they're devastated, unable to believe that the heart palpitations, light-headedness, disorientation, and sense of doom were "all in their mind." Later in this chapter, you'll meet Howard and Tammy, whose fear of flying illustrates why panic attacks are often described among the most terrifying of all human experiences.

Given extraordinary circumstances, panic attacks aren't that unusual. Someone yelling "fire" in a crowded movie theater might create a chain reaction of panic in much of the audience. Panic in a traumatic situation is normal—and quite contagious. If you're a worrywart, living your life primed and ready for panic, well, let's just hope no one is between you and that exit door. The biggest problems worrywarts face aren't fires or traumas, however; they're things such as elevators, bridges, open spaces, flying, driving, speaking in public, taking tests, and other common circumstances. In fact, sometimes nothing at all may precipitate a panic attack—at least not something you can readily identify, not yet.

Remember the classic children's tale, Chicken Little? In the story, when an acorn hits Chicken Little on the head, he, in true worrywart fashion, becomes convinced the sky is falling. Running hysterically through the streets, he begins to infect the likes of Henny Penny, Ducky Lucky, and Cocky Locky with his panic. Chicken Little and his band of worrywarts find out, it's their panic that provides Foxy Loxy with a meal ticket. The moral of the story for you: When panic takes over, you can be devoured by it.

There Is a Better Way

In any given confrontation, if you remain relatively calm, not only will you think more clearly, but you'll also become more instinctual about protecting yourself. Rather than confining the reactions of your worrisome Insecure Child's distorted, hand-wringing thoughts, doesn't it make more sense to trust your psyche's instinctive ability to do what's necessary? It sure does. Remind yourself that anticipation and worry are only abstractions: "If she says that, then I'll say such and such. . . ." When, instead, you risk trusting your instincts, you rely on actual here-and-now, Self-talk cues.

If you're a worrier, you may understand this concept, but you won't trust it. You're wedded to the belief that you can make it through life only if you've braced and rehearsed for it. According to the twisted thinking of your Insecure Child, this can happen only if you worry. Let's say I were to initiate a rather preposterous experiment where, without any provocation, I threw a pillow at every worrywart who entered my office. It wouldn't surprise me if there were a few who would be convinced they should somehow have been able to anticipate that I might do that: "Why did I let that happen?"

Worrywarts believe (or at least act as if they believe) that life is a kind of mathematical code that *what-iffing* can—if they work hard and long enough—break. When something surprises them, they shake their heads and say, "I should have known that was coming." Worrywarts leave no room for messing up—it's too dangerous: "What if he throws a pillow next session?" Unfortunately, worrying generates anxiety, tension, apprehension, and depression—proven antagonists to clear and effective thinking.

The simple truth is that if you choose to handle yourself in a rigid, narrowly defined, or rehearsed way, you become less effective—one more victim of control. A better choice is to "let go, let life." Without the logjam of twisted, worried thinking, you can begin to risk living more naturally and effectively. There's no better way to liberate your thinking than by straightening it out.

If God Wanted Us to Fly, He Would Have Given Us Wings

No discussion of worry would be complete without a look at one of its more familiar, if not most highly publicized manifestations—fear of flying. Fear of flying (or, as I was corrected by one of my patients, "It's not a fear of flying, it's a fear of crashing!") happens to be the quintessential metaphor for any true worrier. This fear is phobic: Phobias are identified anytime your fear has a specific hook, such as planes, elevators, bridges, and so on. Because of its phobic nature, fear of flying has particular relevance for all control-sensitive people, especially those who have a tendency to panic. Even if you love the wild blue yonder, this section can offer valuable insight into the tunnel-visioned nature of control, so buckle up.

Fear of flying has managed single-handedly to expose more worrywarts than perhaps any other insecurity (fear of public speaking may be more prevalent but can often be avoided and hidden from others). Claiming many sufferers each year, fear of flying has become big business. Books, tapes, seminars, even therapies ranging from desensitization to hypnosis have sprung up all over. Sooner or later, the pressure to fly reaches just about everyone, whether it be taking the kids to Disney World, a sales meeting across the country, or a honeymoon.

Fear of flying has emerged as a significant problem afflicting thousands every day. Some people, including one famous sports announcer who manages to traverse the country on his specially equipped bus, simply avoid the problem. This is fine if you can afford it. Others capitulate to family, friends, or bosses and arrive at the dreaded airport panicked, riddled with tension and fear. These are the "white-knucklers" who somehow manage to get through their flight on a combination of cocktails, prayers, and holding their breath. They manage but will tell you without hesitation, it was pure hell.

First off, fear of flying has nothing to do with flying. That's right, fear of flying isn't about flying or crashing; it's about control. When it comes to finding a suitable hook for your Insecure Child to hang his or her projections on, flying is a veritable coat closet. With your feet no longer on the ground, you find yourself unable to control your immediate destiny. "What if something goes wrong?" Thoughts of lightning, wind shear, engine failure, wing-icing, mechanical malfunction, or even hijacking all converge in your head. These things can—and do—happen. We call it fate. To a worrywart, fate is always a dreaded and malevolent dictator.

You can usually get white-knucklers to admit, although very reluctantly, that worrying can't really avert an air tragedy. Worrying is an attempt to do something, anything, to feel less vulnerable. Even though they may have to accept fate's worst, at least they can try to improve their chances of survival. "What if that bozo doesn't know how to open the exit hatch, should I push him aside? Where should I sit? Is it safer to sit over the wing? Where are the life preservers . . . the oxygen . . . is my seat belt tight enough?" You may be tempted to think that all this planning how to tiptoe through a tragedy should be reassuring. The truth is, worrywarts are anything but reassured.

Not all fear of flying is focused on a plane crash. For some, it's the closed-in feeling, the fear of airsickness, or in Tammy's case,

> It's those bathrooms. There's always a line. I mean, what if I really
> had to go? Sometimes I go into the bathroom when it's empty,
> just in case. If I'm in there . . . you know, if nature calls . . . at least
> I'm there!
>
> There's one seat on the plane, in front of the galley, right across
> from the bathroom, where you can see the door when it opens.
> Just as the person leaving clears the aisle, you could be in position
> to get into the bathroom . . . you know, if you had an emergency
> and had to cut the line.

I remember one time I was sitting in the front of the plane, I asked this guy sitting in that seat if he would mind switching with me. He said no. Flat out, "no!" I actually began pleading with him until he finally called the flight attendant, who asked me to go back to my seat. If I hadn't been so anxious, I would have been embarrassed. Looking back now, the way that guy was protecting his seat, I wouldn't be surprised if he were a bathroom freak, too. There are probably a lot of us out there.

You and I can agree that a bathroom accident certainly can't be compared to the catastrophe of a plane crash, but a worrier, whose thoughts get distorted, can become very susceptible to the trap of tunnel vision. If you are a worrier, you become obsessed with your panic, to the exclusion of everything and everyone else around you. Whether you're worrying about crashing, being hijacked, or not getting into the bathroom, panic is panic.

Tammy's bathroom "hook" is only casually related to flying. A more traditional example would be Howard's experience. Howard, a freelance cinematographer, was ecstatic when he was hired to fly to Kuwait to film a documentary on the troops returning from Operation Desert Storm. After three years of covering local news events, this was his big break. Twenty-six years old, gregarious, extroverted, and considered by all to be a take-charge type of guy, he seemed ideal for such an important assignment. Ideal, with one exception: He had a fear of flying.

Two weeks before the flight, Howard called me. He was frantic, insisting he had to see me as soon as possible. We met that afternoon, and he wasted no time telling me he had to get on that plane, "I don't have a choice. My career depends on it. I'll never have an opportunity like this again. You've got to help me!"

Howard had flown before, but until recently, he felt only a vague discomfort, a kind of unsettled feeling. Over time, he noticed that his discomfort had changed to apprehension, then anxiety. At first, he felt anxious only while in the air, but lately, he began to experience it days, even weeks leading up to a flight. He had gone the route of taking a fear-of-flying seminar, had tried hypnosis, and on his last trip had taken an anti-anxiety medication prior to the trip. I represented his last hope: He wanted to understand "why" he feared flying.

"The last trip was a nightmare, even with medication," Howard said. "It took me a week to get over it. Now with this trip coming up, I can't sleep, I'm not eating. What am I going to do? My seminar taught me that flying is the safest form of travel and statistically you have more of a chance of dying in a car accident, but it doesn't change how I feel. Nothing does."

Realizing we had only two weeks before his flight, I wanted to get right to the point. I had to convince Howard that his fear of flying had nothing to do with flying, and everything to do with the twisted, childish thinking so typical of control. He was interested. It was one approach he had never considered.

"That makes sense," he said. "The plane only represents my fear, it *isn't* my fear! I always thought it was because I didn't trust planes . . . kind of superstitious, that something really bad would happen. But what you're saying is it's not the flying that I fear, it's giving up my usual control. I guess if I hadn't been driving cars all my life, I might feel the same way about them."

Howard learned that his preflight anxiety was clearly a case of *what-iffing*. He also had no problem recognizing his basic distrust of life, his insecurity. The equation became obvious: basic distrust + fear of losing control + what-iffing = fear of flying. Fortunately, we had enough time to get into some Self-talk, and he was also able to notice the unique, childish quality of his reactions, "Sometimes I feel so small, like the others on the plane are grown-ups and I'm this little boy . . . this terrified little boy." Howard was right at home with Self-talk, recognizing that his Insecure Child was in the background fanning the fires of his insecurity and panic.

We were able to meet five more times prior to his flight. The progress was evident in our last session:

> The one thing that helps me most is realizing that the problem is inside me—my Insecure Child—not outside me. It really has nothing to do with the plane. This is comforting. Guess I feel less like a victim. Sometimes I still have apprehensive thoughts, but I'm a hell of a lot better at not following them. Just like we discussed, I've been taking each thought, one by one, and straightening them out. I do have to keep reminding myself, "it's not the plane, it's my insecurity," but that's okay, I need practice. I'll get there. At least I know it's the truth. I guess I just needed to see things more clearly.

A few months later, I met with Howard after his assignment. He had, in fact, white-knuckled it to Kuwait, but he was proud of the fact that he hadn't panicked and never once felt he was going to lose it. The worry thoughts were there, but he was able to return their volley with a consistent Self-talk effort. Although we hadn't had time to work on his directed Self-talk technique, he finally realized he had a choice.

❖ ❖ ❖

TRAINING SUGGESTION

In order to facilitate your Self-talk efforts, it's essential that you become familiar with how and why you worry. Because worry is the cornerstone of both anxiety and depression, you'll need to work hard at isolating this damaging habit. Use the following chart as a template for listing and redirecting your worries.

Worry Thought	Insecure Child Elaborations	Directed Self-Talk
I don't want my daughter to go on that class trip.	I know something will happen to her. What if she gets lost? No one will watch her the way I do.	I'm not going to let my Insecure Child ruin this for my daughter. If I'm that uncomfortable, I'll call the school and discuss my concerns.
I don't want to get sick.	I haven't been sick for months. I know I'm due! My worst fear is throwing up. Now I've done it. You know what they say about jinxing yourself. Now for sure I'm going to wind up with a stomach flu!	No one likes to get sick—especially me. It does me absolutely no good to ruminate about such "what-ifs." I refuse to allow myself to think that by worrying, I can control my fate.

❖ ❖ ❖

13

Self-Coaching for Hedgehogs

Before being influenced by our discussion on Hedgehogs, take the following self-quiz to assess any tendencies you may have. Answer each question as being either mostly true or mostly false.

T	F	My feelings often leap from dislike to hatred.
T	F	If people get too close, they will hurt you.
T	F	I often feel threatened.
T	F	I usually have to get even.
T	F	I often feel attacked.
T	F	I feel safest when I'm left alone.
T	F	I have trouble trusting people.
T	F	I'm too negative.
T	F	I'm too suspicious.
T	F	My relationships are often filled with resentment.
T	F	I'm often jealous.
T	F	I often feel rejected.
T	F	I often harbor anger that gnaws at me long after an infraction takes place.
T	F	I'm too competitive.

If you scored between 11 and 14 true, you possess strong Hedgehog tendencies and need to recognize the importance of not letting these particular habits persist without some Self-coaching intervention. A score between 8 and 10 true suggests moderate Hedgehog tendencies. Be aware of the warnings in this chapter, and don't allow any progression toward Hedgehog hostility to develop. A score of 4 to 7 true indicates you have few significant Hedgehog tendencies. You may, however, be prone to occasional Hedgehog defenses when dealing with stress. A score of 3 or fewer indicates no significant Hedgehog tendencies.

Don't Tread on Me

Have you ever found yourself snarling at someone in the express checkout line because the person's cart had too many items? How about on the road? Do you blast your horn at another driver who's poking along when you're in a hurry? If someone hurts your feelings, do you retaliate? What about if someone criticizes you, does that person become your enemy? Is your motto, I don't get mad, I get even? If any of this describes what you do, or what you want to do, you may have a pattern of distorted thinking I call Hedgehog tendencies.

Ever seen a hedgehog? It would be hard to find a more adorable creature. A tranquil hedgehog held in the palm of your hand offers a wonderful experience of silky-soft comfort and cuteness. In contrast, however, when riled up and defensive (which doesn't take much for these wary little fellows), they roll up into a ball, forcing countless porcupinelike spines to project out in all directions. In this configuration, hedgehogs become unappealing to all the world.

A hedgehog protects itself by repelling danger. A control-sensitive person may use this same defense when feeling insecure and out of control. A normally amiable person may suddenly recoil with hedgehoglike spines of hostility. Hostility has a predictable effect on people—it repels and discourages them. Keeping people at arm's length is a Hedgehog way of controlling—creating either physical or emotional distance. Hostility has many forms. It can be passive, aggressive, abusive, obnoxious, resistant, or just plain cantankerous. The result is usually the same: "No one's going to take advantage of me!"

A Hedgehog defense is of particular importance because of the profound effect it can have on your personality. While most people would agree that worrywart or mountain-out-of-molehill tendencies are negative and upsetting, Hedgehog tendencies are more insidious. They tend to be long-standing, relatively unnoticed, and better tolerated. This is especially true when hostility is passive. Clenched teeth, a strained voice, and a confrontational attitude may be a more traditional image of hostility, but there is another form, equally as unpleasant, but much less in-your-face. This is passive hostility. It's a favorite defense of children and of adults who act like children. Ask passive-hostile Hedgehogs a question, and you may find them pretending they can't hear a word you're saying, leaving you frustrated, angry, and powerless. Whether your hostility is obvious or passive, either way, it still hurts.

Part-time Hedgehogs

Many fledgling Hedgehogs are only part-timers. Because their confrontations are few and far between, part-time Hedgehogs have the ability to keep their spines covered up most of the time. This can be a problem, especially when it masks the burgeoning adoption of a Hedgehog way of life.

If Sam and I hadn't been working on the nature of his Insecure Child only the week before, he might never have noticed his tendency toward Hedgehog hostility—or if he did notice, he might have quickly swept it under a rug of denial.

Sam, a thirty-six-year-old accountant, had been coming to therapy feeling mildly depressed and "aimless." Sam and his family had flown to Disney World for a long weekend. Upon arrival at the rental-car booth, he was told that the van he had requested wasn't available. Seeing the frustration on his wife's face and the impatience of his kids, something snapped in Sam's normally mild-mannered approach:

The girl was telling me she was sorry about the mix-up and how she couldn't do anything about it. I was annoyed, but not upset. Then I hear my wife grumbling. She was obviously tired and frustrated. For some reason, hearing her complain made me feel threatened. I can't explain it, not clearly. I kind of felt I had to be more of a man. My family needed me! That's when it started. All of a sudden I was feeling hostile: Who the hell does this woman think she is? No one treats me this way!

At first, my anger was controlled: "This is unacceptable," I said. "I don't want to hear any excuses, I want that van." The girl smirked, giving me an I-don't-need-this attitude. She was definitely challenging me! That's when I went into the red zone. In a much louder voice, almost shouting, I went on: "I want to speak to the manager, call your manager. Just because you don't know what you're doing doesn't mean I have to tolerate it!" As my anger grew, my thinking became more muddled. I was saying things that were totally ridiculous, like, "You think I'm a fool, well you're the fool . . . I'm going to sue . . . you just wait until I call my lawyer!"

When I saw my wife's embarrassed look and my kids cringing in disbelief, my tirade ended as quickly as it started. It was like I got hit over the head with a two-by-four. I became immediately quiet—and upset. I don't even know what the girl was saying at that point. I only wanted to get out of there. It was terrible, I was so embarrassed.

I was only trying to be strong and not let anyone take advantage of me. I wound up feeling awful. What the hell is wrong with me? I've always thought of myself as a nice guy. Yet I can turn into this monster. That girl didn't deserve what I said to her. Once I lost it, there was nothing I could do. I was totally exposed, embarrassed, humiliated. I felt like crawling under a rock!

Sam's outburst was 100 percent, grade-A Hedgehog. The sales-girl's attitude of indifference was the last straw. Sam's manhood was put on the line along with his status as father and husband. He felt he had no choice; he had to put her in her place. His thinking proclaimed, No one is going to get away with cheating my family! What was most upsetting to Sam was the eventual loss of control he felt.

The truth is that Sam did have a choice. He could easily have protected his family without hostility. Unfortunately, Hedgehogs have little trust. They believe that people will take advantage of you unless you go on the defensive. What began as an attempt to demand control and protect his turf ended up as Sam's worst nightmare—he was embarrassed and exposed to all the world.

In the past, similar experiences had left Sam crushed and depressed for a while, but that was it—nothing learned. With each confrontation, Sam was becoming more convinced he was inadequate. Life was beginning to feel like a pack of vicious dogs nipping at his heels. He was worried and tired about the progression of his negativity. He was also primed and ready for a little Self-talk.

Here is a condensed version of Sam's Self-talk work:

Self-Talk Step 1 Review. Learn to Listen

Practice hearing your thoughts. Ask yourself, "Does what I'm hearing sound mature, rational, or reasonable, or does it sound primitive, excessively emotional, childish, and insecure? Is it me, or is it my Insecure Child talking?"

Keeping Step 1 in mind, Sam and I reviewed his narrative. The earliest hint of insecure, childish thinking was when Sam felt threatened about not being more of a man. He could recognize the primitive, insecure flavor of his reaction, especially by the time he arrived at the specific thought, "Who the hell does this woman think she is?" Sam, reviewing his reactions, had no trouble recognizing the presence of an Insecure Child who was about to have a tantrum.

Self-Talk Step 2 Review. Learn to Stop Listening
When you realize that your Insecure Child is speaking, decide not to listen. Then make yourself stop listening!

Sam had not only listened to his Insecure Child; he had allowed himself to become his Insecure Child. He now understood that what he needed to do in that moment of conflict was to pull away from the confused avalanche of childish panic and demand a more adult response. For example, he might have said to himself, "This isn't life or death!" Then, after a deep breath, "I *will not* let my Insecure child confuse me!"

Self-Talk Step 3 Review. Direct Your Thinking
After you stop letting your Insecure Child steer your thoughts, do something about it. Direct your thinking toward a healthier perspective.

Sam also found that by personalizing his Insecure Child, he was in a much better position to anticipate his Hedgehog reactions. He did this by calling his child Travis. It was from one of Sam's favorite movies, *Taxi Driver,* with Robert DeNiro. The character, Travis Bickle, was a tortured, paranoid, self-appointed vigilante—a perfect match for Sam's Insecure Child. Travis's famous line was "Are you talking to me?" Whenever Sam caught himself sounding like Travis, he would immediately recall the sick, demented character from the movie and have no further trouble distinguishing Travis's voice from his own healthy, more mature voice.

Sam began to understand that his hostility was based not on actual threats, but on perceived threats—served up on a platter by his Insecure Child. Understanding this simple truth allowed him to begin directing his thinking toward more reasonable ways to handle conflict. Once he stopped listening to his Insecure Child, he began to see other options. Referring back to the example with the salesperson, Sam had the following insight:

> I wish I could go back and handle that situation with the car rental differently. I would have insisted on not taking things so personally. When you think about it, it was so ridiculous. Travis [Sam's Insecure Child] convinced me that my manhood was at stake. I just let him manipulate me. From now on, I call the shots, not Travis! The only reason I went crazy was because I let myself get convinced I was being attacked.
>
> I'm starting to get the picture—finally. I had an opportunity this morning at the mall. I was about to pull into this parking spot, and out of nowhere, this guy coming from the other direction pulls in my spot. Travis was ready to jump out of the car, but I pushed him aside, took a deep breath, told myself that I'm not going to permit myself to act foolish, and drove off. It took a minute or so, but then I felt pretty darn good. It wasn't much, but it sure convinced me that I have a choice.

Full-time Hedgehogs

Unlike Sam, who was able to interrupt the progression of his Hedgehog evolution by using Self-talk, some people allow their hostility and negativity to go on too long. Whereas a part-timer such as Sam may have some capacity for amiability, full-time Hedgehogs, even when feeling in control, tend to be chronically nasty. Take one look at Sally, and you'll quickly understand why you need to halt the progression.

Sally is a third-grade teacher who had had many reprimands from her principal for repeated negligence, such as coming to school late, leaving her class unattended, and so on. Sally came to therapy enraged: "I work with morons," she told me. "At the last faculty meeting, I gave them a piece of my mind. There are a lot of teachers who aren't very professional. Why should they single me out? I named names! I don't care who gets in trouble. I don't care who likes me. I shut my door when I go in, I do my thing, and I leave at 3:30." Sally was controlling the situation with her anger, and her hostility got her exactly what she wanted—everyone avoided her.

Hedgehogs live in a world divided into two kinds of people—those who threaten and those who are potential threats. It's a bunker mentality, where the enemy can be anyone—a neighbor, a boss, or even a spouse. From their dark bunkers, Hedgehogs peer out at life through small window slits. With such limited perspective, traps such as tunnel vision, black-and-white thinking, or mind reading are common.

Sally, our black-and-white thinking, tunnel-visioned example, relied on her hostility to isolate her from her accusers. If you're generous—very generous—you might say it was self-defense. Sally felt she needed to defend herself against the assault of her colleagues, but the real problem wasn't coming from her coworkers; it was from within. She was unable to recognize her own irresponsible, childish behavior. Sally needed to come out of her bunker and see the bigger and more objective picture—she needed not only to straighten out her thinking, but to straighten out her perceptions and tuck in those sharp spines.

Ask yourself, has your view of life become too narrow? Are you beginning to see more negatives than positives, more threats than friendly gestures, more enemies than friends? Are confrontations becoming routine for you? Are you beginning to live your life in a bunker, overly protected and leery of attack? Most importantly, is hostility becoming a part of your steady diet? If so, it's time to get serious about this altogether avoidable habit.

Don't be seduced by hostility's quick-fix way of controlling a situation. Eventually, all this repelling leads to tension, irritability, sleep disturbances, social and marital conflict, negativity, and, because of the intense defensiveness of this reaction, depression. Like it or not, hostility turns you into a bully. What begins as a simple attempt to escape anxiety hardens over time into a resistant personality pattern wrought with anxiety and depression. Patti can tell you all about this progression. She married a part-time Hedgehog who, in two years, progressed into a real bully.

Do You, Patti, Take This Hedgehog?

Jim and Patti, married only two years, came to therapy because, as Patti put it, she couldn't take Jim's resentment any longer. At our first session, she got right to the point:

> Jim has become a complete stranger to me. We had a whirlwind romance and got married impulsively, but back then, he really seemed to care. He used to trip over himself trying to please me: flowers, romantic trips to the beach on weekends, poems, the whole nine yards. I have no idea who he is anymore. I know he's not the Jim I married two years ago.
>
> The only way I can describe it is that he's not a very nice person. Sure, there were a few ugly incidents back before we were married, one where he almost got into a fight with a waiter, another with a neighbor, but I never suspected anything. Believe me, if I'd known he was going to turn into a tyrant, I wouldn't have been so quick to get married. I keep hoping I'm going to wake up and all of this will be a bad dream.

Patti's biggest mistake was to assume that her infatuated, romantic image of Jim was the whole picture. She thought she was marrying a wonderful, loving, sensitive guy, but instead, she found herself married to a Hedgehog. Two years earlier, when they met, his spines were tucked in as he rode the crest of their wave of infatuation. Jim's Hedgehog personality had been evolving for years, long before he met Patti. Unfortunately for Patti, during their courtship, she saw Jim only in a buoyed-up state of mind brought about by the security of being in love. When not threatened, Hedgehogs can be quite charming.

"He seems to resent everything I do," Patti went on. "Yesterday, I thought I'd be nice and get the car washed. When I get home and tell him, what does he say? He gets angry at me for wasting money, that the brushes at the car wash will ruin the paint job, and I should've got home earlier because he was hungry. That's been Jim—selfish, rude, insensitive." Patti began shaking her head, looking frustrated and spent.

> Whatever I do, he has a problem with it. And it's not just me. He seems to have a problem with everybody. I really believe he's a hateful person. You should hear what he says about my poor mother. I'm too embarrassed to repeat it. Like I said, it's everybody, his sister, his boss . . . Ruth, our neighbor, called last week and asked if we wouldn't mind picking up her mail because they were going away for the weekend. You'd think she was asking for Jim's right arm. He starts ranting and raging, "Who does she think she is? That all I've got to worry about is her mail. Why can't people just leave us alone?" Does this sound like a sane man to you?
>
> I've had it. My mother keeps telling me to ignore it, to just let him blow off steam. She doesn't know what I'm putting up with. Tonight, for example, driving over here, someone cuts us off and

Jim begins following him, flashing his lights, cursing. I'm trying to calm him down. He really scares me. At this rate, he's going to have a heart attack before he's thirty. I just can't go on living with this.

The Truth about Jim's Problem

In spite of Patti's early frustration and doubt, things actually progressed quickly once Jim began to work his personal training program. Working with the follow-through part of his program, Jim came to the conclusion that he expected people to hurt him. This insight led to an immediate recollection: "I was a sickly kid, frail, slight build, you know, kind of timid. Not qualities that make you popular in the neighborhood. I got teased a lot . . . beat up some. The worst was the time I was held down by these three kids. There was nothing I could do to stop them."

With some effort, Jim realized that he used hostility as a shield to protect himself from the hurt he expected. "My childhood taught me a lot," he said. "Now, you might say I'm trying not to get beat up by life." He shook his head, then continued, "If no one gets close, then no one hurts me. Right? Yeah, that seems to fit. Actually, it's not like I'm thinking all this. I just do it. I'm not planning it. I'm not saying, 'Now I'm going to get beaten up so I'll avoid it by being hostile!' It just sort of happens."

The fact that Jim was being ruled by his old feelings of inferiority didn't escape him. "I guess I feel like a dog on a leash." The irony, which I pointed out, was that there *wasn't* any leash. Because of his old patterns, Jim just acted as if there were. These tugging, leashlike feelings of insecurity, rejection, and fear were being thrown at him by an inner bully child (Jim felt that his Insecure Child bullied him into his hostile interpretations) that was dictating and destroying his life—and Patti's. By recognizing that there was no leash, that his bullying Insecure Child was the tugging force of his insecurity, he finally understood that he, separate from his Child, could be different. He had a choice.

Capitalizing on Jim's insight, I said, "Let's take Patti. You always assume she's doing something to make your life miserable. You and I have both heard her explanations. To me, they sound reasonable and believable. In fact, she seems very distressed that you don't realize she really cares about you. It seems to me she would welcome the opportunity to love you. You just keep making things miserable through your negativity. You make it impossible because you keep allowing your leash to pull you in the old direction of telling yourself that you're different, not as good as others. Not only are you on that leash, but you're acting like you're beaten down—there's no fight left in you. Given the chance, you still believe that people are going to hurt you."

I had Jim's full attention. He appeared to hang on my every word. Compared to his usual arrogance and detachment, now he was more accessible, relaxing his spines. He was ready for my pep talk.

I went on, sounding every bit like a coach before the big game, "The bottom line is you're not that vulnerable child anymore. The truth, the real truth, is that you, your life, everything has changed—except you! You just refuse to accept it. Why? Because you're still listening to your bullying Insecure Child. To make matters worse, you listen to your Child's drivel, then you allow yourself to contribute additional insecure thoughts. That's called piling on, and just as it's illegal in football, it's illegal here. If your Insecure Child's going to talk, the very least you can do is to not help him out! It's one thing for your Child to twist reality—after all, he's a child—you're not!

My final plea: "Ask the question, What if you were to reject your Insecure Child's confused view? Can you accept the notion that things have changed, that you aren't that frail, vulnerable child any longer, that things can be different? What do you have to lose?"

Jim thought about this for a long moment. "You're right," he said. "The problem is I just can't believe it . . . somehow I can't trust it could really be true. Patti, for example, could be saying all that stuff because it sounds good. Maybe she's not admitting that she wishes she had married someone else, that she made a mistake. Maybe she's deceiving herself."

"But what if, and I know it's a big if," I said, "what if she's really telling the truth? What if you're wrong and she truly loves you? Sure she hates your hostility and would rather live without it, but mostly she feels cheated out of the romantic lover she once knew. Step apart from that bullying Insecure Child, and ask one question: What if you really are enough for her?"

At first, I thought Jim was getting angry. His face reddened, then I noticed his eyes welling up. He started to get up but then sat back down. He began to cry. For once, Jim was letting go and allowing that which he had denied all these years: vulnerability.

When he was able to talk again he said, "I'm scared."

Once Jim understood that his hostility was his bullying Insecure Child's worn-out, overused leash dragging him in outdated directions, Jim and Patti went on to do quite well. He realized that his projection of inferiority just didn't make sense in the context of his present life—at least no common sense. Because his feelings of inferiority were initiated by his Insecure Child's convoluted thinking, it was, after all, childish. Once Jim saw how ridiculously he had been behaving, he began to invite, rather than repel, life. Rather than continuing to distance himself from what was good and healthy in his life, he began to embrace it.

Hedgehog Traps

In Chapter 6 you learned about various insecurity traps to avoid (should statements, what-iffing, etc.). Hedgehogs show a particular vulnerability toward certain traps: jealousy; bigotry, racism, and prejudice; competition and threats, fears, and intimidation. These traps, or hooks, can snag an unsuspecting Hedgehog with considerable force. They are linked by a common tendency to see people as the enemy.

1. Jealousy

Jealousy is a curse in any relationship, and Hedgehogs, because of their anticipation of rejection, are particularly susceptible to it. Because Hedgehogs usually expect the worst, they live in a state of constant imbalance—a state of disequilibrium that quickly becomes intolerable. In their attempt to control, Hedgehogs then become hawkish in their jealousy. Bottom line: Jealousy is just another word for control— oppressive control.

2. Bigotry, Racism, and Prejudice

Bigotry, racism, and all forms of prejudice are particularly troublesome Hedgehog problems. These problems are distinctive because they involve anonymous people or groups, not individuals with whom you have had conflict. These anonymous people or groups have the dubious honor of having your insecurity projected outward and attached to them. Living with projected hatred and hostility is an attempt to distance yourself from those who you feel will hurt you. In reality, it's an attempt to distance yourself from the insecurity within yourself that you feel will hurt you.

3. Competition

Even though Hedgehogs seem to thrive on competition, they really hate it. When challenged in any real or imagined way, they feel trapped. Why? Because all challenges are experienced as a threat to their control. Whether it's competing with a friend at tennis or with a coworker for the boss's praise, Hedgehogs can quickly lose perspective, becoming extremely tunnel visioned and intense.

4. *Threats, Fears, and Intimidation*

Just as competition can ignite a knee-jerk hostile response, threats, fears, and intimidations are equally toxic to a Hedgehog. These intentionally aggressive experiences demand quick, compensatory reactions.

Am I a Hedgehog, or Am I Just Angry?

How can we tell when our hostile feelings are appropriate? Clearly, there are times when anger is an appropriate reaction. When someone hurts, insults, humiliates, or embarrasses us, it's only natural to feel anger. When anger is coupled with insecurity, however, hurt, insult, humiliation, or embarrassment takes on a whole new meaning. Now anger festers. Long after the affront, we are still stewing in the juices of our hostility. Festering emotions are one reliable tip-off that Hedgehog insecurity is involved.

I'm reminded of a story about two Zen Buddhist monks walking along a stream. Coming upon a young lady in distress, the older monk inquires as to her problem. The young woman needed to cross the swiftly moving stream, but confessed she was frightened to make the attempt. The older monk took the young lady in his arms and carried her across, letting her down on the far bank. Later that afternoon, the two monks, having been walking in silence since the incident, stopped to rest. The younger monk couldn't contain his anger any longer and blurted out: "I can't believe you picked up that young woman, allowing yourself such physical contact." The older monk replied, "I carried the woman only for a moment; you've been carrying her all afternoon in your mind." The young monk was angry, not at the old monk, but at his own suppressed desire to touch the woman. The old monk's actions were hitting too close to home, and it was too much for him.

If ever you encounter a situation where anger doesn't dissipate rapidly but instead seems to get under your skin, beware. As with the young monk, there's usually more to it. Rather than suspecting the other fellow's shortcomings, suspect that your own insecure personality is leaving you feeling out of control.

Self-Coaching Reflection
Anger that festers is driven by insecurity.

❖ ❖ ❖

TRAINING SUGGESTION

Tape-record your reactions to any specific situation that has caused disruption, difficulty, anxiety, or depression in your life. Doing so can really give you the flavor of your Insecure Child. When trying to express or write down your thoughts, you're often not tuned in to the nuances of tone, feeling, and spirit that reflect the essence of your Child. This is particularly true for any Hedgehog recollection. Hearing the hostility and negativity of your Child can really be an eye opener.

Although it's not necessary to make recordings every day, I do recommend it for any significant Insecure Child encounters. Once you begin to really hear what your Child sounds like, you won't need to rely on your tape recordings.

❖ ❖ ❖

14

Self-Coaching
for Turtles

Take a look at the following self-quiz to determine whether your natural Turtle tendencies (i.e., occasional respites from stress) are moving in a direction of unnatural avoidance and control. Answer each question as being either mostly true or mostly false.

T	F	I prefer to avoid confrontation.
T	F	I prefer being alone.
T	F	I don't have many interests or hobbies.
T	F	I watch too much TV.
T	F	I prefer working alone.
T	F	Relationships are mostly problems.
T	F	I hate phones.
T	F	I don't have many friends.
T	F	I hate social commitments.
T	F	I struggle at parties.
T	F	I'm usually late.
T	F	I am more comfortable with things rather than people.
T	F	You can never be too safe.
T	F	I don't take criticism well.

If you scored between 11and 14 true, you have definite Turtle tendencies and need to recognize the importance of not letting these particular habits persist without some Self-coaching intervention. A score of 8–10 true suggests a moderate tendency toward Turtle living. Be aware of the warnings in this chapter and don't allow any progression toward Turtle escapism to develop. A score of 4–7 true indicates few significant Turtle tendencies. You may, however, be prone to occasional Turtle defenses when dealing with stress. A score of 3 or fewer indicates no significant Turtle tendencies.

Me, a Turtle?

When you think of a Turtle, what comes to mind? Its shell, right? When life gets too rough for Turtles, they just pull inside their old shells and wait for better times. Humans don't have shells, but sometimes they act as though they do. Anxiety and depression can encourage Turtle behavior. For the overly anxious person, pulling into a shell of avoidance may provide an effective vacation from chronic or intense stress, and for the beleaguered, depressed person, crawling into a shell can provide a sanctuary that makes the intolerable tolerable.

All Turtle experiences have one thing in common: They allow you to retreat from some aspect of life where you feel a loss of control. Once in your shell, you feel protected and secure—in control. Arguably, one of the most famous—albeit bizarre—Turtles in history was the brilliant inventor and shrewd businessman, billionaire Howard Hughes. In order to ensure his complete isolation, especially in his final years, Hughes descended into a Turtle shell of paranoia and drug addiction. From his black-curtained luxury hotel rooms, the emaciated and deranged Hughes slipped further and further into a self-created Turtle world of fanatical control. One of Hughes's aides, for example, was reportedly summoned on Easter Sunday morning to chase a fly that infiltrated Hughes's sanctuary. With all the money in the world, Howard Hughes found he couldn't buy what he wanted most—absolute control.

No one, not even a billionaire, can build a perfect shell. There will always be a fly buzzing around somewhere. Clearly, not all Turtle behavior is as obvious or eccentric as Howard Hughes's. In fact, most

Turtle behavior is no different from normal, everyday behavior. I know this sounds confusing, but it really isn't. All you have to know is that Turtle behavior is defined not by *what* you're doing, but by *why* you're doing it. Take, for example, watching TV, listening to music, or just reading a good book:

- If the reason *why* you're engaging in these behaviors is to relax and unwind, then you aren't behaving like a Turtle.

- If the reason *why* you're engaging in these behaviors is to control some aspect of life by providing a haven, an escape, or an insulation, then you are acting like a Turtle.

Turtle behavior is simply any behavior that allows you to retreat from, rather than deal with, life. Who doesn't need to kick back and retreat from stress once in a while? Clearly, by this definition, a little Turtle behavior can be perfectly normal, and at times a necessary part of living. We all act like Turtles sometimes. Hey, it's why we have vacations, right? Like most things in life, Turtle behavior in moderation won't harm you. Nor is it true that a little Turtle behavior now and then will make you a Turtle. Like all the traps of insecurity mentioned earlier (what-iffing, mountain-out-of-molehill thinking, black-and-white thinking, Hedgehog defense, etc.), Turtle behavior becomes problematic only when used as an ongoing strategy (not an occasional respite) to control life.

When used occasionally to recharge your psychic batteries, Turtle behavior can actually be beneficial. Unfortunately, an innocent tendency to "kick back" and regroup, especially when combined with insecure thinking, can progress into a serious habit of avoiding life's demands. Be clear on this point, however: It's not life's demands that cause excessive Turtle reacting; it's your Insecure Child's interpretation of these demands, followed by toxic thoughts of being overwhelmed. This is what instigates most avoidant responses.

Because life's demands can—at best—only be postponed, never eliminated, Turtle behavior is a habit that inevitably generates considerable anxiety and depression. Once anxiety and depression get thrown into the mix, Turtles may mistakenly think the only way out is not out, but further in—into their shells. When this happens, you've reached the point where insecure, Turtle thinking has concluded that life is too difficult, too hard, and too impossible. "I just need to be left alone."

Self-Coaching Reflection
Life can be avoided but never escaped.

When we are overwhelmed, the sanctuary provided by a shell becomes more and more inviting. Why wouldn't it? It's a seductive place of quiet, peace, safety, and relative control—but don't be fooled. (Self-coaching healing principle 4: Control is an illusion, not an answer.) For humans, a Turtle shell is an illusion of safety created by avoidance. No matter how thick your shell or how secure you feel tucked away inside one, at some point, you must poke your head back out and deal with life. Of course, none of this is a problem if your shell experiences are used sparingly to provide a bit of relief from a specific stressor, such as a bad day at work or a fight with your spouse. Here, once you've licked your wounds, you're up and out of your shell in no time. It's only when occasional relief turns into frequent escape that poking your head out causes significant anxiety or depression—sometimes both.

Turtle behavior, aside from contributing anxiety and depression to your life, also has a tendency to become addictive. For example, you might notice that one day you're staying in your shell a little longer than necessary, avoiding a bit of responsibility, copping out, or just "forgetting" about an engagement. The more you become acclimated to your shell, the easier and more attractive it becomes to stay there.

Blame it on insecure thinking. Insecure thoughts are the reason why you have a shell, the reason why you get addicted to staying inside your shell, and most importantly, the reason why you suffer. Procrastination is one common example of the type of insecure Turtle thinking that can leave you feeling overwhelmed and pressured. "I heard you, damn it! I said I'd do it later." Once you begin to sidestep a demand, pressure begins to build. When a Turtle says, "Yeah, yeah, I'll do it tomorrow," it's the Turtle's Insecure Child hoping against hope that, given enough time, the demand will just go away.

Your Insecure Child prefers procrastination because it's safe. Because the Child already feels overwhelmed and vulnerable, it only makes sense to avoid any more responsibility and further depletion. Unfortunately, however, procrastination, rather than decreasing pressure, actually increases it (because life can only be avoided, not escaped). You eventually wind up damned if you do and damned if you don't. Like plants in a hothouse, depression and anxiety thrive in this atmosphere of ambivalence.

If you're already depressed, any and all Turtle behavior becomes magnified. Depression can make you feel there's no choice but retreat. Because you feel you can't deal with life anyway, going into a shell doesn't sound like such a bad deal. In fact, it may sound very appealing. Like most deals that sound too good to be true, however, they are. Turtle living may begin as a haven, but it always winds up a prison.

Self-Coached Turtles

If you suspect you have Turtle problems, then it's time for some Self-coaching. Using what you've learned thus far, you'll need encouragement to poke your head out of your shell and challenge the insecure thinking that leaves you feeling overwhelmed. Self-talk will allow you to pull away from your Insecure Child's panic and to risk believing the truth. The truth insists that there's no reason why you can't begin to handle life outside your shell. The truth says that if you want real protection, you're not going to find it locked up in a prison of a shell. The truth affirms that power, real power, is the legitimate capacity to trust your own resources to handle life. The truth allows you to see that avoiding life is never a satisfactory answer—only a sidestep.

Use the case studies presented in this chapter to get a feel for applying your own Self-coaching techniques. Although these are examples in which I coach patients, recognize that my interventions represent what you'll be doing with your Self-coached program. It's not that hard. With a little practice and repetition, the techniques will become predictable.

Is It Heaven or Is It Hell?

Lest you begin to ascribe Turtle symptoms exclusively to oddball billionaire types or weirdos, let me introduce you to Tom. Although his behavior is clearly excessive, it has elements most of us can relate to, especially the tendency toward avoidance. Tom, a thirty-three-year-old single automobile mechanic, was an avid movie buff. Piece by piece, he began to construct an expensive home theater system. It started with a 40-inch TV, followed by a DVD player, then a surround-sound speaker system, and finally the pièce de résistance, his $2,000 shiatsu-massage leather recliner, about which Tom couldn't say enough. "It was actually designed by NASA to provide a zero-gravity position during lift off!" Tom was truly at one with his entertainment center—and that's precisely what turned out to be the problem.

That was a year ago. When I first met Tom, guess what was bothering him? For starters, he had gained 40 pounds, was staying up all night watching TV, having a hard time at work because he was so tired, and feeling mildly depressed and anxious. "Once I get in that chair, that's it for the night. Things got really bad when I bought one of those satellite dishes: 500 channels. Now I just can't turn the damn thing off. I don't get to bed before two or three in the morning! I never go out. Look at me, I'm a slob. I'm not taking care of myself, not paying bills. All I do is come home and plop in my recliner. What scares me most is I just can't seem to change my behavior."

A big problem for Tom was that every time he tried to break his nighttime ritual, he became more anxious. Once his efforts were sabotaged by anxiety, he just wanted to sink further and further into his surround-sound equipped shell. A decent block-buster movie was all it took to melt away his discomfort. Then, at least for the duration of the movie, there was no struggle—only his zero-gravity state-of-the-art media environment.

Unfortunately, the further he sank, the further out of control his life became. He had to stay constantly entertained to avoid feeling anxious. When on the job and away from his addictive lifestyle, Tom felt miserable. Life was passing him by, and he was—very literally—a spectator. His anxiety was shifting quickly to depression, especially when he considered the lack of intimacy in his life. It was this growing dissatisfaction, powerlessness, and fear that led him to me.

Tom entered therapy with some insight. He knew, for example, that just because you retreat into a shell doesn't mean life will wait for you to come out. Jobs, bills, social responsibilities, and physical and psychological demands such as diet, exercise, and relationships were all suffering. Whenever your capacity for handling life's responsibilities erodes, problems that were once easily sidestepped become highly exaggerated and overwhelming. An addictive cycle begins:

❖ ❖ ❖

The more you retreat ▶ the more life's demands pile up ▶ the more overwhelmed you feel ▶ the more the incentive to avoid ▶ the further you retreat

❖ ❖ ❖

Intellectually Tom knew what he had to do. Instead, however, he listened to his Insecure Child, who convinced him that he was too weak, too tired, too powerless to change his behavior. Interestingly, when his Insecure Child's struggle would become intense, Tom usually wound up heading for the kitchen for cookies and milk, just as he did twenty-five years earlier, when his mother upset him by making him finish his homework. (Some habits have very long tails.) Night after night, Tom found himself no match for his Insecure Child, as he allowed himself to sink further and deeper into his world of avoidance. And the more he sank, the more depressed he became. Poor Tom, his hi-tech sanctuary was supposed to bring years of bliss. As they say, watch out for what you wish for!

Shell-shocked

Using Self-coaching, Tom and I began to look at his Insecure Child–perpetrated, insecure thinking. He had become convinced that he, unlike a normal person, was too weak to handle life. Actually, at this point he was right. Once depressed, Tom began to feel emotionally and physically drained. The further he went into his shell, the more inactive he became, and the more fatigued he felt. He recognized that his lack of exercise, weight gain, loss of sleep, and depressed mood were all contributing to his mental and physical malaise. From inside his dark shell, however, doing anything about his predicament was just too much to ask, "It's too hard!" No wonder Tom reported feeling drained and tired.

Initially, Tom thought the only reason he was having problems was because he had become addicted to his TV and had let too many things pile up. This was a fairly accurate snapshot of Tom's dilemma. Using Self-coaching's follow-through, however, we were able to establish that it was his entire lifestyle—long before his TV addiction—that instigated the construction of his elaborate shell.

As far back as he could remember, Tom had never had any luck dating. This, more than any other factor, was an enormous stressor that played heavily on Tom's mind. The months leading up to his TV purchase were filled with insecure and panicky ruminations about never finding a wife and spending the rest of his life alone. He had begun to drink, not excessively, but nightly. He knew he needed to do something about his anxiety and depression but didn't know what. It was during this tailspin period that Tom happened to walk past a surround-sound home entertainment center set up at a local electronics store. His decision was made on the spot.

Tom was a loner from as far back as he remembered: "When I was in school, I stayed to myself. I wasn't a joiner. Maybe I was shy, or maybe I was just insecure." Tom was finally starting to nail down the "why" aspect of his behavior. He now recognized that his media addiction was both a compensation for and a distraction from the life he wasn't living. This left him with a lose-lose choice: Poke his head out into a world of frustration and rejection, or stay in his shell getting more and more depressed. The answer we came to was simple and straightforward. Poke your head back out into the world, but instead of living with distorted, Insecure Child thinking, replace it with effective Self-talk.

Tom never enjoyed being a Turtle. He always wanted to be part of the world. He just never felt it was meant to be. His recliner and his home theater were really just extensions of a shell that had been thickening for years. His self-image had suffered as he unwittingly, over the years, accepted a pattern of insecure, self-defeating thinking.

Even as we progressed, Tom would continue to fall prey to his Insecure Child's toxic perceptions: "I'm thirty-three years old; I've had only a few relationships, and they weren't serious. Any woman's going to think I'm a freak. It's such an embarrassment. Eighteen-year-old kids in high school are more experienced than I am!" Tom just couldn't bear to face being exposed for what he felt were his inadequacies. He originally entered therapy to break his habit of excessive TV watching, but instead, he was introduced to a pathetic, Insecure Child-Turtle, trying hard to avoid life by never taking responsibility for it.

Tom had grown sloppy with his thinking, especially his acceptance of self-condemnation. He had to get disciplined with his

Self-talk workouts. We agreed on a zero-tolerance approach to his Insecure Child. Tom began to fight back. He began to appreciate how his indulgent, avoidant lifestyle was directed by his Child's incessant doubts and fears. He had no trouble hearing his Insecure Child and decided he was ready to stop listening. Rather than trying to limit the amount of TV time and struggle with his ambivalent, whining Child, Tom found it easier not to argue—he just turned the TV off. Of course, this made him anxious, but he was willing to accept this discomfort rather than to be ruled by his Insecure Child.

Tom wound up responding with one of the most constructive decisions of his life. Recognizing that breaking his habit caused anxiety and provoked addictive desires, he decided to join a local gym and get physical about his resolve. He began to come home from work, and instead of turning on the TV and fighting with his Insecure Child thoughts, he would head right over to the gym. He would make himself stay at the gym until he felt better about himself. This usually didn't take long.

Self-Coaching Reflection
If your Insecure Child senses strength and resolve,
the Child will back off. If your Insecure Child senses
weakness, the Child will take over.

Within months, Tom began to regain, not only a life, but also his strength and his physical shape, to boot. His newly found confidence was an asset in maintaining his Self-talk program. He had absolutely no tolerance for a self-defeating Insecure Child. Thoughts that once Ping-Ponged around in his head were stopped dead in their tracks. In the past where he would listen to these thoughts and even contribute a few doubts of his own, now, as soon as he determined it was his Child trying to get his ear, he automatically chose the opposite path—the path of directing his thinking toward responsibility and engagement. He challenged himself to sustain eye contact with women, then he progressed to talking, and eventually he began flirting. What his Insecure Child had always seen as impossible became possible as Tom abandoned his shell once and for all.

Self-Coaching the Right Attitude

Tom wound up meeting someone at the gym, and guess what? Not only did she never notice his lack of experience, but to her, Tom was absolutely perfect! He didn't need experience to be loved; he just had to be courageous enough to be himself.

Your Insecure Child, by undermining your confidence, always prevents you from learning how effective your natural, spontaneous personality can be. Like Tom, in order to get beyond your Insecure Child's stranglehold, you have to be willing to risk finding out the truth. There's no other way. You might feel it's reckless to leap off that cliff of self-doubt and timidity into the unknown, but this couldn't be further from the truth. You'll find that the cliff that you thought was so impossible, so dangerous, isn't much of a cliff at all. In fact, it's only an illusion. Your Insecure Child created the illusion, and you, over time, sheepishly accepted it.

Just as Tom did, you will reach a point where you'll need to turn off the TV and take the action necessary for that leap of faith. You need to be reckless enough to risk believing in yourself. Make the decision now! Decide to be reckless enough to be okay. If it's a turtle shell you're worried about missing, think again. The only reason you cling to your shell is because you don't allow yourself to believe in a life outside of it. Know anyone who wants to buy a 40-inch TV?

Shells Come in All Shapes and Sizes

What about you? Are you building shells right now? In order for any behavior to be considered your Turtle shell, it must show an attempt to avoid some aspect of life in order to feel more in control. As a rule of thumb, any excessive behavior should be questioned as a possible deflection or avoidance of life. Here are a few common examples of what shells are made of:

- Watching TV, listening to music, reading
- Emotional withdrawal
- Social isolation
- Shyness
- Internet overuse
- Compulsive eating
- Use of alcohol and other drugs
- Gambling
- Compulsive running or bodybuilding
- Excessive or compulsive pursuit of a hobby
- Overworking
- Hypochondria (illness-focused withdrawal)

Why Turtles, Hedgehogs, and Other Opposites Attract

You would think that Turtles and Hedgehogs, being such opposites, would naturally repel each other. This is far from the truth. As long as neither poses a threat to the other, Turtles and Hedgehogs often find themselves attracted to one another. An overwhelmed, beleaguered Turtle may look to the Hedgehog's aggressiveness for strength and security. The Hedgehog, on the other hand, recognizing how threatening people can be, appreciates the passivity and calm of the Turtle. Insecure people are generally attracted to anyone who promises to bring more control to their lives. All you have to do is find someone who promises the gift of control and marry that person. As long as both partners find their relationship to be benign, the free ride can go on for a long time—sometimes years. If either partner begins to feel threatened, however, then watch out. What may have started out feeling like a team effort designed to fend off life's slings and arrows quickly turns into a competition, and with a Turtle and a Hedgehog, things can get pretty ugly.

Anyone who has worked with married couples can tell you how the qualities that initially attract a couple often become the poison that repels them. The shy, insecure husband who marries the extroverted wife because she brought excitement to his otherwise dull life finds that he can't stand his wife's constant nagging to go out, to socialize, to travel. The confused, doubtful, timid wife who married the headstrong macho man because of his unwavering convictions and certainty about life finds that she can't stand his pig-headed, black-and-white rigidity. If you are prone to insecure thinking, you must be cautious about what attracts you. Once again, let me warn you to watch out what you wish for. If your thinking is distorted by your Insecure Child, you might get what you wished for—and regret it ever after.

In general, the attraction of opposites often makes for interesting and balanced relating. A healthy person may be attracted to an opposite type, not as a tool for control, but as an enhancement and complement to the healthy one's personality. Choosing an opposite type becomes a problem only when one or both partners are ruled by insecure, unconscious thinking. Because your attraction is based on your Insecure Child's longing for control, you will inevitably be disappointed. Why? Because no one can do your work for you. The sooner you realize, accept, and risk believing this, the more quickly you will progress. If you refuse to believe that you alone are responsible for your well-being, then disappointment will come knocking at your door, and disappointment has a nasty habit of quickly turning into resentment: "I feel so cheated." You'll feel cheated because you weren't rescued from your insecurity.

Take a look at Sherry and Brett's marital problems. They entered therapy at the point where disappointment had long since turned to resentment. Sherry had no idea that she was married these past four years to a Hedgehog. Rather than face the fact that her husband was abusive and obnoxious toward her, she instead passively agreed with his assessment that it was all her fault. Sherry was a Turtle who couldn't bear to confront the real problems in her marriage. According to her Insecure Child, if she could just be more tolerant, more in touch with his needs, less emotional, things would be okay. Brett handled things; he was tough, never wishy-washy; and Sherry needed that—at least that's what she thought when she married him.

When I first met Brett, I was taken by his gracious, friendly smile. He certainly seemed eager to work things out, especially, as he put it, "To help his wife get better." Brett was an elected local official who struck me as wanting to win my vote. As I soon found out, he wanted my vote that he was a wonderful husband who was only asking that his wife not drive him crazy. I must tell you, he was intense, like a phone salesperson trying to sell you a subscription. He wasn't interested in what I had to say, only in getting me to agree with him. I could see why he was such a successful politician. Nonetheless, it wasn't long before his holier-than-thou arguments led me to suspect that Brett was simply an opportunist who wanted to manipulate and control others. At this point, I didn't yet suspect that he was a Hedgehog. I hadn't seen his spines.

It was only our second session when things deteriorated for Brett, and his true colors began to bleed through. Sherry was talking about how Brett yelled, scolded, and frightened her much of the time. Looking at Brett, I sensed his wheels turning. His eyes, darting back and forth from Sherry to me, were trying to assess Sherry's bombshell revelation. (I later found out that he had warned Sherry not to discuss his behavior.) Although he was inappropriately smiling and feigning patience, I noticed his face reddening, the veins in his neck protruding, and the hinge of his jaw twitching spasmodically. This inconsistency had to be addressed. I asked him what he was feeling.

In a practiced voice of control and calmness he said, "Sherry is too sensitive. She distorts things. Sure I may have criticized her for forgetting the dry cleaning or getting the car inspected, but I wasn't yelling! She's just too sensitive. She exaggerates. I'm sure you would feel the same way. Honestly, Doctor, I think Sherry has a problem with reality. Isn't there any medication you could suggest?"

Brett's Hedgehog spines, still neatly concealed—but twitching—behind his veneer of civility, were his last line of defense. He resorted to them only when all else failed. Two sessions later, all else failed. Sherry was discussing Brett's chronic absence. According to her, he was out every night, all weekends, playing golf, taking trips; they had no marriage. Brett, feeling cornered, began to redden again. For the first time, his voice began to show a strain, his eyes narrowing, as he leaned forward toward Sherry in a menacing manner.

For once, Sherry didn't retreat or back down. She told him of how unhappy she was and how lonely she had been for years. That was the last straw. Brett snapped. He abandoned all pretense of civility and plummeted into a Hedgehog assault. He had had enough of this; he needed to restore control now, before things deteriorated any further. He stood up, looming over Sherry, violently screaming at the top of his lungs, "You're crazy! I don't know what you want from me. All you do is whine. You're crazy!" Watching Brett glaring and screaming at Sherry, I felt he might physically act out. He was truly frightening. He was violently taking control in a Hedgehog manner—at least he was trying to. I stood up and put myself between Brett and Sherry. I insisted that Brett calm down. Reluctantly, he slowly sat back down, humiliated, angry, and exposed.

Next, he turned his spines on me, telling me what a terrible psychologist I was for not seeing his wife's problems. Ouch! I, of course, had a much different agenda. I wanted to help Brett recognize what was going on for him and suggested that he and I have a separate session to talk about his rage. He just glared at me with burning eyes, refusing to cooperate any further.

For the next two appointments, Sherry showed up alone. Brett was too "busy" to join her. Eventually, he told Sherry that she was the only one who needed therapy, and he wouldn't be coming any longer. I called Brett and tried to encourage him to come in. He was apologetic, as he told me he was too busy to fit therapy into his schedule, and he urged me to help his wife (spines neatly tucked away). I expressed my concern about the loss of control I had witnessed. He quickly shot back, "No offense, Doctor, but you were just missing the point with Sherry's problems! I'm not trying to tell you how to do your job, but as far as I'm concerned we're wasting our money with you." That was it; Brett used his spines to dismiss me. He walked away, convinced that my words were meaningless and my inadequate psychological training was the cause. Spines can do that. One sure tip-off to a Hedgehog: They are never, ever wrong.

Sherry and I discussed Brett's potential for violence. I told her I was uncomfortable with the extent of what I had witnessed and suggested that she carefully consider her husband's potential for violence. We talked about her options. Sherry said she was going to lay low for a while. She was going to retreat into a Turtle-like defense and try to avoid conflict. She, like Brett, had had enough. Unlike Brett, she sought to retreat rather than to repel. She longed for the quiet of her protected shell. Rather than facing the truth, Sherry decided to stop therapy.

In time, Turtles can become lulled into a false sense of security because of the relative calm of their shell-protected existence.

Almost two years later, I got a call from Sherry. Disregarding the concerns I had expressed about Brett, she had poked her head out of her shell. Unprotected, vulnerable, without defense, she tried to take on Brett's hostility. In the crisis that followed, he broke her arm and her jaw.

Although Brett and Sherry represent extreme—and sad—examples, their story conveys the destructive potential created when opposites insist on using their relationship as a tool of their Insecure Child. This destructive potential isn't limited to physical abuse. Psychological violence, abuse, or intimidation are all possibilities. Although a Hedgehog may clearly represent a greater potential for acting out, Turtles can also become abusive. The abuse of the Turtle is passive rather than active. By retreating and withholding emotionally, Turtles can inflict a very different form of destructiveness on a relationship.

I always tell couples when we first begin therapy, don't look to your partner to change. Don't point a finger of blame. Look to yourself. Ask yourself, "What do I need to do to be a better person?" If both partners take on the responsibility of Self-coaching, things will quickly improve. Each partner, by becoming better, healthier, less insecure, can then bring to the relationship a genuine capacity for relating—not the defensive, clinging kind dictated by the Insecure Child.

Brett, aside from his violent acting out, also represents the worst-case scenario. He pointed his finger at Sherry and saw her as crazy, as the problem, and the reason why his life was miserable. When you believe that someone else is so responsible for your misery, how can you love that person? Instead, you're likely to wind up resenting, if not hating, the person. Nothing positive can happen when you allow insecure, tunnel-visioned thinking to endure.

Heads and Tails

Just as heads and tails represent opposite sides of the same coin, so too do Hedgehog and Turtle behavior represent opposite sides of the same goal—control. As different as Turtle and Hedgehog behavior may seem, they're joined by a need to control. That's why it's possible to be a Hedgehog sometimes and a Turtle at other times. At work, for example, a husband's Turtle attitude may prevail as he avoids conflict, hides in his office, and desperately tries not to make waves. When a Turtle husband comes home, however, where he feels safe, he may become a Hedgehog around his wife and kids, snarling, attacking, and attempting to keep them and their needs at arm's length. "Get away from me, I've had a rough day!"

Not all defensive behavior is predictable. External circumstances may precipitate a surprise noxious response. Depending on these circumstances, one minute you may repel, and at the next retreat. If nothing else, control-sensitive people are consummate opportunists. Control is all that matters. I'm reminded of the agnostic's prayer: "Dear God, if there's a God, hear my prayer." This prayer was clearly penned by a control-sensitive person—cover your bases, don't take any chances, and if there's a God, please let me feel I'm in control.

Your unique personality will steer you more toward certain strategies of defense rather than others. Based on your strengths and weaknesses, through a process of trial and error, you have come to learn what works for you and what doesn't. What works for you will be practiced over and over again by your Insecure Child. Do keep in mind, what works *for* the Insecure Child works *against* you.

✤ ✤ ✤

TRAINING SUGGESTION

Take a look at the common shell experiences listed on the left of the chart on page 186. Next to each tendency, you will see a scale ranging from 1 (Never) to 5 (Often). Grade yourself regarding any Turtle behavior that you've noticed in yourself within the past three months.

If you've listed any Turtle tendencies, include this self-assessment in your training log. As you progress with your Self-coaching program, you'll want to periodically (I suggest once a month) retake this quiz to assess the effect your program is having on these tendencies. Scoring is a simple matter of totaling all your responses and then comparing this number with the previous months' tallies.

Turtle Tendencies	Never		Occasionally		Often
Watching TV, listening to music, reading	1	2	3	4	5
Emotional withdrawal	1	2	3	4	5
Social isolation	1	2	3	4	5
Shyness	1	2	3	4	5
Internet overuse	1	2	3	4	5
Compulsive eating	1	2	3	4	5
Use of alcohol and other drugs	1	2	3	4	5
Gambling	1	2	3	4	5
Compulsive running or bodybuilding	1	2	3	4	5
Excessive or compulsive pursuit of a hobby	1	2	3	4	5
Overworking	1	2	3	4	5
Hypochondria (illness-focused withdrawal)	1	2	3	4	5
Miscellaneous withdrawal	1	2	3	4	5

❖ ❖ ❖

15

Self-Coaching for Chameleons

Most people are familiar with chameleons—perhaps not with the actual pocket-sized, arboreal lizard whose tongue can snap a bug from a distance of one and a half times the length of its body, but at least with the chameleon's distinctive ability to change the color of its skin. Calling someone a chameleon is usually derogatory and suggests that the person changes his or her personality according to circumstances. Chameleons, aside from their trademark defense of camouflage, are also secretive, solitary, aggressive, territorial, and bad-tempered—an interesting but not very appealing list of attributes, especially when found in humans. Although human Chameleons may share some of these traits, one in particular stands out—the ability to manipulate how they are perceived. In lizards, this is called protective coloration; in humans, it's called being a fake, phony, or fraud.

In the wild, protective coloration is often found among the most helpless creatures—those who have little or no other means of defense. (Although protective coloration can benefit predators such as a tigers or cheetahs, I'm referring to animals that use it strictly for defense.) Although not as glamorous a defense as claws, wings, teeth, or poison, it's nevertheless extremely effective. (Just try to spot a snowshoe hare lying in the snow 50 feet in front of you.) Although human Chameleons don't change color, they can be shifty and deceptive, and like their lizard counterparts, they can be extremely effective at manipulating a situation. Chameleons come in three varieties, which I call the Swindler, the Politician, and the Diplomat. Each one attempts to control by either adjusting the context of a situation (how you see her or him) or the content (what the person tells you). Nothing is sacred to the Chameleon—except being in control.

By now, you probably recognize that control is an illusion. Chameleon solutions are no more effective at offering control and stability to your life than any of the other control strategies mentioned thus far. Also, like all the other expressions of control mentioned in this book, the opposite always remains true: Rather than lessening your debilitating symptoms, these strategies only feed your Insecure Child, the source of your chronic anxiety and depression.

The Swindler

Chameleon traits are difficult to detect because they are protected by a veneer of rationalization and denial. Most Chameleons have become so knee-jerk in their deliveries that only under unusual circumstances will they begin to see, much less question, their own behavior. As with any control strategy, the more extreme the defensive expression, the more resistant it becomes to treatment. Also because Chameleons are so effective at manipulation, they aren't looking to change a good thing—hey, if it works, why fix it? Over time, however, this shallow, empty, and superficial way of life begins to generate depression. One thing about depression, it gets your attention, and it humbles you. Even the most hard-boiled Chameleon begins to question his or her way of life when depressive symptoms start to trip up the Chameleon. This is the point where Self-coaching can really help.

Of the Chameleon's three expressions, the Swindler has the dubious honor of being the ugliest strategy. The Swindler has only one ignoble goal: cheating you. It's a defense where the end (control) justifies the means (cheating you). The *end* that most Swindlers seek is usually financial, resulting in status, power, or some other acquisition. It's their "now you see me, now you don't" attitude that gives Swindlers such a bad name. Take a look at one of the Swindlers I've had the misfortune to run into.

The Watch Incident

I couldn't have been more than ten or eleven years old. I was standing in front of my house, which happened to be located right near an exit from the George Washington Bridge, when a guy in a big car with New York plates stopped and called me over to his car. This was the 1950s, when kids were taught to be polite to strangers. He told me that he had a "deal" on women's watches. I, coincidentally, had been pondering how I would spend the ten dollars that I had saved from snow shoveling the previous winter for my mother's birthday present.

He showed me the watch. It was the most beautiful thing I had ever seen—clearly worth much more than I could afford. I told him I was looking for a present, but there was no way I could afford such a watch. He asked me how much money I had, and I told him. He asked me if I could go inside and find any more. I said I didn't think so. He seemed a little annoyed, and after a momentary pause, he let me know that if I wanted the watch, he would take the ten dollars for it. He also let me know that he wasn't happy about it, though: "Ya know, kid, I could get ten times that amount for this beauty." I knew he was right, just seeing the sun sparkle off of the gold casing. Before he could change his mind, I ran inside for the money, unable to believe my good fortune. What luck!

That night, I gave my mother the watch. She opened the box and was, to my delight, quite shocked. Taking the watch out of the box, she stopped before placing it on her wrist. She looked at me and then solemnly said, "Do you know this watch has no insides?"

She handed me the watch (which I had never removed from the box)—it was almost weightless! She was right. I'm not sure what was said after that. Now I was the one who was shocked.

How could this happen? Didn't that man realize how many long, cold hours I had shoveled snow at twenty-five cents a driveway? Didn't he know how important that gift was? Could there be people this mean and rotten in the world? No. No. Yes.

Call me naïve, call me simple, but until that moment, I had never been stung by such overt maliciousness. I had been swindled, plain and simple. I'm sure the guy pocketed the ten-spot and drove off feeling not particularly good or bad; it was all part of a day's work for him. He was a Swindler living in a dog-eat-dog world and had just become the dog that ate the dog.

The Pinhole View of Life

A very interesting aspect of chameleons (the lizard kind) is that their eyes are covered by the same kind of skin that covers their bodies. There's one tiny pinpoint hole in this membrane, through which the little fellow sees. I think there is an apt parallel between chameleon lizards and Chameleon Swindlers. Swindlers see life from one, tiny, tunnel-visioned perspective—greed. (Pinhole view and tunnel vision are the same. I use the term pinhole thinking here because it gives the reader a better image for the specifically narrow, self-centered, lizardlike view of the Swindler.) Money represents control, and control is all that matters. That's the pinhole view of life.

When an Insecure Child becomes threatened or panicked, a pinhole perspective can lead the way to control. Whether it's money, power, or status, if you have what the Swindler needs, the Swindler sees nothing wrong in taking it from you. Recall the Swindler's credo: The end always justifies the means. This belief is supported by the attitude, "a guy's gotta do what a guy's gotta do." Swindlers feel little or no remorse taking from you "what's necessary." Swindlers see cheating, stealing, and tricking as part of their necessary behavior in the quest for control.

The Insecure Child rationalizes swindling as self-defense. When panicky or insecure, you, like each of the people mentioned in this chapter, are more likely to stray from your moral center and become pinhole visioned. Sometimes, you can wind up with a complete loss of perspective as your Insecure Child focuses only on what you *must* have to regain control. In some cases, the consequences for such manipulations can be serious, if not criminal.

In situations where you excuse yourself and allow a Swindler mentality to prevail, you are allowing an Insecure Child's pinhole view to guide you. As seduced as you may be by such a quick fix to your stress, recognize that whenever you allow your Insecure Child to *run* your life, you invariably open the door for the Child to *ruin* your life! Live by the Child, die by the Child. Because the Swindler's solution to any problem satisfies only a momentary need for control, the Swindler becomes a target for long-term anxiety and depression. Why? Because the Swindler's not actually doing anything to feel more secure, only making the Insecure Child stronger and more powerful. Keep in mind, an Insecure Child with a little confidence is likely to repeat what works. What was an isolated Swindler's solution to a specific problem can become a regular habit of control.

Self-Coaching Reflection
Security can come only from your moral center,
never your Insecure Child.

The Politician

A second type of Chameleon, the Politician, is slightly less offensive than the Swindler—slightly. Politicians aren't necessarily going to bilk you out of your savings or perpetrate a scam, but they are going to try to manipulate you and the truth. The highest ambition for a Politician is converting you to her or his point of view—getting your vote. They're usually debaters who are much more comfortable with thoughts rather than feelings, and they are never, ever wrong about anything. For them, it's all a matter of perspective—theirs.

I don't know about you, but when I listen to an elected official, I usually wind up fatigued trying to figure out the truth lying somewhere under all the self-serving platitudes. Where, oh where is the truth? Perhaps the single most archetypal political comment ever made was during President Clinton's videotaped grand jury testimony. When asked (regarding a previous statement about a sexual relationship with Monica Lewinsky), "Is that correct?" Mr. Clinton responded, "It depends on what the meaning of the word 'is' is." This one statement, in my mind, will forever define the essence and soul of all politicians—even the Chameleon kind. There is no center. Truth, guilt, morality, and reality are all relative. It's a matter of interpretation. I'm not trying to take anything away from President Clinton. Far from it, I feel he is what he has trained to be all his life: a consummate politician. We expect as much from our political figures and our political system, but we are usually less adept at recognizing or dealing with Politicians (the Chameleon kind) in our everyday life.

You Just Don't Understand Me!

George is a thirty-seven-year-old, single insurance salesman who happens to be a Politician. He was part of a counseling group I was running a few years back. No matter what the group threw at him, he, being a Politician, would skillfully deflect it and wind up sidestepping any and all responsibility. Needless to say, things got a bit testy one night when the group demanded some accountability for George's constant lateness (he would show up at least fifteen minutes late for every session). George responded,

> I can understand why you guys are upset with me for coming in late . . . has it really been every week? I don't think that's particularly accurate, but if you say so, I'm willing to accept it. I'm not trying to make excuses, but take tonight for example. I was at work late and had to call a few clients. As much as I value this group and each of you, I still have a moral obligation to my clients. I really did the best I could to hurry my calls. I could have spent another hour with those calls, but you guys are too important. I cut my calls short and got here as quickly as I could. I even risked getting a speeding ticket, which I would have gladly accepted, rather than having to be one minute later than I was.

The group, tired of the same old, same old, wasn't happy with George's nondenial denial. Sensing this tension, George throttled up to a higher gear:

> And I bet each one of you has already eaten supper, right? I could have stopped for a burger, but I didn't. Guess I'm trying to tell you how hard I'm trying. I'm really doing the best I can. Maybe you can put yourselves in my shoes. I'm sure if you did, you'd quickly realize I'm putting as much into this group as you. Actually, considering how much I sacrifice to get here, I'm probably guilty of being too involved with this group. I really think it would be great if you guys would cut me a little slack.

The group reluctantly accepted George's political mea culpa for the time being. After a while, however, it wore thin. He continued to show up late, and he always had a reason, always had an excuse. Even when George was eventually backed into a corner by the group's unwillingness to accept any more excuses, he didn't flinch. He stuck to his guns and just kept letting the group know what a wonderful, albeit misunderstood, guy he was ("it depends on what the meaning of the word 'is' is").

Political Relations

Although most of us may get a headache listening to politicians debate, just imagine what it's like to be married to a Politician. Let me tell you, it ain't easy. The lopsidedness of the relationship responsibilities drives most such couples to counseling or divorce court.

Stephanie and Ray are an example. Stephanie is a successful trial attorney who would have done equally well pursuing a career in politics. Ray is a mild-mannered, sensitive kind of guy who has been bouncing from one failed career move to the next. According to Ray,

We've been married for four years, and things have been getting pretty rough lately. Steph has a difficult job and a lot of pressure, I know that. But she expects too much from me. I know I'm not working, but I'm looking. I'll get something soon. Steph wants me to handle everything around the house: shopping, cleaning, yard work. She does nothing. Well, I shouldn't say nothing, she does anything that pleases her. Last weekend she wanted to do some gardening and went out and bought some flowers. If she gets a whim, she does it. I'm not allowed to have whims; I have chores.

When I try to talk to her about the imbalance, she tells me I'm being unfair. She makes it a point to let me know that her income is how we're living. If I ask her for help, she might agree, but she always winds up too busy, or too tired, or something. Last week, I asked her to pick up a bottle of wine on the way home from work, to go with the spaghetti I was making. She, of course, didn't have time, and when I showed my annoyance, she turns it around. "I know you're trying hard to get a job and things are frustrating, but don't take it out on me. My job takes so much out of me that I have to tell you, stopping for a bottle of wine just isn't that important."

I can't ever win. If I weren't feeling so insecure about my career, maybe I'd be more inclined to stick up for what's fair. Sometimes I believe Steph is right and I'm wrong. She's very convincing. The only thing that leaves me suspicious is the fact that she's never wrong. No one can be right all the time. Can they?

I know it's a cliché, but the other night I went to brush my teeth, and the cap was off the toothpaste. I went to bed and casually mentioned to her that the toothpaste was all crusty and to try to remember to replace the cap. She tells me it's impossible for me to understand how distracted she is because I have no pressure in my life, and if the toothpaste bothered me that much, it was an indication of just how petty the pressures of my life were.

The Teflon Defense

After just three sessions with Stephanie and Ray, I was convinced that Ray's perceptions weren't an exaggeration. If anything, he was underestimating his wife's Teflon persona—nothing ever stuck to her. Stephanie was a consummate Politician, whose Insecure Child used a pinhole view of life to justify her every action. In counseling, she readily admitted to being a star (it's a lot easier to accept being a star because of the positive associations we have to successful people), but she just couldn't see herself as a Politician (because of the negative implications of being deceptive). According to her view, it was Ray's petty bellyaching that needed to be scrutinized, not her behavior. Her heels were dug in, and she wasn't about to give an inch.

In therapy, she was masterful at deflecting criticism, insisting that the only reason she was ever negative, rigid, or arrogant was because Ray provoked her. She really believed she was without blemish. "If only Ray wasn't such a whiner; he brings out the worst in me." It was obvious that Ray couldn't win. No matter what he said or how he said it, Stephanie turned it inside out. "If you weren't so insecure and jealous you'd be able to see things more clearly." One time when Stephanie accused Ray of whining, I stepped in, "Ray wasn't whining, he was simply asking whether you felt you were being fair in the relationship. Are you?" Stephanie, slightly red-faced, but true to form, responded, "Do you realize what I've done for this man? What I've given to this relationship? If it weren't for my job, Ray would have a lot more problems than the cap being left off the toothpaste." Nothing sticks to Teflon.

Because Stephanie's pinhole view of life left her unaware of the bigger defensive picture, it was apparent that before any Self-talk confrontations with her Insecure Child could take place, some Self-coaching was needed to set the stage. Based on the fact that

Stephanie appeared to have a hard time with criticism, I encouraged her to consider whether this difficulty could be a defensive strategy designed to protect her from vulnerability. I obviously struck a chord, because rather than deflecting my suggestion as I anticipated she might, she agreed to give it some thought.

Our next session produced a surprise. Stephanie had, in fact, done her homework. She noticed (admitted) that she wasn't well-liked at work. She went on to describe how at luncheons and social gatherings, she often felt isolated and excluded. She managed to bottle these feelings up, protecting herself with a dismissive, "They're such idiots!" Stephanie needed to be applauded, and although Stephanie was tops at the firm and applauded for her skills, she was a social outcast. This was the chord that I had struck—the truth that she was struggling with feelings of vulnerability, lack of acceptance, and deflated self-worth.

For the first time, she became curious about Ray's perceptions. Other than beefing up her existing defenses, which further alienated everyone around her, it never occurred to Stephanie that there was anything she could do about her experiences of rejection. It was staggering for her to realize that her behavior (i.e., trying to insulate herself from rejection) made it impossible for anyone to approach her. She acknowledged that she had an expectation of rejection and was not about to let herself be hurt. Ray's plea, "I don't want to hurt you," brought a slight moistening to her eyes—which she quickly wiped away.

Rather than challenging her insecurities, Stephanie instead chose a life of protection and control, and it was the anticipation of rejection that instigated her pinhole view of life. Her Teflon defense, so characteristic of Politicians, allowed her to deny her pain. One thing about Teflon: Nothing sticks to you, not even rejection or abandonment. If nothing sticks, nothing can hurt you. Finally, Stephanie was widening her view. With Ray's assistance, she was now fully accepting her pinhole perspective, along with her Teflon defenses of arrogance, her black-and-white thinking, and her need always to be right and in control.

Stephanie was well-guarded and had long ago buried her feelings about being displaced by the birth of her younger brother. Her brother was born with a major birth defect, requiring an inordinate amount of attention and energy from her parents. Stephanie, who had been the only child for five years, wasn't in a position to understand their almost complete abandonment of her. Only after many major surgeries—and years—did her brother finally improve. By this time, Stephanie had already perfected her plan of self-protection: Stop feeling, and start performing.

Her efforts didn't pay off, though. Her parents were just too preoccupied. Stephanie did her best to stave off her mounting insecurity and panic. Unfortunately, she did this by developing a veneer of arrogance and aloofness. She made herself better than everyone else. Although unpopular socially, she was a star performer for her teachers. By the time Stephanie was in college, she had managed to rise above her feelings of vulnerability. Only now, years later, in therapy, did she begin to realize that by rising above her feelings, she had become inaccessible to being loved. Ray had been trying to tell her so for years.

At this point, considering Stephanie's straight thinking success, Stephanie's Insecure Child didn't have a chance. Whenever she caught herself doing her Teflon dance, she would stop, often midsentence, and make herself respond more truthfully to the situation. Just because her Insecure Child wanted to be aloof, Stephanie didn't have to agree to be aloof. She began to become more legitimately involved in all her relationships, especially with Ray. Thrilled with the reception she got, Stephanie became convinced that being more sensitive, involved, and vulnerable wasn't the deficit she had always—in her pinholed view—thought it was.

Politician Self-Quiz

Because Politicians are usually unaware of their political defenses, a self-quiz may help you detect whether your Insecure Child is political. Answer each question as being mostly true or mostly false. If you're not sure, leave the question blank.

T	F	I have to be right.
T	F	If criticized, I can usually turn things around.
T	F	Thinking is a much more valuable trait than feeling.
T	F	I have to be liked, admired, or appreciated.
T	F	In an argument, I'm not likely to give in.
T	F	Even if I don't believe in what I'm arguing, I still have to win.
T	F	I don't take criticism well.
T	F	When threatened, I become shrewd and calculating.
T	F	Feelings often get in the way.
T	F	I have a hard time admitting I've done anything wrong.
T	F	I can always justify my actions.
T	F	I would rather convince than defeat an opponent.
T	F	I often see people as adversaries.
T	F	You can never be too safe.
T	F	I'm generally quite persuasive.
T	F	I don't let people affect me.
T	F	I would rather win than be right.

If you scored between 13 and 17, you possess strong Politician tendencies; between 8 and 12, you have mild tendencies; between 4 and 7, weak tendencies; with a score lower than 4, you have little or no Politician tendencies.

Diplomats

The last category of Chameleon is the Diplomat, also known as the Yes person. Unlike the Swindler, who wants to cheat you, or the Politician, who wants to convert you, the Diplomat wants to appease you. Before you feel flattered, keep in mind that your appeasement has little to do with your well-being or happiness; it's all about the Diplomat's control. When you're pleased with a Diplomat, you're not going to be a threat. If you're not a threat, the situation is controlled. "That's right, Officer, I was going over the speed limit. I'm really sorry to have troubled you. Your job is difficult enough without having to chase after someone as careless as me."

The worst-case scenario for Diplomats is having someone get angry with them. When people are angry, who knows what they'll do? It's this uncertainty that leaves Diplomats feeling insecure and out of control. Diplomats can get pretty paranoid about offending someone.

Looking for Peace

Take a look at Rudy's reaction to a coworker who tried to flirt with his girlfriend Mary:

Ever since I called him and told him to stay away from Mary, I've been going crazy. I was so panicky last night, I asked my mother for one of her tranquilizers. I just keep asking, "Why? Why? Why?" I don't know what came over me. I should have ignored him. That's what Mary wanted. Why didn't I listen to her? I just seemed to snap. I remember yelling and cursing at him, I'm not even sure what I said. He never reacted to me; he just had this smirk on his face . . . what was that all about?

It was so out of character for me, so stupid. There's nothing I can do now. How do I know I haven't provoked him into something? I always thought he was a little strange. Who knows, maybe he's the type that could be waiting for me with a baseball bat, or maybe he'll try to hurt me some other way. I don't know, maybe call my boss and start a rumor, threaten my girlfriend, trash my car. Who knows what he's capable of? I don't see how I can ever put my guard down. It could be months before he decides to take *action*. When will I feel safe again?

Poor Rudy was not used to risking his feelings. From the magnitude of his paranoid reaction, you can understand why. Look at the fallout! Rudy's experience (i.e., yelling at this cad) was out of character for him. It was, in fact, undiplomatic! He was used to controlling a situation and minimizing consequences by not making waves—not even ripples. "Give 'em what they want, and they'll leave you alone" has been a motto that served him well. Rudy's anxiety suggested a solution (unfortunately it was his Insecure Child's solution):

I'm tempted to talk to him, you know, let him know that I'm cool with the situation. I'll offer to shake hands. Ask him to understand why I got so upset. I'm beginning to feel better already.

Rudy was feeling better because he just found a way (his Insecure Child's way) of restoring control. It has nothing to do with what Rudy believes or wants. It has to do with trying to mollify his antagonist with a diplomatic solution—not very satisfying, but safe. It's true that being a Diplomat can eliminate all but the most difficult of conundrums, but at what price?

Throughout this book you've been shown how control is always a shortsighted attempt to feel secure. Rudy can go on for a long time pleasing everyone, walking on eggshells and trying to avoid conflict, but the real question is, can someone like Rudy ever find true peace in a world that requires complete acquiescence? Peace maybe, but no solace.

Saying Yes When We Mean No

Diplomats are Yes people who have a hard time saying "no" to anything or anyone. It doesn't matter that this strategy burdens their lives with added responsibility and demands—they just can't say no. Well, that's not entirely true. If their refusal isn't their fault—"I'd love to help you out, but I have to go on an interview and won't be in town"—then it's okay. In this case, the Diplomat feels blameless and therefore insulated from your anger.

Matt, a fifty-three-year-old social worker, was having a hard time saying no. Everyone loved Matt. And why shouldn't they—he was a pleaser. Ask him to do anything, and chances are he'll do it with a smile. Don't let that smile fool you, though. Inside, he was a cauldron of conflict and anxiety:

> I told my boss that I'd fly with him to Chicago the end of next week to work out the specifics on a deal we'd been working on. Last night, my buddy calls screaming with excitement that he just got a couple of tickets for the World Series, and he's counting on me to go. The tickets are for the fifth game of the series, which is when I'm supposed to be in Chicago! What's wrong with me? I'm on the phone, I know I have to refuse the tickets, I know I have no choice, and what do I say? I told him it was fantastic and that I couldn't wait. I'm insane! I just couldn't say no. You know what's even crazier? Not only wasn't I saying no, but I found myself trying to get my buddy all pumped up about the game. I'm either crazy or stupid!
>
> The tickets are for the fifth game of the series. If the Yankees sweep, I'll be okay. Then I'm off the hook and can fly out first thing in the morning and meet my boss. If the Yankees don't sweep, I'm dead. I really don't know what I'll do.

Fortunately for Matt, the Yankees did sweep the series, and he was off the hook. Did he learn anything? Yes, he did. One thing he realized was that his World Series dilemma wasn't unusual. Looking back, there was a whole history of similar predicaments.

Some of these were resolved naturally (like the Yankees' sweep), others by worming his way out (feigning sickness or injury), and still others remained unresolved, leaving a trail of scars and hard feelings.

Matt was particularly vulnerable to invitations. Over the years, there were many things he did that he absolutely hated. Matt's essentially a beer, hot dog, and ball-game kind of guy, yet over the years, he's allowed himself to be coerced into attending the opera, the ballet, and a guided tour through the Metropolitan Museum of Art. Lately, Matt's noticed that his sleep is generally interrupted and that he has become more moody over the past year. When Matt and I started talking, he was flirting with a Turtle solution to his problems. He was, quite literally, trying to hide from everyone.

Luckily, Matt and I began to talk before he had a chance to create a formidable shell around himself. He was still ready and desperate to learn how to say no. We began with Self-talk. He had no problem seeing how his Insecure Child (aptly called "Wimpy") would begin to panic whenever someone made a request of him. "You're right, I feel just like a child who's afraid to say the wrong thing because I'll get in trouble." Matt had to assimilate the notion that just because his Insecure Child couldn't say no, that didn't mean *he* couldn't. Although it was terrifying for Matt to consider not being a Diplomat any longer, the notion of being able to do what he wanted appealed to him.

We did some role playing where I would pretend to ask Matt to join me at different functions. Rather than having him listen to his Insecure Child, I wanted him to get used to hearing his more healthy, mature self. Matt enjoyed this exercise. In this no-risk environment, he found that saying "no" wasn't so strange or— once he got the hang of it—difficult. He couldn't help smiling as he would tell me, "No, I'm sorry, Doc, I can't join you this weekend." He was smiling because he loved how it felt—saying what he wanted to say. Just trying on this more honest persona had a liberating, energizing effect on him. He left our session almost hoping for an opportunity.

It didn't take long. The very evening after our session, Matt was sitting with his wife when his sister called to invite him and his wife to their daughter's piano recital on Saturday. This wasn't an easy challenge, but Matt was primed, practiced, and ready to try.

As it turned out, he had been looking forward to playing golf on Saturday with an old friend and really didn't want to spend it in a hot, stuffy auditorium looking at his watch. (Matt wasn't a Beethoven or Mozart kind of guy.) Matt stifled his Insecure Child, who was wanting to blurt out, "Sure, Sis, we'll be there." Instead, he swallowed, told Wimpy to back off, took a deep breath, and made himself say, "I'm sorry, Sis, I've already made plans that I can't break." The next part was just as hard for Matt. Now he had to fight an intolerable Insecure Child urge to take back his refusal: "Well, maybe I can break my plans, I'll let you know." He stuck to his guns, said no to Wimpy's panic, and made himself sit through a difficult moment of silence. His sister, a little shocked at this refusal (after all, no one in recent memory could give you an instance where Matt had said no to anything), said she understood and hung up.

Matt had mixed emotions. He was elated that he was going to do what he wanted on Saturday and that he didn't have to sit through any of that long-haired music, but he was also feeling panicky. When we talked about the panic in our next session, Matt realized that he wasn't used to feeling out of control. Refusing his sister had left him feeling vulnerable to her anger or resentment. By being the Diplomat, he had escaped ever feeling this vulnerability. It took some straight thinking and Self-talking for Matt to recognize that his vulnerability was only a habit—a habit with no here-and-now business, other than to screw up his life.

As Matt continued his "saying no" practice, he still needed to do something about his anxiety. It was hard for him to trust that he really could be a more secure person. At first, saying no was bittersweet. He liked being liberated but was still getting hammered with anxiety about being vulnerable. There was no objective basis for Matt's insecurity. His anxiety and panic were echoes of a long-past skirmish with his parents—echoes that continued to reverberate throughout his life.

Early on in our sessions, one thing that kept tripping Matt up was that he was paying too much attention to his discomfort. Rather than dealing with his Insecure Child more directly and forcibly, he was becoming worried about his worry, "I don't know, I'm not sure this is working. I've been feeling shaky inside. I think I'm getting worse. I shouldn't be feeling shaky, I should be feeling better. What's wrong with me? Why am I worrying so much about all this?"

I told Matt to treat his symptoms as he would any cold symptom—a stuffy nose, a sore throat, a headache—uncomfortable yes, but nothing to worry about. "When you have a cold, the less you focus on your symptoms, the better you feel. Sometimes, you even forget you're sick. It's the same with anxiety. The more you focus on your symptoms, the more nervous you get. Accept your symptoms as you would a runny nose. Forget about them, and focus on working with your Insecure Child. That's the only important thing. Your symptoms aren't important, your Child is."

Matt's progress was steady and uneventful. He worked hard and finally overpowered Wimpy. Once he liberated himself from his habit of insecurity and found that he didn't have to please everyone, Matt found that taking care of himself and living a more honest life was actually quite easy—and very natural. He also found that saying no and being more up-front with the world didn't make him a bad person. He could actually be himself and still be worthwhile. Diplomats don't understand this simple truth. They are forever hiding what they see as their unacceptable desires.

❖ ❖ ❖

TRAINING SUGGESTION

Chameleon tendencies are difficult to detect because they are protected by a veneer of rationalization and denial. Reread the sections on the Swindler, the Politician, and the Diplomat, being as objective as possible. If you may have Chameleon tendencies, it really helps to solicit the opinion of others. A spouse, friend, or relative can be helpful with this assessment. Sometimes, specific behaviors patterns or habits, such as saying "yes" when we mean "no," can point to a Chameleon tendency.

Chameleon tendencies are difficult to rate objectively. Do your best to (a) isolate specific Chameleon tendencies, (b) subjectively decide how often these tendencies occur (use the following scale), and (c) periodically reassess these tendencies to chart your Self-coaching progress.

Chameleon Frequency Scale

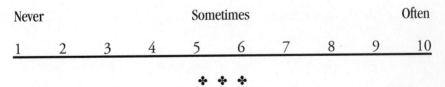

Never				Sometimes					Often
1	2	3	4	5	6	7	8	9	10

❖ ❖ ❖

16

Self-Coaching
for Perfectionists

Let's start out by assessing your level of perfectionism. Answer each question as being either mostly true or mostly false.

T	F	Whatever I do, it has to be done just so, or I can't put it down.
T	F	I have no tolerance for getting ill.
T	F	I have an image to maintain.
T	F	I get anxious when things go wrong.
T	F	I'm usually right.
T	F	Details are a very important part of life.
T	F	I've been called a control freak.
T	F	I hate when things are out of place.
T	F	If you want to get a job done right, you have to do it yourself.
T	F	I have trouble being on time.
T	F	I have to win.
T	F	I have a hard time letting someone else drive my car.
T	F	I tend to overdo everything.
T	F	I'm never caught off guard.
T	F	I have no tolerance for mistakes (mine or other people's).
T	F	I fuss too much when I'm getting ready.

T	F	I've been accused of being too neat (or fanatical, or obsessive).
T	F	I've been told I'm too rigid.
T	F	Whenever I get involved in something, it has to be 100 percent.
T	F	I'm more intellectual than emotional.

If you scored from 16 to 20 true, you have definite perfectionistic tendencies and need to recognize the importance of not letting this particular style of defense persist without some Self-coaching intervention. A score of 11 to 15 true suggests a moderate tendency toward perfectionism. Be aware of the warnings in this chapter, and don't allow any more rigid, compulsive behavior to develop. A score of 6 to 10 true suggests few significant perfectionistic tendencies. You may, however, be prone to occasional perfectionistic defenses when dealing with stress. A score of 5 or fewer indicates no significant perfectionistic tendencies. In your case, continue maintaining your natural tendencies to handle, rather than control, life's demands.

Anything but Average

There are three kinds of Perfectionists: the Star, the Fanatic, and the Control Freak, but they all have one thing in common: They all believe that if you're willing to work hard enough, you can eliminate your vulnerabilities. The logic is simple: If you and what you're doing are perfect and no one can find fault, then no one can hurt you. As long as all your ducks are lined up neatly in a row, you feel completely in control.

Perfectionism isn't a personality trait for the lazy or less motivated; it's a full-time job that takes full-time commitment. Whereas Hedgehogs are defined by their hostility, and Turtles by their retreating, Perfectionists are defined by their excessively high standards and unflagging effort. Whether it be cleaning a closet, taking a test, or influencing someone else's opinion, Perfectionists have no choice: They have to perform flawlessly—each and every time.

Perfectionists are also snobs—control snobs. It may be okay for other people to come in second, to flub an exam, or to ignore stains on their blouses, but not for a perfectionist. There is no flexibility—you must be first, the best, and without blemish. Perfectionists venerate their compulsive way of life, seeing it as a higher calling. They are elitists who see mediocrity as a curse. If you want to see perfectionists cringe, just call them "average." The A-word automatically gives rise to anxiety or depression, followed by fanatical efforts to reverse this abhorrent stigma. "Me, average? Never!" For the Perfectionist, winning isn't everything, it's the only thing. It's a life of compulsive effort, driven by black-and-white tunnel thinking.

Perfectionists know only one happiness, which is defined by the philosophy that living flawlessly is the only way to ensure control and mastery over life. There is a grain of truth to this perception, but there is a big down side, too. Once you believe that flawless, perfect living will steer you away from vulnerability and insecurity, you wind up with no choice—you either live flawlessly, or you suffer. It's no different from any other dependency or addiction (alcohol or other drugs, gambling, spending money, overeating, etc.). When you rely on externals to make you feel better, you unwittingly create a *have-to* mentality. Just like drug addiction, perfectionism will leave you with tunnel vision, insisting that all your ducks have to not only line up in a row, but also stand at attention.

To all the world, Perfectionists often do appear perfect. Their homes are immaculate, their cars are freshly waxed, they tend to dress impeccably, never run out of gas, and, especially Stars, are winners and leaders. Whatever they do, they never skimp on energy or effort. For the Perfectionist, "Ain't no mountain high enough!" They often appear as superhuman beings. And why not? They usually accomplish more in a day than most people do in a week. They make the rest of us seem lazy and ineffective in comparison. Don't be deceived by the perfectionist's flurry of accomplishments, however. Take a closer look.

Perfectly Miserable

The key to understanding the dark side of perfectionism is the realization that perfectionism isn't really striving for perfection. It's actually the avoidance of imperfection—and herein lies the problem—for many, the curse. A hair out of place, a spelling error on a report, or spots on the silverware can all generate intense anxiety. This is a terribly stressful way to live, always being on call, maintaining control, and never being allowed to mess up. Living with the intensity of perfectionistic demands means living with anxiety and pressure.

If you are a Perfectionist, you have an apprehensive way of life that eventually depletes and depresses you. Unfortunately, as with all control strategies, the more anxious and depressed you feel, the more likely you are to intensify rather than moderate your controlling efforts. The cycle of control, as you've seen expressed in previous defensive strategies, becomes an upward spiral.

❖ ❖ ❖

Feeling out of control ◗ perfectionistic striving ◗
maintaining perfection produces anxiety or depression ◗
anxiety and depression produce loss of control ◗ intensification
of perfectionistic striving ◗ feeling out of control

❖ ❖ ❖

When caught in a control cycle, Perfectionists who seek therapy won't want to be liberated from their Insecure Children's perfectionistic ways. Far from it—they really want to become better and more perfect neurotics. They're only looking to give their defenses a lube and oil, not to abandon them. Perfectionists have a particularly hard time believing—and risking—that perfection isn't the answer. In fact, in therapy, they often want to be perfect patients. They bring notes, write down their dreams, ask for homework, and hate to leave at the end of the hour. The Perfectionist, especially the Star, wants to become your favorite patient and secretly wants you to give up the rest of your practice so you can appreciate just how wonderful they and their problems can be.

Self-Coaching Reflection
Perfectionism isn't a desire for perfection.
It's a desire to avoid imperfection.

Philosophically speaking, why would striving for such a noble and exalted goal as perfection be such a problem? Simple answer: Nature abhors perfection—at least as the Perfectionist defines it. Although Perfectionists like to believe they're pursuing a lofty, esthetic ideal, in reality, they're only looking for a tool with one mundane application—control. No doubt it's this exalted illusion of complete and perfect control that gets so many people hooked. You know how wonderful you feel when you manage to get that room cleaned up just so, or serve that perfect dinner, or make that perfect impression. You're on top of the world, feeling fulfilled and satisfied. It's normal to enjoy success and to relish having things work out.

If you're prone to perfectionism, you're not surprised by your success. You're a firm believer that you make your own luck. You approach every task with a single-minded certainty. You have no choice, you *have to* succeed—perfectly. The flowers that have to be arranged just so, the dessert that must melt in your mouth, and the clothes that must be impeccable—these are all expected, demanded. Don't misunderstand, it's not all work. Perfectionists do get to enjoy their moment of glory and accomplishment, but it's a fleeting moment at best. The next challenge is already knocking at the door, with another not far behind—and another after that.

All That Glitters Is Not Gold

Generally speaking, Perfectionists tend to be quite successful. Because of their many and varied accomplishments, they are often admired, even envied by others. When I was in graduate school, my wife and I were friendly with another couple, who could only be described as a "supercouple." Both husband and wife were Perfectionists whose lives, by any standard, seemed extraordinary. Aside from having three kids, they had an immaculate house, ever-shiny cars, always-blooming perennials, weedless grass, and (my envy) a garage where every nail, screw, and tool was not only hung and in its place, but also labeled. The husband, who held a challenging position at the university, somehow managed to be at every Little League game, volleyball match, and parent-teacher conference. The wife, who worked part-time, was a class mother, Parent-Teacher Association (PTA) president three years running, a world-class cook, and a black belt in karate. My wife and I felt our lives paled in comparison.

The supercouple seemed to possess an energy and ability far beyond our reach. Years after we lost contact, my wife and I would occasionally lament our disordered lives and wonder why we couldn't be more like this supercouple. My garage (to this day) is an obstacle course, my lawn supports a nation of grubs, and our home rarely approaches perfection. For many years, we just assumed it was because we were less motivated, less perfect.

My wife and I have matured, and now we have a different perspective on our so-called shortcomings. Our epiphany came a few years after I finished graduate school and we moved back east from California. I got a call from one of our superfriends' teenage daughters wanting to know if I could do anything to help. It seems that the husband had been drinking heavily and the wife had slipped into a depression. I spoke to the husband, and he admitted that both he and his wife were burnt out, that they didn't want to go on together any longer.

They seemed so perfect. Regrettably, maintaining their illusion of perfection took too much out of them. They were perfect but got too tired staying perfect. Yes, it's possible to maintain an illusion of perfection, success, competence, or omnipotence if you desire. All it takes is effort, vigilance, maintenance, tenacity, fear, compulsion, stress, and complete dedication—twenty-four hours a day, seven days a week. Are you sure it's worth it?

What may be confusing is that not only are you convinced it's possible to have it all, but you've proven over and over again that you can have it all. So what's a little effort? This conclusion is dangerously shortsighted. Sustaining these unnatural efforts (i.e., living flawlessly) will eventually bring you face-to-face with a more important reality—you can never be happy unless you're perfect. It's a scary world where one glitch, one faux pas, one stumble leaves you depressed and anxious, scurrying to reclaim your throne. It's unnatural to live with such demands. Rather than focusing on being perfect, ask yourself why you need to be so perfect. If being imperfect causes you to feel anxious, suspect that your life is being ruled by your Insecure Child.

Three Expressions of Perfection

Perfectionists fall into three major groups: the Star, the Fanatic, and the Control Freak. Each of these groupings behaves with a perfectionistic style of black-and-white, tunnel-visioned rigidity. Because of this similarity, there is overlap among groups, but there are also some interesting differences:

- *The Star*—Stars want one thing: to be applauded. If people are impressed with you (and what you do), they're not going to hurt you. This is control. The Star is convinced that everyone loves a winner. Stars are usually in successful, spotlight positions. They are typically leaders not followers and are always trying to impress the world.

- *The Fanatic*—Fanatics are what we think of as the classic perfectionist. Fanatics may enjoy the applause of others, but unlike the Star, approval is only a secondary pursuit. For them, the primary objective of their fanatical way is to rise above vulnerability by eliminating all flaws. (If someone happens to applaud this effort, that's a bonus, not an essential.) Fanatics are typically obsessive and compulsive about some or all aspects of their lives, such as keeping fanatically neat closets, cars, or personal appearance. Sometimes, Fanatics become fanatical about their pursuits, hobbies, clubs, religions, or exercise. They are typical overdoers who can't do anything halfway.

- *The Control Freak*—Control Freaks differ from Stars and Fanatics in one essential way: They are socially oblivious. Whereas Stars insist on winning the acclaim of others, and Fanatics are often (although not exclusively) driven by their image and what others may think, Control Freaks are only concerned with absolute control, rather than with being liked. Whether it be controlling others, things, or events, the Control Freak leaves nothing to fate. Everything must be controlled.

The Star

Stars are leaders, presidents of clubs and organizations, winners, high rollers and risk takers. They work hard to keep the spotlight on themselves. As long as everyone is applauding, the Star is content. Because Stars believe "Everyone loves a winner," they are driven to succeed, whatever the cost. Losing ground, fading into the background, and not being noticed is a frightening loss of control. It's one step away from being forgotten and rejected. The Star's Insecure Child has a fragile self-image that constantly needs to be shored up by everyone's admiration.

Sometimes, the Star's perfectionism is diffuse and hard to detect. Gary was shocked to hear that his Star efforts were hurting him. Gary, a twenty-four-year-old man I was working with, had the following (abridged) list of accomplishments to report, "I don't understand why I don't make a better impression on women. I'm a college graduate, I play the piano and trumpet, I'm well read, I have a good job, I'm an athlete, I'm a photographer, an artist, a writer. . . . What's wrong with me? I think I'm a pretty good catch. I'm even thinking about going back to school." Gary was trying to be everything. He wanted to become the perfect person. His Insecure Child had him convinced that the more accomplished he became, the more irresistible he would become.

What Gary needed wasn't more school, or another accomplishment—he needed some Self-coaching. First, he had to stop listening to his Insecure Child's insistence that in order to be appreciated, loved, liked, and valued, he had to be better than everyone else. According to Gary's Insecure Child, the equation was simple: The more you're admired, the better you are. If you're better than other people, then you're controlling how people feel about you. A + B = C, where C, of course, stands for control.

Using the follow-through part of his training program, Gary was quickly able to hit the mark. In his words, "I have a 'little man' complex." Although this admission wasn't buried too deeply, it was nevertheless very upsetting for him to discuss. Actually, he sounded and acted more like a man confessing a murder. After all, it had been Gary's deep, dark secret for many years.

"Everyone thinks I'm the most secure, positive person they know," he said. "They wouldn't believe how messed up I am." He seemed to have made a pact with the devil: "Let me be a Star, then people won't notice how short I am." His Insecure Child was hopelessly trapped in an adolescent struggle for power, potency, and virility. Because he was doomed to be a "little man," no matter what he did, he would never be—nor could he ever be—enough of a man. This was Gary's life sentence, and it depressed him.

When Gary started his Self-coaching program, he didn't have to look far to discover his Insecure Child's influence. He was constantly finding fault with himself, or trying to tear himself down. His Child provided ample opportunity for practice. If, for example, someone were nice to Gary, showed him some respect, or applauded his accomplishments, rather than feeling a sense of relief, Gary's Insecure Child would grow anxious. After all, success was temporary, and he couldn't rest on his laurels.

Gary was on a treadmill, powered by the belief that unless he maintained his stellar performance, he would be minimized (pun intended). Once, early on, I asked what was actually so terrible about being short. Gary, reacting with his Insecure Child as if I'd just punched him in the gut, winced. "If you really want to know, I feel like I'm only half a man!" I almost jumped out of my seat, "That's absurd! You're acting like half a man if you allow your Child to get away with this farce. Enough is enough! It's time to become a whole man."

Gary had no trouble recognizing that he was being a wimp. When his Insecure Child talked, he would hang his head and, as he put it, "accept my fate." Eventually, it dawned on him that he was buying his Child's "half man" notion without so much as a whimper. He tried to get motivated by recalling my words, "Enough is enough!" He was enthralled by the notion that if he could fight off his Insecure Child, he might feel okay about himself—enthralled, but far from convinced. He met stiff resistance from his Child, who kicked, screamed, and tantrumed for weeks. The harder Gary came back with some directed Self-talk, the more his Insecure Child would throw up a barrage of insecurity, "I can't change. Who am I kidding, nothing's going to change the fact that I'm a shrimp. All the therapy in the world isn't going to add an inch to my height."

Gary, however, quickly developed enough muscle to not let his Insecure Child have the last word. On a page in his training log, Gary wrote, "It's not me, it's my Child who's hung up on my height. I think I really understand this now. My choice is to go along with this view and hate myself or fight. I choose to fight! Yes! I've got to see that I'm more than my height. That sounds so stupid when I write it—of course I'm more than my height! Somehow I've got to own this insight. I think if I could say, 'I'm tall enough,' I'd be cured—say it and believe it!"

It was imperative that Gary continue to be tough with his Insecure Child. Typically, the Insecure Child will intensify its sabotage when fighting for its life. I helped Gary realize that this was an indication that he was getting to his Child. "Don't let up," I encouraged. "You have absolutely nothing to lose except your insecurity." He didn't give up. Working on his motivation, Gary developed his own pep-talk slogan, "I don't need to grow taller, I need to grow up!" He would use this affirmation every time he confronted his Insecure Child.

Gary's perfectionistic lifestyle was an attempt to overshadow his insecurity by molding the perfect persona. His truth could be stated simply: I don't have to be perfect, I just have to become more secure. This wasn't security from the outside in (i.e., through accomplishments), but from the inside out—"I don't need to grow taller to be okay. I need to grow up." There was no rational reason why he had to go on looking at the world through the eyes of an adolescent Insecure Child.

Self-Coaching Reflection

It's useful to try to assess the age of your Insecure Child. A tantrumy attitude, for example, may suggest a very regressed Child whose style is reminiscent of a two- or three-year-old, "No, just leave me alone. I won't say a word!" One tip-off that you're dealing with an adolescent Child is a hypersensitive focus on physical concerns. It's during adolescence that physical attractiveness becomes all-encompassing. It's what teenagers obsess about.

The Fanatic

Fanatics are your archetypal Perfectionists. They can be fanatical about anything: work, clothes, shopping, eating, cleanliness, exercise, you name it. I ran into a prototypical Fanatic while pursuing my hobby as an astronomy buff. The club I belong to has viewing parties, where the public can come and enjoy an evening under the stars. The first time I went to one of these parties, I was amazed to see the guy next to me setting up. Talk about bells and whistles, this guy's telescope was equipped with a steel-reinforced tripod, dew shield, eyepieces, cameras, light-pollution filters, star charts, even computer-assisted tracking. He wore battery-powered socks, gloves, and a headband with a red flashlight for night vision. A card table and adjustable folding chair were the last to materialize from the back of his station wagon. He proudly let me know that he was fanatical about his telescope.

Maybe you've run into fanatics—at the gym, at the club you belong to, or at your job. You've been to their houses, seen their manicured lawns, or marveled at their elaborate, carefully maintained worlds. Like the couple my wife and I knew in graduate school, however, perfection demands an enormous price on your resources. Like a sprinter, you may look great for the first hundred meters, but you're not going to keep it up for long. You can't—not without serious consequences.

Jack was an anxious and depressed patient of mine who struggled to maintain his healthy lifestyle. He refused to accept the fact that his fifty-year-old body was going to age, sag, or fail him in any way. His waist was a solid 32 inches, he bragged about not having a cold in two years, and he was convinced that for him, aging was "a myth!" He lifted weights, jogged, and was a fixture at his neighborhood health-food store. He was also an avid chef whose tofu dishes, freshly juiced beverages, and organic veggies were worthy of a gourmet restaurant. Jack was indeed fanatical about his health.

When left to pursue his rigorous schedule, Jack felt great. The problem that brought him to therapy was that his wife, kids, boss, bills, and obligations were all competing and conflicting with his ambition to remain forever young. Jack never had enough time. He could never afford to take an afternoon off or stay out late. No one understood his frustrations. Jack also began to become anxious. After a couple of full-blown panic attacks, he gave me a call.

The problem was, rather than trying to juggle the situation and reduce the anxiety, Jack kept adding more to an already choked life. Just prior to our first meeting, for example, he decided that flexibility was the key to the fountain of youth and immediately signed up for yoga lessons (which he attended after his nightly workouts at the gym). Jack was fanatical, tunnel-visioned, obsessed, and compulsed with one thing—control. He couldn't tolerate losing his grip to age.

Jack died of a brain tumor but there was one consolation to

this tragedy. In the months before his death, he came to realize the foolishness of his ways. He could have remained fanatical: At one point, he thought of flying to Mexico for an exotic cancer cure. Instead, however, he chose to open himself to the time he had left with his family and his friends.

I can't say Jack died a happy man, but I can say he died courageously. Perfectionism had wasted much of his life. In dying, Jack learned that life wasn't about control; it was about letting go.

The Control Freak

Control freaks are easy to spot. They're always directing, organizing, steering, meddling in everyone's business, and typically seen as royal pains in the ass!

Clair is a control freak whose confrontations with her teenage son led her to therapy. Tony, her beleaguered sixteen-year-old, had the following complaints about his mother:

> She refuses to give me any space. I have no privacy. Is it wrong to want to close my door? What does she think I'm doing in there? I've never been in any trouble, I don't smoke, I'm not into drugs. Why is she so suspicious? She's always on my back. No matter what I do, she has to correct it. She has to know where I am, who I'm with, what we're doing. If I forget to call home, I'm grounded. If I'm five minutes late on my curfew, I'm grounded. I'm already grounded for the next two months! She insists she has the right to go through my things, read my notes and mail, and even insists that I give her my AOL password. I'm not stupid. I know parents have to monitor their kids, but she's insane!

Clair, after biting her tongue as long as she could, finally exploded:

Look, you're the kid, and I'm the parent. If I say your door has to stay opened, it stays open. I don't need to give you a reason. Whose house is it anyway? And don't think you're so perfect. Your attitude stinks. You haven't been doing your chores, and you're disrupting my house.

Clair was obviously tough on her son, but her control wasn't confined to him. She divorced Tony's father because, as he told me in an earlier interview, he couldn't stand being pushed around by her. When talking with Tony's guidance counselor, I was told—off the record—how impossible Clair was at Tony's school. She was constantly complaining, always snooping around, and never hesitant to cause trouble. For example, when Tony's counselor forgot to call her back one afternoon, Clair reported her to the principal. Clair demanded—and got—a formal apology.

At first, Clair was impenetrable. She did, however, have enough insight to recognize one twisted perception. "I know it's probably neurotic, but I feel that if I relax my grip on Tony, I'm going to lose him." She was terrorized by the thought that he would wind up in a pit of illegal drugs and alcohol. She was convinced, not because of Tony's behavior, but because her Insecure Child told her so—and she listened. It never occurred to her that she might be frustrating Tony to the point where he might begin acting out, that her fears could become a self-fulfilling prophecy. Nor did it occur to her that her marriage, her reception at Tony's school, and even her friendships all suffered under the strain of her constant demands.

One opening came when Clair admitted she might be losing Tony. This turned out to be her Achilles' heel. It backed her off of her bullheaded arrogance and created a different kind of anxiety. Clair was used to feeling anxious most of the time, but this was because her demands caused conflict. Losing Tony was different.

It was one of the few times she felt powerless. After all, she was used to controlling everything and everyone. Anyone she couldn't control, she eliminated (e.g., her husband, Tony's counselor). Now she was backed up against the wall. She couldn't control Tony, and couldn't bear the thought of losing him. Finally, humbled by her anxiety, she realized she would have to change.

Clair and I had a few sessions together without Tony. She recognized that underneath all her fears and doubts about Tony was a profound sense of insecurity that went as far back as her early childhood. Growing up with a volatile, alcoholic father who was always threatening divorce and abandonment, Clair looked for any opportunity to feel more in control. She had to do something—and she did. She began to take charge. As a child, she began to become bossy, aggressive, and tunnel-visioned. It worked. Where she was powerless and weak, she now became tough, powerful, and insensitive. Her motto: "Don't tread on me!"

Realizing the connection between her past vulnerability and her present Control Freak nature was enough to get the ball rolling. To be really secure, she knew she was going to have to risk letting go—well, at least relaxing the reins. Security, as Clair found out, begins with a willingness to believe in yourself. Sure, it took effort, but she finally appreciated what was at stake if she didn't make the effort.

Self-Coaching Reflection
A willingness to believe in yourself promotes healing and security.

Clair's efforts to apply Self-coaching were met with enthusiasm by Tony. Life at home quickly improved. She stumbled along for a while, but Tony realized she was trying, and that was enough for him. Clair did well.

Telling the Difference between *Want-Tos* and *Have-Tos*

If you suspect that your Insecure Child is pushing you into a perfectionistic lifestyle, it's time for straight talk. How can you tell whether your desire to sing in the choir, to decorate your living room, or to run a marathon is driven by a legitimate or a neurotic ambition? In order to make this distinction, you'll need to learn to distinguish between your *want-tos* and your *have-tos*. The essential difference can be stated thus:

- *Want-tos* are driven by a desire for self-satisfaction, not for any ulterior, control-driven motive.
- *Have-tos* are driven by insecurity. They are compulsive, rigid attempts to use whatever you're doing to feel more in control.

If what you want to do is driven by a legitimate and sincere desire, it's going to feel like a *want-to*. If, on the other hand, your Insecure Child is involved, then it's going to feel much more compulsive—a *have-to*. *Want-tos* can be intense and passionate experiences, but they're not perfectionistic because your motive isn't control. That's reserved for *have-tos*. You'll need to decide, "Do I feel I *want to,* or do I *have to?*"

Don't be surprised if at first, *want to* and *have to* seem identical. You may, for example, hear yourself saying, "I *want to* keep my house spotless." Upon closer examination, however, you may detect your Insecure Child convincing you that unless your house is spotless, you can't relax and enjoy it—or worse, you won't be seen as perfect. In this case, the truth would be that in order to feel in control you *have to* keep your house spotless. Be patient, and use all your Self-coaching tools to help you differentiate between whether you *want to* or you *have to* do something.

Larry's Love-Hate Relationship with His BMW

My friend Larry is at the cusp of understanding this *have-to/want-to* dilemma. He's a car fanatic—and he knows it. It's not uncommon for him to wash and wax his BMW daily. He has a camel hair brush for cleaning the air conditioner louvers, and he gets upset whenever he has to use the car because the freshly vacuumed nap on his rugs will be ruined. He knows he's a fanatic with his cars, but he loves the process. Is this a *have-to* or a *want-to*?

For Larry, it's both.

Larry does love cars, always has. He enjoys every aspect of detailing his car. This clearly is a *want-to* aspect—self-satisfaction without ulterior motive. Where Larry's *want-to* crosses the line and becomes a *have-to* is the point where control seeps into the picture. Keeping the car perfect, not allowing it to get smudged or to have the rugs stepped on is both excessive and rigid (i.e., perfectionistic). When, because of a smudge, love can become hate (i.e., black-and-white thinking), we're no longer talking about enjoyment. We're talking compulsive, all-or-nothing control.

Are you too rigid? Are you working too hard for all the wrong reasons? Are your *want-tos* beginning to turn into *have-tos*? Has your life already become a life sentence? What are you waiting for?

✤ ✤ ✤

TRAINING SUGGESTION

In the left-hand column of the chart on page 223, under Perfectionistic Tendencies, list any Star, Fanatic, or Control Freak tendencies. Using the scale to the right, circle the number that corresponds to the intensity of any tendency you've noted (see example) within the past three months.

If you've listed any perfectionistic tendencies, include this self-assessment in your training log, and then on a monthly basis, retake it, in order to evaluate your Self-coaching progress. Scoring is simply a tally of the numbers you've circled. Your total score should be decreasing with your training.

Perfectionistic Tendencies	Intensity Scale				
Example:	Weak		Moderate		Strong
1. I know I'm fanatical about my appearance. I just can't not care!	1	2	3	4	5

	Weak		Moderate		Strong
1.	1	2	3	4	5
2.	1	2	3	4	5
3.	1	2	3	4	5

❖ ❖ ❖

17

Self-Coaching for Guilt-Sensitive People

Everyone feels anxious and depressed from time to time; it's normal. Likewise, everyone feels guilt. Although guilt is a common experience, most people would be hard pressed to describe it. Sometimes, disappointing a friend or forgetting someone's birthday can cause us intense, cramping pangs of guilt. Yet, at other times, we may lie, cheat, or even hurt someone without so much as an afterthought.

The amount of guilt you feel depends on how you interpret what you're doing—or not doing. A soldier in battle may feel little remorse for trying to kill his enemy: "It's my duty." The same soldier, on leave, may be tormented by the way he snapped at a sales clerk, "I feel terrible; she didn't deserve that."

If you were an anthropologist, you'd have to look long and hard to find a culture where guilt is absent. Clearly, guilt appears to be a universal psychocultural phenomenon. What, if any, could be the evolutionary advantage to such a tendency? Because evolution is a process of discarding the useless and perpetuating the useful, we can assume that guilt, because of its sheer prevalence, must play an important role in human development. How can such a scourge be useful? It may be hard to imagine, but guilt may well be the cornerstone of our entire social, cooperative existence.

Are You Guilt Sensitive?

Parents and other authority figures play a critical role in shaping our perception of right from wrong—our moral sense. Children either learn to curb their selfish and primitive desires or to live with the distress of having angry, disappointed parents (i.e., loss of control). Who hasn't seen this scenario played out in one of its many forms? "If you don't stop that, Mommy is going to be very angry!" Or, "I told you to be careful, now look what you did. You broke it!" The Swiss psychiatrist Carl Gustav Jung felt that without guilt, there could be no psychic maturation. In order to go beyond our primitive, egocentric, childish selfishness, we need an internal mechanism to nag us—a mechanism that goads us into doing the right thing. This mechanism is guilt.

If it weren't for our tendency to be ego centered, rather than other centered, we wouldn't need rules, laws, or commandments. In a real sense, we need to be guarded from ourselves. More specifically, we need to be guarded from our inner child, who seeks one thing—self-gratification. It's important to note that not everyone feels guilt the same way. Some people are highly guilt sensitive, while other people are relatively oblivious to their own transgressions, although they may be quick to point them out in others. Each of us is equipped with a kind of guilt thermostat. For some, the thermostat has a low setting that permits guilt to be switched on easily. These are what I call the Guilt-sensitives. In contrast, others have such a high setting that they seem blind to the hurt they inflict. For these Guilt-*in*sensitives, it may take nothing less than a full-blown trauma for them to feel guilty. If you're a control-oriented person who's no stranger to guilt, then you can assume that your thermostat is probably set too low.

What exactly is guilt? Essentially, guilt is that remorseful, loss-of-control feeling you get every time you think you've done something wrong. If you lose your temper and yell at your spouse, you may wind up feeling guilty, depressed, or vaguely uneasy all day. If, on the other hand, you allowed your spouse to berate you in front of your kids, you may wind up feeling guilty about not sticking up for your rights. Don't think guilt is reserved exclusively for those things you do wrong. *Not* doing something can cause guilt, too. You can feel just as guilty over an inadvertent, unintentional gaffe as you can a premeditated one. Here are a few of guilt's more common expressions:

1. *Guilt by commission.* Thus occurs when you're driven by selfish goals to do something you regret. Cheating on a spouse, lying, stealing, hurting someone, or feigning sickness to get out of an obligation are all actions that can leave you riddled with guilt.

2. *Guilt by omission.* This arises when you fail to do what you feel is right. Neglecting a friend's plea for assistance, not working up to your potential, forgetting a birthday or anniversary, or neglecting to return a phone call are all examples of guilt by omission.

3. *Guilt by comparison.* Compared to others, you feel you have too much. Getting a break, having good fortune, inheriting money, or seeing a homeless person may make you feel guilty about how easy you have it.

4. *Guilt by fantasy or thought.* This emerges when you have thoughts or fantasies that are inconsistent with your morality. Improper sexual desires or thoughts of cheating, stealing, hurting someone, or engaging in antisocial behavior can all bring intense feelings of guilt.

5. *Existential guilt.* This occurs when you feel guilty about who you are, what you do for a living, or where you're going in life—such as not living up to some ideal expectation, feeling lazy, being addicted to some harmful substance or way of life, or giving up.

Feeling Guilty for All the Wrong Reasons

The first time I met Pete, he handed me a black-and-white-marbled composition book, filled from beginning to end with a meticulous, almost tortured printing. This was his diary written during the summer of his tenth year. He asked if I'd take a look, indicating that he thought it might be useful for our work. I asked if there were anything significant about that particular summer of 1960. He nodded, only saying that he thought I'd find it interesting reading. He was right.

As far back as Pete can remember, he felt guilty. He felt guilty about his poor grades in school, his inability to please his mother, his looks, and his lack of talent. He even felt guilty because he hated walking the dog. (After all, he was the one who had pleaded for a puppy.) Pete was an only child whose mother relied heavily on guilt as a means of control and education. He was very sensitive by nature, and it didn't take much for his mother to get compliance. If Pete disobeyed, she would usually give him the "cold treatment." This usually consisted of a day or two of silence. It drove poor Pete crazy. "Anything would have been better than the silence," he said. "I couldn't stand it. I would panic, beg, cry for hours. She wouldn't budge; she had to teach me a lesson." Pete was much too dependent on his mother and absolutely paranoid about losing her affections.

All in all, Pete was a good boy who didn't mess up too often. In response to his vulnerable life, he—out of necessity—did manage to implement a few adequate control strategies. By trying to forecast what was expected of him at all times, he effectively lessened the occasions for failure, and thus guilt. In spite of these and other diligent efforts, Pete's life remained hampered by a sensitivity to guilt. By ten years old, he had adjusted to and accepted his rather compulsive, vigilant, and controlling lifestyle. Had it not been for a trauma one summer afternoon, things might have gone on calmly in this manner for years.

It started out just like any other July day in northern New Jersey—hazy, hot, and humid, with the temperature just topping 100 degrees. Pete's mother, having been summoned for jury duty, left strict orders for Pete, "Clean your room, take out the garbage, weed the garden, and make sure you walk Tippy."

Pete had every intention of carrying out her orders. In fact, he had already cleaned his room, taken out the garbage, and was finishing up the weeding when his neighbor Eugene came panting into his yard, yelling wildly, "I got it! I got it! The go-cart, c'mon let's go for a ride." Dusting off his Levi's, Pete was halfway to Eugene's to see the new go-cart when he remembered Tippy. Tippy was the toy terrier that Pete was supposed to walk. Telling Eugene to wait a minute, Pete ran home, got Tippy, tied her to the cyclone fence at the end of the driveway, and then rejoined Eugene and his dad, who were busy gassing up the go-cart.

Where the time went that morning and afternoon, Pete had no idea. At one point, based on the hunger he felt in his belly, Pete knew it must be getting late. He decided he'd better get home before his mother. Not that he did anything wrong—just that you could never be too sure, and with his mother, never too safe. Walking up the driveway, Pete remembered Tippy. At once, a cold, unsettled feeling gripped his stomach as he ran up the driveway. There lay Tippy motionless. Pete convulsed with panic, fear, and grief. Picking up Tippy and bringing her into the house, Pete began to sob, "I forgot to leave water. I killed Tippy!" Then it occurred to him, had he done what he was told and walked Tippy, none of this would have happened. That one thought paralyzed him. This realization caused an immediate seizure of guilt that Pete knew he would never be able to shake off.

As Pete sat there crying, Tippy on the kitchen floor in front of him, his mother walked in. Seeing Pete and the dog, she screamed, "What happened to Tippy?" Pete, looking up through red swollen eyes, hesitated, then replied, "I don't know, she was lying here when I got home."

For days, the only thought pounding in Pete's brain was, "what have I done." Pete was scared and confused. Somehow he had crossed over the line. He had done the unthinkable and then lied about it! What kind of monster was he? He knew he could never go back to his quiet, normal (moderately guilty) life again. If only he could go back in time and undo this terrible trauma. If only.

Already a guilt-ridden child, Pete decided that the only thing he could do was never screw up again. Never again would he be so careless. Never again would he be so impulsive. His guilt thermostat was pushed up to high, his sensitivity to guilt became so acute that he felt compelled to become a master at control. Eventually, his obsessive, controlled lifestyle wore him down. He came to therapy in his mid-thirties—depressed, tormented, and beaten by life. Pete needed help in resetting his thermostat.

Self-Coaching, the Guilt Slayer

Self-coaching taught Pete how his sensitive nature, combined with the guilt-laden strategies of his mother, set him up for feeling chronically off balance, insecure, and out of control. The incident with Tippy only galvanized Pete's already tortured sense of guilt. His guilt became his radar, scanning the world, anticipating and protecting him from messing up:

❖ ❖ ❖

Stray from mother's (or authority's) expectations ▶
feel guilty ▶ alter behavior ▶ reduce feeling of guilt ▶
avoid straying (control) from further expectations

❖ ❖ ❖

Because control is an illusion, not an answer (Self-coaching healing principle 4), Pete was doomed to suffer. He described it himself as "running up a down escalator through life." The effort and energy he spent avoiding problems left him depleted. Although it was now more than twenty-five years since the traumatic incident with Tippy, Pete was still referring to it, still being affected by it, always confirming that he could never put his guard down, relax, or risk being careless. The last page in his composition book was prophetic. It ended with, "I will never, never, never hurt anybody again."

When I met Pete, he was thirty-five years old. Clearly, he still held the same view of the world he had as a child—you can never be safe enough, and any action can prove to be fatal. Pete's obsessive, almost paranoid cautiousness was nothing more than a knee-jerk acceptance of his tormented past, which he now projected onto his present.

Pete realized that he was just too damn sensitive. He needed to update his script and stop reacting to the world like a helpless child whose mommy would punish him if he screwed up. Instead of being ruled by an outdated habit, Pete needed a more reality-based assessment of danger.

Fortified by his Self-coaching work, Pete began to use Self-talk to confront his Insecure Child. He got plenty of practice. In almost every social situation, he heard his Child buzzing in his ear, "Be careful. Don't mess up. Why is he so quiet, what did I say?" Despite this buzzing, Pete did find the courage to take a bold risk. Even though his Insecure Child kept him off balance with panicky remarks, he decided to treat all Child thoughts as simply false. He decided, "I don't have to be careful. I can take risks. If I mess up, I mess up. I can live with that."

He was extremely uncomfortable at first, but he insisted on acting and thinking more maturely. By demanding that he be less sensitive, Pete released himself from his habitual cowering. As his strength grew, so too did his momentum. He was amazed how quickly everything shifted once he chose to see the world from a here-and-now perspective, rather than from the eyes of "Worry Boy" as he called his Insecure Child.

Armed now with an understanding and foundation of confidence, Pete was ready to take on his Insecure Child. Going through Self-talk's three steps, he was amazed how often his Child spoke. "I knew I was a sensitive, but this is unbelievable. I feel guilty about everything. I forgot to hold a door open for this woman at the hardware store the other day, and I heard her mutter, 'Thanks a lot, jerk!' All day long I was crucifying myself for being scolded by this woman. I felt like I did something wrong—just like with my mother! Rather than feeling angry at being called a jerk, or realizing that it was just one of those things, I just wouldn't let it go. It's sick!"

It was Step 2—deciding not to listen to the Insecure Child—that gave Pete the most problems. Pete, told me, "As much as I despise Worry Boy, he just keeps pushing me around. He's paranoid. All my reasonable thinking seems to stop as I fall into this pit of guilt and depression. I hate myself when I screw up. I just can't seem to win." Reading Pete's words, do you detect a need for a pep talk?

Pete and I worked extensively on his motivation. At first, he needed to be encouraged all the time. My coaching strategy was to talk to the mature potential that had become arrested in his development. My pep talk went something like this: "Worry Boy's tough. He's become too strong. But that's okay, you're going to be building some muscle. Every time you dig your heels in and resist, fight back, or just recognize Worry Boy's influence, you're building psychic muscle. Be greedy, grab your exercise every chance you get. See every problem as an opportunity to build muscle. If Worry Boy knocks you down, forget it, move on. You tried, that's all that really matters. It's the experience (and the exercise you get) that's important. Quit worrying about how much longer, or whether or not the program is working. Just focus on today's work. Tomorrow will take care of itself. Right now is what matters. It's all that matters!"

Self-Coaching Reflection
Pep talks are an essential part of Self-coaching. The key to giving a good pep talk is to allow yourself to get into it—really get into it!

See yourself as a locker room coach pacing up and down before the big game. Essentially, it's a matter of letting go and allowing your inner coach to come forward and speak. You'll be amazed how easy, and enjoyable, this part of your training program can be. Start by coming up with a phrase of encouragement. Hear yourself, see yourself, get emotional. Get mad, and get going.

Pete slowly gained an inch of ground here and an inch there. It wasn't long before he reported in his training log: "I think I did it! Worry Boy was all upset with me because I called in sick to work. I hung up the phone and said, 'I have a choice. I can either let Worry Boy make me feel guilty or I can accept the fact that I don't feel well and I'm entitled to a day off. I chose to stay home. And I chose not to feel guilty! Yes! A couple of times I needed to give myself a pep talk, but I was focused, I was tough. Worry Boy was no match for me today. Not only did I stay home, without guilt, but I felt great—in spite of the flu."

One more thing. As Pete gradually extricated himself from the habit of being ruled by his Insecure Child, he finally admitted, "I made a mistake with Tippy. I was ten years old and showed poor judgment. But, as terrible as it was, it's time for me to forgive myself. I'm not a monster, I'm not a murderer. It's time I grow up and realize that I'm allowed to mess up." Finally, after twenty-five years, Pete forgave himself for disobeying his mother that hot, humid July afternoon.

Is Guilt Ever Necessary?

You can see from Pete's story how powerful—and transforming—the experience of guilt can be. Pete is far from being an isolated example. I could discuss many others, such as Sarah, a woman in her early thirties who lived with her suffocating mother and anguished over what a terrible daughter she was for wanting to move out; or Al, a man who wasn't allowed to enjoy life because his wife died—more than two years earlier!

Although guilt is a common aspect of many presenting problems in therapy, keep in mind that not all guilt is neurotic. For example, guilt can keep you on your toes by making you morally responsive to others—lest you do something you wind up regretting. "I really do need to call my sister." "I guess I have been working the kids too hard." "You're right, I've been acting like a fool." Guilt, and at times just the anticipation of guilt, can be a major force in shaping our socialization.

So, what's the verdict on guilt? Evil or holy? Does guilt, in fact, make you a better or a worse person? One thing's for sure, a deeper understanding of the nature and significance of guilt can help you become more realistic about your moral responsibilities—and the more realistic you are, the less you give your Insecure Child to play with.

Morality and Conscience

Standing between your Insecure Child's selfish nature and the social demands of your community is a mediator, an arbiter of balance and fairness we call our conscience. Think of your *conscience* as a security guard (pun intended) who constantly monitors your actions and thoughts. As you begin to drift toward selfish disregard for some aspect of life, your security guard begins to stir. Your guard's single weapon against your Insecure Child's excesses is the ability to generate *guilt*. Because guilt can be uncomfortable, it usually manages to get your attention and interrupt your behavior.

Guilt and conscience represent two sides of a triangle, but there is a third equally important aspect to forming your sense of right and wrong, your personal morality. This third shaping force is *consequence*. From your earliest experiences with your parents, authority figures, and everyday trial-and-error experiences, you've been continually shaped by the formidable effects of consequence. If you break a law, you risk prosecution. If you neglect a friend, you jeopardize the relationship. If you smoke, you risk lung cancer. We're used to, and expect, consequences for our actions.

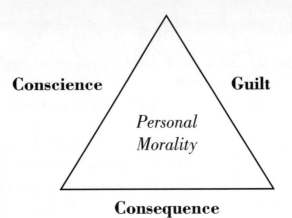

When I was an intern, I ran a therapy group for repeat offenders from Lompoc Federal Prison. The entire group, without exception, had one major failing: Aside from having an exceptionally low guilt setting on their thermostats, they never learned to embrace the concept of consequence. They were just too cool or too smart to get caught ever again. The fact that they had been caught in the past had no relevance to them. They learned nothing—only that next time it was going to be different. They used the irrational reasoning that they could behave the same way, but somehow the results would be different. They were smarter now, and besides, it was just bad luck that they got caught in the first place—certainly not because of their actions.

These prisoners live in a world of consequence just like you and me, but they choose to ignore it. Clearly, all of us can choose to live by our Insecure Children's impulsiveness. You don't have to be a prisoner at Lompoc to break the rules and not feel guilty. Yes, it's possible to ignore consequences, but you can't escape them. If it were any other way, we would be living in a lawless, riotous world where chaos, not moderation, ruled.

Martyrs

No discussion on guilt would be complete without introducing you to another control-oriented type of person, who happens to be a Guilt-sensitive's worst nightmare—the Martyr. Martyrs are particularly adept at manipulating a Guilt-sensitive's weakness. They are perpetual victims who absolutely thrive on guilt. "Oh no, dear, I don't mind if you go to your meeting. Somehow I'll manage the kids, even if my back is killing me. And who knows, maybe my headache will get better." The Guilt-sensitive person, driving off to the meeting, is thinking, "Damn, I'm being so selfish. I should be home helping out. How can I be so insensitive?" Martyrs, like all the other expressions of control mentioned in this book, are driven by insecurity. Turtles, for example, control through distance, Hedgehogs through hostility, and Martyrs through manipulation. Guilt-sensitive people are easy pickings for Martyrs.

In our earlier example, you saw how Pete's mother's "cold treatment" was an effective tool in shaping his compliant behavior—effective but not humane. Less sophisticated mothers and fathers, especially those frustrated and unable to teach the appropriate response, will rely on guilt to coerce and control their children. If a parent happens to be a Martyr, it's particularly devastating for the child's development.

Henry, a fifty-six-year-old patient, recalls his mother:

> As far back as I can remember, my mother was sick—at least that's what she always told me. Whenever I'd do anything wrong, like be late for dinner or not get my homework done, my mother would remind me of her bad heart and how it wasn't good for her to get upset. I lived with the belief that she was this delicate flower, and at any moment, my actions could kill her. It was terrible. She made it much worse by always walking around muttering how no one cared if she got sick. The worst for me was when she would say, "When I'm not around, then you'll be sorry." That used to tear me apart.
>
> Once, I couldn't have been more than six or seven, I was playing with a friend in the yard, and she asked me to go inside and get her an orange. Then I forgot all about the orange. Later that

night, I guess she was trying to teach me a lesson, "One day, when I'm not here, you're going to remember that I asked you to do me a favor," she said. "You're going to remember that orange and how upset you made Mommy." I felt terrible, I tried to apologize to no avail. She only said, "It's too late for that, you can't fix the hurt you caused me."

She was right about one thing. Look—I'm fifty-six and I'm still talking about that goddamn orange! The irony is that my mother's now eighty-four years old (Amazing how long a delicate heart can survive!), and she's still doing it to me, "No one calls, everyone's too busy . . . " And now the new thing is, "I'm so depressed, if I could find a way to die . . . " I know she's being ridiculous but I still feel terrible. I'm so afraid that she's going to die and I'm going to regret not doing the one thing she might ask. You know, like getting the orange.

Henry was depressed and beaten down by his guilt. It had long ago generalized to others—his wife, children, and even friends. Recently, Henry felt anguished when his brother-in-law called to tell him he had two tickets to a football play-off game. Henry hated football, had mounds of work to get done around the house, and didn't want to sit in a crowded stadium in 30-degree weather—but he couldn't say no. It was his mother's orange again. After years of guilt with his mother, Henry wasn't about to let someone else get mad at him. He felt anxious, not because saying no was wrong, but because if he did say no, his brother-in-law would be angry. It was this consequence that Henry couldn't live with.

(Recalling the morality triangle, your eventual decision of what is "right" and what is "wrong" can be influenced by one or all of the three shaping forces: guilt, conscience, or consequence. Henry went to the football game, mostly because of his fear of the consequence if he didn't—namely, his brother-in-law's anger. Henry was becoming more and more of a Turtle, trying to distance himself from the demands of others. Because he couldn't say no, avoidance seemed the only way to avoid conflict.

Henry's Self-coaching program was straightforward. He had to recognize that his mother was a Martyr who manipulated and coerced him. He also needed to understand how his Guilt-sensitive personality was the result of her incessant undermining of his security—screw up, be a little selfish, forget a chore, and you wind up killing your mother! Henry's Self-talk invariably pitted him against a hand-wringing, remorseful Insecure Child who was terrified about doing the wrong thing. Henry began confronting his Child, insisting that if he was ever to feel better about himself, he would have to risk taking a stand. I wholeheartedly agreed.

As harsh as it sounds, I told Henry that one day, if he were to separate himself from the shadow of his mother's manipulation, he would—quite literally—have to risk "killing" her. Henry understood immediately, "You're right, at some point I have to say, 'Enough!' If she dies because I didn't have time to call her, I have to accept that. Hey, if she dies, it's because she worked herself up, not me. I can't be responsible for her neurosis!"

Henry, after fifty-six years of guilt-ridden obedience, finally stepped out of his mother's shadow. She didn't die, and Henry began to live.

Martyrs Make Strange Bedfellows

Don't think parents are the only Martyrs. When a Guilt-sensitive person winds up married to a Martyr, the web can become very tangled. This alignment isn't as strange as it sounds. The Guilt-sensitive person is drawn by the desire to rescue this poor, helpless victim. And why not? Saving someone can make you feel quite powerful and potent. The Martyr, on the other hand, like a card shark, is attracted to easy pickings. The Guilt-sensitive spouse can be manipulated with ease.

Tony and Kerry's relationship gives you a flavor of this lopsided alignment. During a marital session, Tony explained, "Kerry says she never tells me what to do. What she doesn't understand is that she makes me feel so guilty that I wind up doing exactly what she wants."

Kerry interrupted. "No, no, that's not true. Tony has trouble with my being honest. I never try to manipulate him." "What?" Tony fired back. "You think when I say I'm going bowling it's okay for you to tell me how you never get out, how you have nothing to do, and how bored you'll be—isn't that manipulating?"

Kerry began to let her Martyr show. "No matter how hard I try to be honest, I get in trouble. Guess I'm not allowed to have an opinion. Fine, if that's what you want, I'll just be quiet, it doesn't really matter what I want anyway."

Tony was exasperated. "Forget it, forget it. I can't stand it any-more. Whatever you want, I'll quit the damn league! I just can't go on feeling torn apart all the time."

Both Kerry and Tony were being ruled by their Insecure Children. Kerry's Insecure Child insisted that she steer the relation-ship through her fictitious suffering (although fictitious, she—like most Martyrs—allowed herself to believe her suffering was real). She got what she wanted: control. Tony's Guilt-sensitive Insecure Child, on the other hand, only wanted to avoid conflict and be a good boy.

Therapeutically, we had our hands full. Kerry was totally unconscious of her Martyr role and needed a quick Self-coached education. Unfortunately, her lack of insight made it impossible for her to see her behavior clearly. She needed to hear Tony's assessment of what expressions of control were contaminating her life. He (after some follow-through exloration) pointed out that she tried to control everything he did with her suffering. "Whenever I want to do something, you have some kind of problem. Your headache, your back, sometimes you're too tired, or too upset. You always tell me it's okay, but it's really never okay. I get so confused because I wind up feeling so guilty. You never let me decide anything. Unless you're calling all the shots, you develop some kind of problem."

As for Tony, feeling guilty was a way of avoiding conflict. Understanding where this habit came from required some follow-through. He came from a broken home where he was shuffled from grandma, to aunt, back to his now single mother. All the while, he lived with the notion that his parents divorced because of him. This wasn't all together false. His mother was seventeen-years-old when he was born, and his father had to quit high school to work. The demands of marriage and family proved too much for this young, immature couple. Tony, at the ripe old age of seven, had witnessed countless screaming matches where he was the object of contention. Tony lived with the unbearable (although shortsighted) guilt that he had ruined his parent's lives.

Tony rebelled in high school—not caring, getting into drugs, anesthetizing himself from his previous torment. Rebellion worked for a while, then it turned sour. He got into trouble with the law, was forced into rehab, and eventually was put on antidepressant medication. As he pulled out of his destructive period, Tony, now unable to hide in a shroud of drugs, went back to his Guilt-sensitive ways. He became compulsive in many ways, trying hard to control life before it ruptured again.

As Tony and Kerry became more and more steeped in each other's training, they began to help each other out. They got particularly good at pointing out each other's Insecure Child and then giving a critique of what they perceived to be the Child's intentions. What was most important is that they did this in a constructive, therapeutic manner. Nothing is accomplished if one partner uses an insight to attack the other: "Stop feeling sorry for yourself. You're just a pathetic Martyr, and I'm not going to let you tell me what to do." A more constructive, therapeutic response would sound more like, "You're saying it's okay for me to go bowling, but I'm hearing your Insecure Child talking. Why do you think your Child is feeling so vulnerable? Come on, let's talk."

As neurotic as a relationship can get, the opposite is equally true—a relationship can become an ongoing source of accurate feedback and insight. If both partners are willing to share their training efforts with each other, the results can be remarkable. I suggest that both partners read this book, sharing any thoughts or observations along the way, and then routinely exchange training logs, followed by a feedback session.

❖ ❖ ❖

TRAINING SUGGESTION

If you're using Self-coaching to deal with relationship issues, keep in mind that the feedback your partner gives you is extremely valuable. Assuming that the feedback is given in good faith, you need to accept the possibility that your partner may see aspects of your Insecure Child that you can't see, won't see, or haven't taken the time to see. Don't waste a golden opportunity to progress by being defensive or tunnel-visioned.

❖ ❖ ❖

❖ ❖ ❖

TRAINING SUGGESTION

Make an assessment as to whether you think you are Guilt-sensitive (i.e., due to your Insecure Child). Under the headings listed on the left, list the type of guilt expressions that you're prone to. Rate each expression using the scale on the right. On a regular monthly basis, check to see whether your Self-coaching work is reducing your sensitivity to guilt.

	Mild		Moderate		Extreme
Guilt by commission example: lying, cheating, hurting someone					
your example:	1	2	3	4	5
Guilt by omission example: forgetting or neglecting something					
your example:	1	2	3	4	5
Guilt by comparison guilt in comparison to others					
your example:	1	2	3	4	5
Guilt by fantasy or thought thoughts or fantasies inconsistent with your morality					
your example:	1	2	3	4	5

Existential guilt
guilt about
who or what you are

your example: 1   2   3   4   5

❖   ❖   ❖

PART V

Self-Coaching
for Life

18

Self-Coaching and Letting Go

In the introduction, I mentioned that I had been on a high school football team. My decision to join the team wasn't an easy one. At 102 pounds, I was scared to death. If you recall, the only reason I joined was to give the impression that I was a tough kind of guy. In spite of my trepidation about playing, however, something quite remarkable happened. This "something" is important for you to understand, and it has nothing to do with football and everything to do with self-liberation.

The first day of practice, I was handed my equipment—shoulder pads, hip pads, thigh pads, knee pads, helmet, mouthpiece. Never before had I seen such paraphernalia. Coming from a neighborhood where old baseballs were typically wrapped in electrical tape, I thought this was impressive stuff! I sat in the locker room, mesmerized. As I began adjusting the massive array of plastic, rubber, and foam armor onto my body, a strange feeling began to emerge, one I had never experienced before. I can only describe it as a profound serenity, tranquility. Considering the horsing around and general mayhem of the locker room, my mood was certainly curious.

Completely dressed, I stood in front of the locker-room mirror. I saw not a skinny kid, but someone transformed. I was gigantic. Not only were my shoulders as big as a house and my legs bulging with foam pads, but I had grown a full inch and a half taller, due to my cleats—this was definitely good. Walking onto the field, I realized that

I was completely protected and insulated from harm. My skinny body was no longer vulnerable. I was encased in an exoskeleton that left me feeling confident and secure. What was really startling, however, was that for the first time I didn't have any doubts or fears! None! Zero! This was an amazing awakening. No one could hurt me. I truly believed this, and this is what set me free. For the first time in my life, I felt liberated from insecurity.

I came to love football, and for four years, I played with reckless abandon. It never occurred to me (in spite of my teammates' injuries) that I could get hurt. Here's my point: It wasn't my pads that made me invulnerable; it was my willingness to believe in those strategically placed pieces of armor that allowed me to let go of all my fears. Put simply, I trusted those pads.

Before you run out and purchase shoulder pads, recognize that if you can learn to trust—yourself, your world—then you're free to discard insecurity, anxiety, and depression. Self-coaching can teach you to trust again, perhaps for the first time. Once you believe in yourself, once you trust your natural resources to handle life rather than to control it, then you're ready to experience that almost transcendent feeling of serenity, the one I first tasted in that locker room many years ago.

Habits Were Made to Be Broken

So often, patients want me to know how screwed up they are, how "mental" they are, or how crazy they are. I never accept these dire perceptions. From the beginning, I insist, "The only thing wrong with you is that you have a bad habit, a habit of insecurity." Like any habits, whether they be nail biting or cigarette smoking, your habits won't be easy to break—but they are breakable. Your Insecure Child has gained habit strength—your Child has become your nicotine, your booze, your weakness.

Self-talk is your tool to dislodge your destructive Insecure Child habit and replace it with a life-sustaining habit of natural, instinctual functioning. Don't be naïve; don't think you're different—expect a struggle. Habits, by their very nature, resist change. Mark Twain, referring to his smoking habit, said that smoking was the easiest habit in the world to break—after all, according to Twain, "I've stopped thousands of times!" Breaking old habits requires an ongoing effort. Your Insecure Child must be challenged, not just today, but every day until you're liberated from all anxiety and depression. Pep talks, Self-talk, and your systematic daily training efforts are all necessary components designed to kick the habit of insecurity.

I've mentioned that it's up to you to develop your own positive affirmations. After many years of helping and coaching patients to shed the skin of anxiety and depression, I've found one positive affirmation (derived from Self-Coaching healing principle 5) I use more than any other, and I want you to add it to your list. Whenever I'm with a patient who's starting to overly dramatize her or his struggle, I make sure I point out, *"It's just a habit!"*

I want you to repeat this often: It's just a habit. I want to remind you, again and again, you're not up against anything supernatural, demonic, or mysterious—it's just a habit! Nothing else. You've probably given your symptoms too much respect. As my patient Ira once told me, "You don't understand, Doc, this is a depression I'm talking about!" Ira was totally awed by his depression. He wasn't seeing it as just a habit. For Ira, it was a matter of deflating his depression, seeing it for what it was, and then, using Self-coaching, breaking the habit of depression and insecurity.

Perhaps you're a bit like Ira, looking at your problems as being more than you can handle. As long as your ability to function and feel safe aren't in jeopardy, however, it's up to you to stand nose-to-nose with your struggles and decide that you're going to trust your Self-coaching program (remember my "pads").

Trust is a willingness to believe. Don't take my word for it. You decide. Review the chapters in this book, and ask yourself, "Does this program really make sense of why I'm suffering? Does understanding my Insecure Child's need for control explain my anxiety and depression?" If your anxiety and depression can be explained, if you can actually see the effects of your Insecure Child and your Child's many nefarious strategies for control, then why not take that next and last leap of faith? Why not admit the one thing that will start you on the path of true liberation? Why not admit that what you're suffering from is just a habit—a habit of insecurity. While you're at it, you might as well admit another truth: *Habits can be broken.*

Some Realities

I remember running a marathon when I was forty-five years old. For much of the race, I kept thinking, "I'm getting too old for this." I'm sure these thoughts eroded my efforts and diminished my performance. That night, while I was sitting home watching the local news coverage of the marathon, three old men were being interviewed. These old men had finished the marathon. These old men were each over ninety years old. On my next marathon, I didn't feel too old.

What does this have to do with you? Just be careful with negatives. Realize that negatives, as rational as they may seem, can always be challenged. Negatives are part of your Insecure Child's habit of keeping you off balance and perpetually insecure. At forty-five, I wasn't too old. Guys twice my age were competing. I was listening to my Insecure Child.

I don't have much more to tell you about beating anxiety and depression. You're going to need to be patient and realistic about your goals and expectations. Impatience will bury you just as well as negativity; both are poisons. If you were quitting cigarettes, you'd have no problem telling yourself that a destructive attitude was, "just the nicotine talking." When it comes to negativity, impatience, laziness, doubt, or distrust, do the same as you would with nicotine: "That's just my Insecure Child talking."

Muscle Building

You need to stick with this program long enough to develop positive and healthy emotional muscle. Your muscle-bound Insecure Child has weakened you. In order to change the balance, you'll need to exercise your mental muscle every day, through your training program. There's no shortcut. To break a habit, you're going to have to reshape your thinking and perceptions, especially about yourself. As you develop your muscle for self-trust, everything else will follow. Stick with the truths laid out in the seven Self-coaching healing principles:

1. Everyone has a legacy of insecurity, the Insecure Child.
2. Thoughts precede feelings, anxieties, and depressions.
3. Anxiety and depression are misguided attempts to control life.
4. Control is an illusion, not an answer.
5. Insecurity is a habit, and any habit can be broken.
6. Healthy thinking is a choice.
7. A good coach is a good motivator.

The program will work if you work it!

Letting Go

There's one final step to Self-coaching: letting go. In jogging, the parallel would be to go out for a 20-mile run, putting all your training insights together (monitoring your split times, using a heart monitor to stay in a tight aerobic heart range, etc.), and then coming home, getting into a hot tub, and allowing your thoughts to melt away. With Self-coaching, it's important for you to train vigorously and subdue your Insecure Child's sway over your life, but after a period of intense effort, you need to let go and head for that tub.

Sometimes, you need to let go following a prolonged skirmish with your Insecure Child. At other times, it may be beneficial after a brief encounter where you find yourself becoming too anxious or upset with your training. At still other times, you may simply need a well-deserved rest from your training. When running a marathon, sufficient rest is just as critical to your success as your days of long grueling runs. It's the same with Self-coaching. Once in a while, find that hot tub in your mind, kick back, and let yourself enjoy the lack of effort.

The single best way of letting go is to be in the moment. One of my favorite Zen Buddhist stories is of a monk who, walking along a mountain path, encounters a tiger. Seeing a vine growing on the cliff face just below his path, the monk leaps off the edge, grabbing hold of the vine.

The vine begins to loosen, and in the frozen moment before his fall and death, the monk notices a strawberry growing on his vine. The last words the monk speaks before his death are, "What a magnificent strawberry. I think I'll eat it."

This story illustrates being totally in the moment. No past, no future, no abstractions such as doubt, worry, or fear, only that pristine moment filled with an appreciation of that magnificent strawberry. As you become more proficient at separating from your Insecure Child, you will think less and feel more. You will let go of your struggles and efforts, to be with the wonderful strawberries that populate your world.

Letting go takes practice and patience, especially because much of your training has been a cognitive effort to free yourself from your Insecure Child's distortions. Nonetheless, you'll find that as your Child's influence diminishes, your capacity to let go increases. You will begin to grow in confidence and self-trust. Once you're no longer living in chronic fear, you can risk letting go of any struggle and become totally engrossed in watching a sunset, listening to an opera, playing with your children, or soaking in a warm bath.

How do you let go? There's only one way. First, through your Self-coaching efforts, you lessen your Insecure Child's compulsive grip on your life. Then, periodically you begin to practice being in the moment. You let go of thoughts as you become immersed in whatever activity you're involved in. It doesn't matter what activity it is: You can be raking leaves or eating supper; practice being totally in that experience—the sensations, impressions, sounds, tastes, and sights of the moment not your thoughts. This is letting go. In time, you will experience more and more of your life outside of your head. Anxiety and depression don't exist outside of your head, so remember to take a break once in a while and eat a strawberry.

Ready, Coach?

That's all I have to say. It's all I need to say. You have everything you need to insist on a life free from anxiety and depression. If I had one wish, it would be for you to find out just how simple all this really is.

It's never been that complicated. It only felt that way. Your Insecure Child's days are numbered as you prepare to live the life you were meant to live. Remember that Self-coaching isn't just for your acute pain; it's also a way of life. Just as I get up and jog every day, you can adopt Self-coaching as a way of maintaining balance, clarity, and spontaneity throughout your life. There will always be challenges, anxieties, and depressions; that's life. With Self-coaching, however, you'll always have a way to get back to your center.

Training Log Format

Designing Your Training Log

There is no right or wrong way to set up a training log. It's up to you to be as elaborate or as simple as you want. One thing I can promise: Your efforts will not be wasted. Experience has demonstrated that the feedback, insights, and reinforcement you get from a training log cannot be duplicated in any other way. It's the single best way to provide an ongoing, objective, and systematic way of beating anxiety and depression.

Although any suitable notebook will do, I suggest a three-ring binder. The advantage of a three-ring binder is that you can make copies of the exercises presented in the appendix and insert them, as needed (or pull them out for comparison). You can reproduce the exercises exactly as I've presented them, or (where applicable) you can just record the scores from each, with an attached note of explanation. Either way, you'll have a means of evaluating the effects of your training program over time.

Remember, it's your Training Log—make it personal. It's up to you to personalize and use your log in whatever way you can to motivate and instruct yourself.

I suggest that your training log contain the following four sections:

1. A section for Self-talk efforts
2. A section for follow-through
3. A section for specific incidents, insights, or daily observations
4. A section including pertinent exercises reproduced from this book

Section 1: Self-Talk

Self-Talk Review

Step 1. Practice hearing your thoughts. Ask yourself, "Does what I'm hearing sound mature, rational, or reasonable, or does it sound primitive, excessively emotional, childish and insecure? Is it me, or is it my Insecure Child talking?"

Step 2. When you realize that your Insecure Child is speaking, decide to stop listening.

Step 3. After you stop letting your Insecure Child steer your thoughts, do something about it! Direct your thinking toward a healthier perspective.

Describe any encounters with your Insecure Child, including a step-by-step analysis of your efforts:

_____

_____

_____

_____

_____

_____

_____

_____

_____

_____

_____

Section 2: Follow-through

What expressions of control contaminate my life:

_____

_____

_____

_____

_____

Clues—past or present—to explain my Insecure Child's habits:

_____

_____

_____

_____

Finding my truth—recognizing any choices:

_____

_____

_____

_____

Additional insights or observations:

_____

_____

_____

_____

Section 3: Daily Observations

Insights, feelings, incidents, and observations:

_____

_____

_____

_____

_____

_____

_____

_____

_____

_____

_____

_____

_____

_____

_____

_____

_____

_____

_____

_____

_____

_____

_____

_____

_____

_____

Section 4: Exercises

In this section, you can include any or all of the training suggestions listed at the end of each chapter. I've divided these exercises into three categories:

1. *Daily*—You should make every effort to include these exercises as part of your daily log entries.

2. *Monthly*—this category is used mainly to help you monitor your Self-coaching progress over time and should be periodically included in your log.

3. *As needed*—This category should be used at your own discretion.

Here is a list of all the Self-coaching exercises and assessments available. You will find these listed at the end of each chapter, as indicated.

Daily

1. Experiences where you felt a loss of control (Chapter 6)

2. Thinking traps (Chapter 6)

3. Charting follow-through efforts (Chapter 10)

Monthly

1. Assessing depressive symptoms and their severity (Chapter 4)

2. Assessing natural and destructive anxiety symptoms (Chapter 5)

3. Assessing Turtle tendencies (Chapter 14)

4. Assessing Chameleon tendencies (Chapter 15)

5. Assessing Perfectionist tendencies (Chapter 16)

6. Assessing Guilt-sensitive tendencies (Chapter 17)

As Needed

1. Inner-outer experience: Learning to get out of your head (Chapter 1)

2. Determining whether your struggles are rooted in anxiety, depression, or a combination of the two (Chapter 3)

3. Healthy versus insecurity-driven need for control—telling the difference (Chapter 7)

4. Differentiating among directed Self-talk, undirected thoughts driven by insecurity, and neutral undirected thoughts (Chapter 8)

5. Assessing your Self-talk reactions (Chapter 9)

6. Changing channels (Chapter 9)

7. Looking for hook experiences (Chapter 10)

8. Working with proactive and passive thinking (Chapter 10)

9. Using pep talks (Chapter 11)

10. Determining how and why you worry (Chapter 12)

Index

action, 134–35, 178
adrenal glands, 53
affirmations, 23, 247
alcohol, 77–79
Alcoholics Anonymous (AA), 78, 79
American Psychiatric Association, 37
analytical therapy, 6
anger, 153–60, 166, 167. *See also* hostility
antidepressant medications, 39, 40, 45–46, 58
anxiety, 50–59. *See also* depression
   depression and, 27–28
   destructive forms, 53–54
   effects of, 51–52
   eliminating, 6
   energy and, 28
   natural forms, 53–54
   social forms, 57
appeasement, 199
asking "why", 118–19
attitude
   adjusting, 129–31
   definition of, 129
   positive thinking, 131, 248–49
atypical depression, 40, 48
avoiding conflict, 236–37, 239
avoiding imperfection, 209. *See also* Perfectionists
avoiding life, 169–71, 174–75, 179

behaviors, 36
bigotry, 165
bipolar depression, 48
black-and-white thinking, 68, 159, 197, 208
Bully Child, 101

Chameleons, 2, 101, 187–205
   manipulation, 187–88
   tendencies of, 205
cheating, 188–90
Chicken Littles, 101, 143, 144–45
choices, 4, 31–34, 39, 118–19
clues, 124–26, 128
competition, 165
conflict, 236–37, 239
conscience, 233–34, 236–37
consequences, 233–34, 236–37
control, 3, 21–22
   as an illusion, 21–22, 69, 171, 188, 229
   insecurity and, 74–83, 121–22, 179–80
   losing, 61–63, 70–72, 146–50, 169, 218, 225
   strategies of, 21, 63, 114–16, 188–91
   traps to avoid, 64–69, 73
Control Freaks, 101, 102, 207, 212, 218–20
control-insecurity connection, 74–83
   quiz on, 74–75

Index

control-sensitive people, 62, 69,
    76–77
  choices, 118
  hostility, 153
control-sensitive personalities, 60–73,
    81
  quiz on, 60–61
criticism, 195, 196

demands, 218–20
depression, 13–14, 37–49
  anxiety and, 27–28
  atypical forms, 40, 48
  bipolar forms, 48
  causes of, 41–42
  destructive forms, 42, 43
  dysthymic forms, 47
  eliminating, 6
  energy and, 28
  evaluating, 43–44
  insecurity and, 43
  major forms, 40–41, 47
  mild forms, 40, 43
  moods and, 45
  natural/destructive forms, 43
  natural forms, 42–43
  postpartum forms, 48–49
  quiz on, 40
  seasonal affective depression (SAD),
    47–48
  severity scale, 44
  types of, 46–49
destructive anxiety, 53–54
destructive depression, 42, 43
Diagnostic and Statistical Manual, 37
Diplomats, 101, 199–205
directed imagination, 13
distorted perceptions, 34–35, 50–51,
    63–64
  threats, 158, 159
distrust, 51, 97–98, 156
dopamine, 45
drug abuse, 41, 77–79

dysthymic depression, 47
dysthymic disorder, 40

environmental stress, 41–42
escaping from life, 169–71, 174–75,
    179
exaggerating, 118–19, 121, 123–24,
    142
experiences, interpreting, 29–30

fact from fiction, 122–23
family history, 41
Fanatics, 102, 207
  perfectionism and, 212, 216–18
fears, 146–50, 166
  of flying, 146–50
  letting go of, 249–51
fight-or-flight response, 52–53, 56
flawless living, 207–8
follow-through, 114–28
Freud, Sigmund, 4, 5
Frightened Child, 101
full-time Hedgehogs, 158–60
functioning ability, 37–39

general anxiety disorder (GAD),
    54–55, 58
Generation Insecurity, 75
greed, 190
guilt
  by commission, 226, 241
  by comparison, 226, 241
  conscience and, 233–37
  consequences and, 233–37
  definition of, 225
  by existentialism, 226, 241
  by fantasy, 226, 241
  martyrdom and, 234–40
  morality and, 233–37
  by omission, 226, 241
  removing, 229–32
  by thought, 226, 241
  understanding, 233–34
  wrong reasons for, 226–27

Index

Guilt-insensitive people, 225
Guilt-sensitive people, 101, 102,
    224–41
  Martyrs, 101, 102, 234–40
  removing guilt, 229–32

habits
  breaking, 17, 22, 42, 94, 116–17,
    246–48
  insecurity and, 22, 42, 71, 94–95,
    116–17
  persona and, 33
have-tos, 67, 208, 221–22
healing
  principles of, 19–23, 90–92, 94–95,
    116–17, 125, 171, 249
  specific personality types, 139–241
Healing Your Habits, 13
healthy choices, 4, 39, 118–19
healthy thinking, 22, 91, 94, 117,
    248–49
Hedgehogs, 101, 102, 152–67
  full-timers, 158–60
  part-timers, 154–58
  quiz for, 152
  tendencies of, 152–53
  traps to avoid, 165
  Turtles and, 179–85
Helpless Child, 102
hooks, 123–27
Hopeless Child, 102
hostility, 153–60, 166, 167
  understanding, 162–63
Hysterical Child, 101

imperfection, 209. *See also*
    Perfectionists
Impulsive Child, 101
inertia, 134
Inner child, 225
inner talk, 18. *See also* Self-talk
Insecure Child, 19–23, 79, 125
  changing channels, 102–5, 114

fears and, 146–50
identifying, 101
Self-talk, 88–91, 94, 114–28,
    175–77, 214–15, 230–31, 246–47
thought patterns of, 98–100, 106,
    171, 172, 184
traits of, 100–102
trust and, 97–98
tuning out, 102, 157, 163, 175–78,
    231
insecurity, 19–23, 29–30, 90
  anxiety and, 51
  control and, 74–83, 121–22, 179–80
  depression and, 43
  fears and, 146–50
  habits and, 22, 42, 71, 94–95,
    116–17
  help for, 39
  hostility and, 166
  perceptions of, 63–64
  quiz on, 74–75
  resolving, 81–82
  thoughts of, 171, 172, 184
insight, 4, 76–77, 116–18, 120–21
instinct, 53
interpreting experiences, 29–30
intimidation, 166
intuition, 12

jealousy, 165
Jung, Carl Gustav, 4, 5, 12, 225

leaders, 213
letting go, 4, 146, 218, 249–51
listening, 97–98, 156–57
living in the moment, 92, 249–50

major depression, 40–41, 47
manipulation, 101, 187–88, 191,
    238–39
Manipulative Child, 101
Martyrs, 101, 102, 234–40
medical conditions, 35, 41, 58

medications, antidepressant, 39, 40,
    45–46, 58
mind reading, 66–67, 159
misery, 208–10
moods, 45
morality, 233–37
motivation, 23, 95, 129–38, 231

name calling, 68–69
natural anxiety, 53–54
natural depression, 42–43
natural/destructive depression, 43
near-death experience, 53
negative patterns, 54–57
negative thoughts, 31–34, 42, 76, 248
neurotransmitters, 45–46
New York City Marathon, 15
norepinephrine, 45

obsessive-compulsive disorder (OCD),
    56–57
Occam, Sir William of, 6
Occam's razor, 6
opposites attracting, 179–85
Overwhelmed Child, 101

panic attacks, 51, 55–56, 144–45, 218
Panicked Child, 101
part-time Hedgehogs, 154–58
passive hostility, 154
passive statements, 117–18, 127–28
peace, 199–200
pep talks, 131–34, 138, 231–32, 247
perceptions, 31–35, 50–51
    insecurity and, 63–64
Perfectionists, 75–76, 102, 206–23
    examples of, 212
    fanaticism and, 212, 216–18
    illusions of perfection, 211
    quiz for, 206–7
    success and, 210–11
    tendencies of, 212, 222–23
persistence, 95–96

persona, 33
personality types, 139–241
phobias, 57, 146. *See also* fears
phototherapy, 48
physical conditions, 35, 41, 58
pinhole thinking, 190, 195, 196–97
planning versus worry, 143–44
Politicians, 101, 102, 191–98, 205
    manipulation and, 191
    quiz for, 198
    relationships and, 193–95
    tendencies of, 198
positive attitudes, 131, 248–49
positive thinking, 131, 248–49. *See also*
    thoughts
postpartum depression, 48–49
prejudice, 165
principles of healing, 19–23, 90–92,
    94–95, 116–17, 125, 171, 249
    for specific personality types,
    139–241
proactive statements, 117–18,
    127–28
problems
    eliminating, 16
    exaggerating, 118–19, 121, 123–24,
    142
    root of, 27–35
procrastination, 171–72
psychoanalysis, 6
psychological factors, 42
Puer Aeternus, 34

quizzes
    control-sensitive personalities,
    60–61
    depression, 40
    Hedgehog tendencies, 152
    insecurity, 74–75
    perfectionism, 206–7
    Politician tendencies, 198
    on Self-coaching, 9–10
    Turtle tendencies, 168

racism, 165
reflections
  anger, 167
  anxiety, 30
  asking "why", 119
  avoiding life, 171
  believing in self, 220
  changing habits, 42
  control, 69, 143
  exaggerating, 142
  healing, 80
  Insecure Child, 177, 216
  insecurity, 29, 42, 76
  pep talks, 231–32
  perfectionism, 209
  security, 191
  Self-talk, 105
rejection, 196
relationship issues, 80–81, 90, 107–10,
    160–65, 180–84, 193–97,
    199–201, 210–11, 238–40
resentment, 160, 161
responsibility, 180, 184
retreating from life, 169–71, 174–75,
    179

safety, illusions of, 69–70, 171
saying "no", 200–205
seasonal affective depression (SAD),
    47–48
self-assessment, 184
Self-coaching, 15–17, 245–51
  breaking destructive patterns, 17
  eliminating problems, 16
  healing problems, 25–83
  for healthy lifestyles, 6, 17, 22, 91,
    94, 117, 248–49
  for life, 243–51
  program, 11–14, 85–138
  quiz on, 9–10
  understanding, 7–23
self-gratification, 225
self-perceptions, 31–35, 50–51

insecurity and, 63–64
self-quizzes
  control-sensitive personalities, 60–61
  depression, 40
  Hedgehog tendencies, 152
  insecurity, 74–75
  perfectionism, 206–7
  Politician tendencies, 198
  on self-coaching, 9–10
  Turtle tendencies, 168
self-reliance, 17
Self-talk, 13–15, 20, 80, 87–96
  basics of, 88
  definition of, 87
  directed thinking, 107–10, 157, 178
  follow-through, 114–28
  Insecure Child and, 88–91, 94,
    175–77, 214–15, 230–31, 246–47
  insights, 116–18, 120–21
  listening, 97–98, 156–57
  motivation for, 23, 95, 129–38, 231
  patience with, 110–11
  review of, 111
  steps of, 97–113, 156–57, 230–31
  understanding, 87–96
  worry and, 145–51
self-therapy, 9–18
self-trust, 97–98, 247, 249
selfishness, 225, 233
sensitive people, 227–31. See also
    Guilt-sensitive people
serotonin re-uptake inhibitor (SSRI)
    medications, 45
"should" statements, 65
social anxieties, 57
Stars, 102, 207, 209, 212, 213–16
statements
  passive style, 117–18, 127–28
  proactive style, 117–18, 127–28
  "should" statements, 65
stress, 30–31, 41–42
Stubborn Child, 102
success, 129–31

Index

suicidal thoughts, 40, 41
Sulking Child, 101
Swindlers, 101, 188–91, 205

taking action, 134–35, 178
teflon defense, 195–97
thinking traps, 64–69, 73
thoughts
  destructive pattern of, 30, 71
  directed thinking, 107–10, 157, 178
  feelings and, 20, 92–93, 125
  healthy thinking, 22, 91, 94, 117,
    248–49
  Insecure Child and, 98–100, 106,
    171, 172, 184
  insecurity, 171, 172, 184
  negativity, 31–34, 42, 76, 248
  passive thinking, 117–18, 127–28
  positive thinking, 131, 248–49
  proactive thinking, 117–18, 127–28
  traps to avoid, 64–69, 73
threats, 158, 159, 166
training assignment, 112
training log, 112, 135–37
  example of, 112, 253–58
training suggestions
  anxiety, 59
  Chameleon tendencies, 205
  changing channels, 113
  clues, 128
  coaching style, 138
  control, 72, 83
  depression, 49
  follow-through, 126–27
  guilt-sensitivity, 241
  hooks, 127
  hostility, 167
  inner talk, 18
  pep talk, 138
  perfectionistic tendencies, 222–23
  principles of healing, 23
  proactive versus passive thinking,
    127–28

relationship issues, 240
root of problems, 35–36
Self-talk, 96
  thinking traps, 73
  troublesome behaviors, 36
  Turtle tendencies, 185–86
  worry, 150–51
transactional analysis, 6
traps to avoid, 64–69, 73, 165
troublesome behaviors, 36
trust, 97–98, 247, 249
  lack of, 51, 97–98, 156
truth, 117–18, 122–23, 191
  believing, 172
  neurotic truth, 123
  real truth, 123
tunnel vision, 66
  Chameleons and, 190
  Hedgehogs and, 159
  Perfectionists and, 208, 217
  Turtles and, 184
  Worrywarts and, 148
Turtles, 101, 102, 138–86
  Hedgehogs and, 179–85
  quiz for, 168
  shell of, 169, 171, 179
  tendencies of, 168–69, 185–86

want-tos, 221–22
what-iffing, 65–66, 141, 143–45, 149
what-ifs, 3, 65–66, 141
withdrawal, 115
worry, 93–95, 141–51
  effects of, 142
  versus planning, 143–44
  reasons for, 142–43
  Self-talk and, 145–51
Worrywarts, 101, 102, 141–51

"yes" people, 199, 200–201